COOKING FROM SCRATCH

By Eleanora Armistead Crane

Edited by Sarah and Adriano Duque

COOKING FROM SCRATCH

On the Insert tab, the galleries include items that are designed to coordinate with the overall look of your document. You can use these galleries to insert tables, headers, footers, lists, cover pages, and other document building blocks. You can use these galleries to insert tables

Printed By:
Amazon

Printed in the United States of America
Free template by: Used to Tech (https://usedtotech.com)

First Printing Edition, 2021
ISBN 9798412660066

1

INTRODUCTION

The main deterrent to good cooking, as I see it, is in never having learned how. While roles are no longer as clearly defined as they once were, a lot is expected of American women. Think about it. We are somehow expected to perform our varied tasks, home, childcare, office and of course the kitchen, with ease and efficiency and when it comes to the latter, with little or no training. No more secrets passed from mother to daughter?

Case in point, my early cooking career has been so traumatic that I feel qualified to advise on errors. Blame these (I like to tell myself) on no knowledge whatsoever of the kitchen, having always been chased out of it when growing up and on a no-nonsense, if-you-can-read-you-can-cook approach. Unfortunately for me, my particular cookbooks, donated by the previous tenant and which I pored over, turned out to be instruction-less collections of recipes, designed for the experienced. They failed to tell me, for example, that it will not work if sautéing fat is not initially sizzling hot nor if food is even slightly damp, that a boiling green vegetable will lose its color if pan is covered, not to mention early soufflés which did not fall as they never rose in the first place-no words on how to fold in beaten egg whites-all mundane omissions but with a profound effect on outcome. My first party livened when I dropped a pan of biscuits. They were so hard and rubbery that they bounced like golf balls as they hit the floor, much to the delight of my guests. In short, I floundered.

Thanks to an unforeseen turn of events, I ended up in a Swiss cooking school, in Geneva, to be specific, where food is taken as seriously as it is in France. I was straightened out, or perhaps vindicated is the better term, on the very day the chef announced that if any of us came up with a well-cooked meal, it would be purely accidental, as none of us knew anything about cooking processes nor the techniques that comprise them. These processes are fairly limited and consequently easy to grasp. What can you do other than braise or stew, boil and related processes (simmer, poach) bake, broil, sauté, fry or steam, not to mention the barbecue and the grill? All cooking, all recipes are based on one of the above and what distinguishes say, one stew from the other, is your choice seasonings. Master these processes and you will be well on your way but keep in mind that good cooking also requires interest on your part, taste, that is, knowledge of seasonings and how they work and of course, fine, fresh ingredients.

Many of us who have been caught up in the cooking mystique tend to believe that there is no other cuisine worth bothering about. I now disagree, finding nothing wrong with good any-kind-of-cooking. That includes good American cooking, simple straight-forward at its best, and so often maligned by Europeans.

Our vegetables are a favorite target (no taste) but again, I disagree. Even if you live in sections that do not enjoy the long growing seasons of say, California and the Deep South, good vegetables are available, not necessarily in your local supermarket but certainly in city vegetable markets or in local farm outlets.

At the risk of flag waving, Oregon fruit, shipped all over the country is exceptional, our beef second to none. Nowhere in Europe can you walk into a supermarket and pick up the tender, well-marbled steak that we take for granted. On the other hand, good veal has to be looked for. Our store bread deserves all the criticism it gets. Remedy this by either making your own (see bread) or by finding a good Italian bakery. No matter what type of cuisine, by all means take advantage of and apply the impeccable techniques, their care and attention, emphasis on freshness and a small amount of their well-known dedication to food.

This reservation came about after a recent visit to a local bookstore, run, oddly enough, by a man, where to my astonishment; I found "The Joy of Cooking" and "The Joy of Sex" back-to-back on the cookbook shelf.

My advice is to continue to cook, taste and season as you go, taking the time to find the best ingredients. Learn from your mistakes. Even the most experienced make them on occasion. However, keep in mind that a cooking error is nowhere as traumatic as a gardening error which might set you back a whole growing season. And what else? Give the baked potato as much care as you give the finest beefsteak and you will not fail.

2

PREPARATIONS

Cooking Processes

When I first started cooking, we used eggs, heavy cream and butter with abandon and without any feelings of guilt whatsoever. They were our mentors and did they not do the same? Do they still not do the same? I can only conclude that their rationale is that nothing can replace the flavor of butter. Obviously neither out cookbooks not they have kept pace with cholesterol findings.

I would be remiss indeed if I did not point out that there are measures which will reduce these levels without sacrificing too much of the flavor. You might begin by substituting margarine for the conventional sautéing mixture of butter and olive oil or like the Spanish, use olive oil all alone. This eliminates cholesterol but not the fat content.

To gloss over this briefly, you might make it a habit to cut all fat from meat, removing chicken skin. Remember that organ meats and shellfish are high in cholesterol. Reduce amount of sautéing fat. Be careful about skimming fat from soups, stocks and stews. The best way to do this is to chill them overnight.

To continue with unpleasant subjects, the current salmonella problem is distressing, and nobody seems to be able to pinpoint when it will be over. Meanwhile forget about hollandaise, béarnaise, Caesar salad, homemade mayonnaise, soft boiled and scrambled eggs, omelets and all egg dishes which are not thoroughly cooked. Products such as egg beaters are not the answer, at least not for me. At the end of this book, there are egg recipes designed to be used when raw of slightly cooked eggs can be eaten again.

There are also salmonella precautions to be taken with raw turkey and chicken. After bringing home either, rinse off under running water, pat dry and refrigerate in plastic bag. When ready to cook, do not let fowl touch kitchen counter. Cover counter with newspaper, cutting board on top. After use, wash board and utensils thoroughly.

It has been well publicized that a turkey, or chicken for that matter, should never be stuffed the night before, but did you know that after a turkey dinner, the bird should never rest on its serving platter while you do the dishes or whatever? Either refrigerate it or put it in the soup pot and start your soup.

Bake and Roast

Your ingredients determine the cooking method, particularly when meat is involved, the tender cuts cooked one way, the tough another. The tender cuts call for roasting, broiling or the sauté, while the tough require the tenderizing effects of long, slow stewing or braising. Do not make the mistake of broiling the tough or braising the tender in the case of the latter, meat will simply fall apart. To differentiate between the tough and the tender when buying meat, see chapter on beef.

Oven Placement

The two terms are more or less synonymous, the differences more a matter of terminology. We speak of roasting meat in the oven and yet when it comes to cakes, pies, breads and the like, we refer to it as baking - same process. You might term both baked ham and roasted beets misnomers. Keep oven in check with oven thermometer. Always preheat to its desired setting some 30 minutes in advance. For air circulation purposes, do not overcrowd oven, not allowing pans to touch oven walls nor each other. If using two racks, arrange pans so that one is not directly over the other.

As for oven placement, foods which need bottom browning go on lowest level, such as unfilled pie shells (known as blind baking); foods to be browned, such as quiche and gratin dishes go on the top level; reserve the center for roasts, puddings, filled pie shells and the like.

Boil

Green vegetables and pasta are initially dropped into rapidly boiling water (later to be turned down). Food to be blanched (see below) calls for the same and this is it for the rapid boil of 212 degrees.

Blanch

To blanch is to drop foods briefly into rapidly boiling water, the purpose of which is to loosen their skins, for instance, onions, garlic, almonds and tomatoes. Recipes often call for blanching or partially cooking a green vegetable, particularly when cooking is to be continued in sautéing pan.

Refresh

Refreshing always follows blanching. This connotes running the blanched food under cold running water. In the case of green vegetables, this stops the cooking and sets the color and in the case of food which requires peeling, it enables you to slip off skins easily.

Simmer, Poach

To simmer is to cook a liquid so slowly, over heat so low, that only an occasional bubble breaks on surface. Soups and stews, stocks are always simmered.

Poaching is something else again. This time liquid is cooked so slowly that you have no breaking surface bubbles but only an occasional shimmer. Fish and chicken recipes often call for poaching. For both poaching and simmering, you may want to invest in an inexpensive gadget known as a flame tamer which will keep wayward stove burners under control.

Braise and Stew

These processes are so similar that it is almost hair-splitting to define the two separately; both designed to tenderize tough cuts of meat by long, slow simmering. For what it's worth, to stew is too first brown small cubes of meat in oil, followed by simmering in a liquid. Braising on the other hand, connotes larger pieces of meat, sometimes browned, sometimes not, a smaller amount of liquid, pan tightly covered, either on stovetop or in oven.

Broil

The best candidates for the heat of the broiler are fatty fish and tender cuts of meat or fowl which contain a certain amount of fat. This excludes veal and lean fish. I personally find broiling a troublesome process, requiring constant watching to ensure that surface does nor char. Always preheat broiler to its highest level 20 minutes in advance but do not preheat broiling pan, my choice of which is the standard slotted broiling pan which usually comes with stove.

For fish, however, I use metal baking pan. If stove is electric, leave oven door slightly ajar when broiling, not necessary with gas. Depending on thickness, food is placed in oven so that its top surface is within 3 to 6 inches from heating element. Allow some 3 inches for a thin fish fillet. If food starts to char, you have two choices: move pan to lower level or turn off broiler and turn on oven to finish the cooking.

Fry (Deep Fat)

Having once set a stove on fire with fat which escaped from skillet, I now recommend the use of an electric deep-fat fryer. Proponents of frying will tell you that if your fat is sizzling hot (in the high, 300-degree range), a protective coating will form around food and no fat will seep in. Even so, I now limit my frying to   fried potatoes.

Sauté

Why so many words on the subject? The sauté is one of the most used processes in cooking and if any of the several steps involved is improperly done, it will not work. Define it as to brown and cook small pieces of food quickly in sizzling hot fat. However, the term is used in two ways. It is applied to an entire process in which food is first browned in hot fat, cooking continued until food is done. Pan can be covered or not covered, a liquid added after the initial browning or at the end, for sauce making purposes. The term is also used (but not by the purist) to describe browning meat quickly, say a steak, or softening or browning onions and garlic. Your fat choices are butter, clarified butter (see butter), oil or a mixture of butter and oil in the proportion of 2 butter to 1 oil (my choice).

Butter used alone burns at a comparatively low temperature. The use of clarified butter will help counteract this as will the butter-oil mixture. In any event, the amount called for is small, to film pan bottom by 1/8 -inch. You can use less if you will or a non-stick pan, but at the risk of sacrificing flavor.Unless food is to be coated (flour, cornmeal or breadcrumbs), make sure that food pieces are thoroughly patted dry or they will not brown. Skillet (hopefully cast-iron) should be the right size, that is, just large enough to hold food pieces comfortably in one non-touching layer. If too small, pieces will steam rather than brown and if too large, fat which is not covered by food will burn.

Directions generally call for adding fat to skillet, heating to desired temperature, and then adding food. I like to do this as follows: warm empty skillet over low heat. Add fat and when it in turn warms up, turn up heat and when at the proper sautéing temperature, add food pieces. Keep in mind the words "warm skillet." If skillet is too hot when fat is added, the fat can conceivably flame. Food pieces should be added to fat when fat is sizzling hot, just short of smoking. How do you determine this? If using clarified butter, it will turn golden, if oil alone, when, as the Spanish say, a light haze forms over skillet, and if the butter-oil mixture, watch for butter to foam and sizzle. At the very moment fat ceases to foam, add food pieces. To avoid splattering when adding food pieces to hot oil, either gently slide food pieces into the hot fat or tilt skillet away from you. Lower heat to avoid burning and when brown on one side, turn and brown on the other.

Softening Garlic

Recipes often begin with sautéing chopped garlic in oil or butter. Care must be exercised as, if the fat is too hot, the process too long, garlic will brown and impart an unpleasant, bitter taste. To this end, sauté briefly - for two minutes or so over moderate heat and be prepared to add the solids called for in recipe, perhaps tomatoes, onions or a liquid, which will take care of browning. Another and perhaps easier way to accomplish this is to quarter garlic slices instead of the chopped. Remove and discard slices after they color slightly and proceed with recipe.

Softening Onions

Countless recipes start with the above, onions sliced or chopped. Two methods are called for, the first to merely soften, cooking until translucent, the second to caramelize until golden brown. To soften, drop onions into moderately hot fat-hot enough to sizzle - immediately turn heat to low, cover pan and cook slowly, stirring up now and then. It should take some ten minutes. To caramelize, cook in moderately hot fat until onions turn brown, stirring up to prevent burning. In either case, season with salt and pepper on completion.

Steam

Steam is to cook over, not in, boiling water. Steaming racks which fit into saucepan are available as are the regulation steaming pans, some of which are layered so that more than one vegetable can be steamed at a time.

Some Unrelated Ingredients
Bread crumbs

Your own breadcrumbs are superior to what you can buy in the supermarket. Hopefully, use your own bread. If not, supermarket breads will do. If recipe calls for fresh crumbs, tear bread apart, remove crusts and process in food processor. One slice should yield roughly half a cup. If dried breadcrumbs are called for, bread can be hardened in 250-degree oven. If crumbing food which is to be cooked or baked, add crumbs to a little hot melted butter plus a little parsley. For the purposes of this book and to avoid repetition, flour, unless otherwise specified, refers to all-purpose unbleached, butter to the unsalted, oil to olive oil, baking powder always to the double acting, lime and lemon juice to freshly squeezed, large, grade AA eggs, both cheese and nutmeg to the grated (by you), pepper to the ground (also by you).

Butter

What can I say about butter other than that nothing replaces its flavor? Tasteless (I say) margarine can be used but keep in mind that while it has no cholesterol, its fat content is high. Olive oil, on the other hand is cholesterol free but its fat content is as high as that of butter. While the excesses of butter, cream and eggs are not in tune with the times, you can moderate. My non-medical feeling is that unless you have been told otherwise, the answer is not total abstinence but moderation. You can not only lesson butter intake but are scrupulous when it comes to degreasing. This will probably involve making stews, soups and stocks a day ahead and chill long enough for fat to congeal on surface. This chilling also improves flavor. If you chill stew in which you have used very little fat, you will be shocked by the amount of fat that congeals in the pan. In sauté pan, butter will burn at a fairly low temperature. So-called milky solids contained in the butter cause this. This can be mitigated by using oil alone, a mixture of butter and oil or by clarifying butter. I personally prefer the oil/butter mixture.

Clarified Butter

To clarify, cut butter into tablespoon bits, always a little more than recipe calls for, as it will dissipate. Heat butter in heavy pan over moderate heat. When melted, take off heat and skim off surface froth and let settle for a few minutes. The clear, yellow liquid on top is your clarified butter. Spoon this off and discard milky solids which will have settled on pan bottom.

Cheese

In this brief section, it is of course impossible to do justice to the many fine cheeses. I can only suggest that you start cooking with such old reliable as the Swiss, Emmenthaler and the Italian Parmigiano Reggiano, then going on to others. I particularly like the excellent cheeses of Spain, France and Italy. There is also fine American cheese. If buying the imported, be sure that it is the real thing. Aged Parmigiano Reggiano, for example, will be so stamped. Save the rind to flavor your long cooking soups. Avoid the tasteless pre-grated and so-called processed cheeses. Wrap and store in warmest part of refrigerator, wrapped in foil rather than plastic. Find yourself a good cheese store which will be able to tell you when your soft cheeses, such as Brie, are ripe.

Cream (heavy)

In this health-conscious era, some of us turn their backs on heavy cream but continue to use butter, perhaps not realizing that if the cream is beaten too vigorously, it turns to butter, six of one and half dozen of the other, as they say. This, I might add, was a real plus during World War II when butter was rationed, but not heavy cream. Even so, I will occasionally use it in a sauce (for which it does wonders) or as a topping for a special dessert. For whipping, a metal bowl is preferable, keeping in mind that cream will double in volume. I use a hand-held electric beater. Bowl, blades and cream should be chilled which involves putting them all in freezer some 20 minutes in advance.

There are two stages of beating, lightly for folding into a dessert, more stiffly to top one. In either case beat slowly, circulating beater around bowl, rotating bowl as you beat. In 3 or 4 minutes, when cream starts to visibly thicken, pull beater across surface. If it leaves light traces, cream has reached the proper folding-in stage. To prevent last minute beating, you can whip cream, say before dinner, placed in sieve over bowl in refrigerator. Forego the ultra pasteurized.

Crème fraîche (French for "fresh cream") is a soured cream, but less sour than American sour cream. It has a comparatively low viscosity and a higher fat content.

Eggs

Due to the current salmonella epidemic, the USDA has recommended that we forgo both raw and slightly cooked eggs for the duration. Eggs should be cooked for at least eight minutes, or to internal temperature of 140 degrees. This effectively takes care of the former two-minute scrambled egg, top-of-the-stove omelet, sunny-side-up, your own mayonnaise, béarnaise and Hollandaise sauces. Commercial egg substitutes are now available in some markets, but I do not find them satisfactory. I have been unable to find pasteurized eggs; however, powdered egg whites, which of course can be used in uncooked egg white dishes such as mousses, are now available. Further recommendations are:

1. buy eggs from refrigerated cases and use within two weeks of purchase
2. refrigerate in there store cartons
3. do not leave at room temperature for more than two hours and finally
4. discard those with cracked shells.
5.

I continue to make custards and baked egg dishes but am careful to cook them to 160 degrees on internal thermometer. For a custard, this is 10 degrees short of curdling.

Flour

Once again, unless so indicated, flour in this book calls for all-purpose, unbleached Southern flour, such as Martha White, which comes from a softer wheat, makes better baking powder biscuits but do not use for bread. For successful cakes, do not substitute all-purpose for cake flour. Unless your recipe calls for sifting, measure flour by scooping out of bag with measuring cup, leveling off with back of knife.

Nuts

Keep in mind that nuts not only add a great deal of flavor to desserts but also to savory dishes. I have in mind particularly pecans, walnuts, almonds and pine nuts. You will read that nuts will keep much better if you buy them in the shell. They are so troublesome to shell that I buy them unshelled, storing in refrigerator until ready to use. To bring out more flavor, before chopping, try toasting them in a skillet. This can be done by placing them in a hot, dry skillet and stirring. This will only take a minute or two.

Wine

It is not recommended that you use your finest wines when cooking. However do not use one so poor that you would not be willing to drink it yourself. This, of course, eliminates the so-called cooking wine, often found in stores. After the alcohol content burns off, which it will, all you have left is the flavor of your wine.

I like to store opened bottles of wine in the refrigerator with the aid of a kitchen store gadget, which helps seal out air. If adding a spirit of high alcohol content, say brandy or a liqueur, or perhaps even a wine, into a hot simmering sauce or perhaps a stew, first move skillet from burner, as it could conceivably flame. If it should happen despite your best efforts, keep a pan lid handy.

Seasonings

When we casually eye the rows of spices on supermarket shelves, we tend to forget their historical background, the years and years of bloody spice-trade wars and the territorial discoveries and acquisitions that took place in their quest. The bottle of peppercorns, which we now take for, granted would have been worth its weight in gold.

We also tend to forget that the Roman soldiers were paid in salt, hence the English word salary. Appreciate them the more. Will future generations regard the current quest for oil in the same casual light?

Herbs

The word herb applies to a classification of plants such as rosemary, thyme, and basil, to name a few. Their fragrant leaves and stems serve to flavor our dishes. On the other hand, the aromatic spices come from the bark, buds, seeds or roots of other aromatic plants. In either case, my feeling is that the proper use of herbs and spices, (that is with a certain amount of restraint) plus your own stock can make the difference between a good and a poor cook.

In this plastic, computerized age, certain products of nature, namely spices and herbs, can create an almost magical effect. When added to a substance, they have the unique ability to bring out the natural flavor of the substance, imposing little of their own. Some say that this is the main point in cooking.

Herbs are available both fresh and dried. Remember that the dried are three times stronger than the fresh, making it all too easy to over season. This works out to 1 tablespoon of fresh to 1 teaspoon of the dried. I like to reduce this to ½ teaspoon.

The shelf life of the dried is short even if kept under the best condition, that is, stored in a dark, cool, dry spot. After 6 months, their flavor will approximate that of dried grass.

The fresh are increasingly available in markets. If not in yours, substitute the dried or you might consider growing your own. If you wish to grow your own buy the small, started potted plants in garden centers. In some areas certain perennials, such as mint, can be wintered over outside.

Grow them on a partially shady windowsill in the summer, sunny in the winter. Better yet, if you have outside space, sink plants in the ground, pots and all, bringing them in at end of the summer. Perennials should survive, annuals, no. Thyme and rosemary, both perennials, are easy to grow, while I am lucky if my basil plants, annuals, last through Thanksgiving. My list of favorites is small, namely mint, sweet marjoram, tarragon, basil, dill, chervil, cilantro, rosemary, thyme, the last two to be used with restraint. This does not mean, however, that you should not try them all.

Surprisingly, I find the dried dill weed (weed, not seed) as effective as the fresh. Do not forget the flavoring possibilities of the ever-present parsley, especially in the winter. The chopped leaves make an attractive garnish but most of the flavor is in the stems. An effective way to store them and all fresh herbs is to place them in a glass of water, cover them loosely with a plastic bag and refrigerate. They should keep for a week.

How are herbs used? Both the fresh and the dried can be used interchangeably except for the noted differences in strength. Herb bouquet or bouquet garni (see below) can be added to long-simmering dishes such as casseroles, stews, and soups, at the start of the cooking. The dried can be added at the beginning of the cooking while the fresh are generally added at the end. The chopped fresh can be scattered over salads, freshly cooked vegetables or over roasts as they go in the oven.

Herb Bouquet (Bouquet Garni)

Emulate the French, and flavor food with what they call a bouquet garni. This generally consists of a bay leaf or two, a few parsley stems, a sprig of rosemary or thyme, tied together with a long piece of string for easy removal or tie dried herbs or spices in cheesecloth bag. Add to long-simmering dishes at start of cooking, removing at end.The Italians have a great last minute way of flavoring stews and soups with what they call a gremolata, a mixture of grated lemon rind and parsley (I add grated garlic), sprinkled over soups and stews at the end of the cooking.

Spices

As pointed out, spices come from buds, seeds, stems and bark of various aromatic plants, often tropical in origin. They can be bought whole or pre-ground. My advice is to buy a spice grinder and grind them yourself, if you will. This has nothing to do with the zealous food writer who claims that grinding your own is a "privilege" but because they are more aromatic and longer lasting. In any event, I suggest that you avoid pre-ground nutmeg, ginger (the roots of which can both be grated) and the powdered bay leaf, all poor substitutes. It is often recommended that whole spices be toasted briefly in a hot, dry skillet before grinding or before adding whole to the dish to bring out the flavor. Indian cooks will often add these spices to the oil in a sauté pan, an effective way of flavoring the oil. If fat is too hot, however, they will burn. Watch this. Store them openly (see herbs). Give them a sniff now and then to make sure they are still aromatic and do not emulate a neighbor who tells me that she has had hers for 12 years.

Allspice, Cumin, Curry Powder

To begin this limited list, allspice is well named, with taste traces of nutmeg, cloves and cinnamon, a great seasoning as are the other spice listed above. Add a pinch of any of them to sautéing fat destined for just about anything. This, plus a squirt of anchovy paste (see anchovy) will give your dish exceptional flavor. Season flour coatings, say for fried chicken, with any of them. Tie the whole spices in cheesecloth bag and insert in long simmering dishes.

Curry, incidentally, is only available in powdered form. True Indian curry is made out of many spices. I suggest that you make your own, if you wish to go through the trouble. You could try the Indian spice mixture Garam Marsala.

Cinnamon, Nutmeg, Cloves

In this country, we generally reserve both cinnamon and nutmeg for desserts. Not so in Europe, particularly Spain where cinnamon is used in anything you can name, too many, I would say. However a good pinch added to a meatloaf mixture is effective. You can also use the whole stick cinnamon. A nutmeg grater is a handy gadget. I use nutmeg in place of mace, its outer cover. As for cloves, I substitute allspice, reserving the so-called nails for studding whole onions which go into long cooking dishes.

Ginger

For any purpose other than baking, I prefer to use the gingerroot. It can be frozen, taken out of freezer and grated into long simmering dishes. Use with restraint.

Bay Leaf

By all means use the leaf rather than the powdered and buy the imported rather than the domestic. If single leaf is inserted into say, a stew, be sure to remove it before serving.

Capers

Capers are the soft buds of a Mediterranean shrub and are effective seasoning when mashed into a sauce or perhaps vinaigrette. Sometimes they are packed in brine or in salt, in which case they have to be first rinsed.

Mustard

Rather than the dry powered try the prepared -type Dijon.

Pepper

Ground peppercorns quickly lose their zip so grind in pepper mill as needed. The white, black and green peppers are berries which come from the pepper vine, each in varying stages of maturity. The white is often used by those who wish to avoid specks of black pepper in a cream-colored dish (this does not bother me). The soft green can be mashed and added to sauces.

As for the commonly used black, let your taste be your guide. The powerful cayenne and pepper flakes come from the chili pepper and along with Tabasco and hot pepper sauce should be treated with respect. Use the last two by the droplet. The mild supermarket paprika serves for little more than a garnish. For flavor, try the hot imported.

Saffron

Saffron comes from the stigma of the autumn crocus blossom. The fact that there are only a few per blossom and very little is called for per recipe. Buy the threads rather than the powdered. Dissolve in a little liquid and add to a simmering rice dish, such as paella and you will not only have added flavor but will have turned the rice a pleasant yellow.

Salt

With current admonitions in mind and my feeling that if you do not salt at the beginning of the cooking, you might as well forget it, I now salt lightly at the start and as additional ingredients are added and also at the end, to taste. While I will use any type at hand - sea, kosher, or the boxed supermarket - my preference is the kosher. It is often pointed out that if coarse salt is used during baking it will not dissolve properly.

The Anchovy

While Europeans certainly know its value, I am not sure that we do. You can use the canned fillet or the more convenient paste. Add a squirt when stirring vinaigrette or to your sautéing fat along with the spices mentioned above. If using the canned fillet, first rinse, dry, chop and more or less melt in the fat.

Try this when sautéing young spinach and I will guarantee exceptional flavor. There is no discernible fishy taste. A recent dinner guest went on about his dislike of the anchovy, only to ask me why the salad dressing was so good. No, I did not tell.

Garlic

For blanching, peeling and chopping, see chapter on how to chop vegetables. When added to a substance, garlic has the ability to bring out its flavor without inflicting any of its own, that is, if used with a certain amount of restraint. While I do not agree nearly as far as some Spanish friends who use whole head daily, I use it every chance I get. For flavor, try adding a whole unpeeled head at start of soup or stew, mashing a clove in the vinaigrette. When boiling potatoes destined for mashing, add peeled clove or two, running through ricer with potatoes.

Many recipes begin with softening a clove of garlic in oil. This has been gone into thoroughly under the heading "sauté." For those who wish to soften the flavor of garlic, their tops can be cut off, drizzled with oil, and wrapped in aluminum foil, and baked in a moderate oven for a half an hour or so to soften. The skins can be easily removed by squeezing each clove. They can then be added to any dish you wish.

Lemon Juice

Always squeeze your own juice, forgetting the bottled. What could be more versatile than lemon (or lime) juice? It keeps simmering mushrooms white, peeled fruit from discoloring. It goes into sauces and can replace vinegar in the vinaigrette. The addition of juice and rind can pep up a "tired" stew or soup. It has a well-known affinity for seafood. If fish is marinated more than a half an hour or so, the juice can start to cook your fish and throw off your timing. Watch this. The South American appetizer ceviche is an example. Raw fish is marinated overnight in lemon or limejuice, and if refrigerated overnight, it will be edible the next day.

Vinegar

Vinegar, too, has properties. It is used to deglaze a sauce, of course in vinaigrette and like lemon juice, to add flavor to a tasteless dish. Some will use the very expensive aged balsamic vinegar. I would settle for the fine Spanish sherry vinegar. You will not find it in your local supermarket but certainly in special shops. As it is expensive, save it for sauces and salads. For other purposes, use a lesser wine vinegar.

Vanilla

Vanilla is something special. It has the ability of making the substance to which it is added taste more so. That is, sweet dishes seem sweeter, fruit tastes more like fruit and chocolate like chocolate. Avoid the artificially flavored in favor of the pure extract. While chefs prefer the vanilla pod, I will settle for the extract. The seedpod will give you a more intense vanilla flavor. Beans are slit and both pods and seeds scraped out and both added to, say, custard. They can be strained out, rinsed off, dried and reused.There are various bottled spices which should not be forgotten: Worcestershire, Tabasco, hot sauce, not to mention juniper berries.

Onions

While onions cannot be classified as herbs or spices, they certainly cannot be omitted under seasonings. They can be used in many ways, raw or cooked. Countless recipes begin with softened or browned onions. (see the section "Sauté.") An effective way to flavor soups, stocks and stews, is to insert whole, peeled onion studded with a clove or two.

Chutney

This is a very effective seasoner. Rather than make my own, I settle for the English Major Grey's Mango Chutney, wonderful in a fruit salad dressing.

Tips on cooking

Serving Tips

Our winter fruits and vegetables are reasonably varied and we have our own fine summer produce to look forward to. Our choice of winter fruit includes pears, melons, and bananas all year round and of course apples. The first crop arrives in the fall and they are then at their best. I see little reason for the expensive, tasteless, shipped-in peaches and strawberries. This also goes for winter ears of corn. For scraped corn dishes, frozen kernels can be substituted. I find frozen peas a treat in January.

Select these fruits and vegetables with care but not necessarily with the same zeal exhibited by the thrifty European housewives who will take the time to go over a bunch of grapes one by one.

Now this is not going to be a down-on-the-farm, mother's chicken-salad sort of thing but what you make yourself is bound to be better than what comes in a can or wrapped in plastic. Furthermore, there are no lists of additives, excess salt, sugar nor fat content. I am not suggesting that you corn your own beef, make your own sauerkraut or even jellies or jams but such relatively simple tasks as your own spaghetti, tomato and chocolate sauces, apple sauce, soups, gravies, your own grated cheese. Do avoid (my pet peeves) bottled salad dressing, minute rice, both garlic powder and salt, bottled lemon and lime-juice.

An attractively served, or, as they say, presented meal cannot make up for the poorly cooked but it can certainly point up a good one. I am not one who believes in reserving the nice china and silverware for the dinner guest.

Watch your color combinations. An all-white platter of, say, mashed potatoes, cauliflower and creamed chicken is not particularly appetizing. Do not overload plates as though serving a noonday farm dinner.

Hot foods should be served hot, cold foods, cold but not too cold. While salad greens should be crisp and cold, they must never be icy. You may have to remove them from refrigerator shortly before serving to accomplish this. The same applies to chilled, marinated vegetables, fruits and cheese. In the winter, heat dinner plates in turned-off oven.

One sauce per meal is ample. Should you top asparagus with a Hollandaise sauce, think twice about serving a custard dessert? If you have sprinkled the veal with cheese, do not do so on the scalloped potatoes as well. Add garnish of chopped parsley to one dish only. In short, do not repeat yourself.

Freezing Tips

Take advantage of meat sales to stock your freezer. Beef, lamb and pork freeze well, much better than chicken or turkey, I would say. Wrap food to be frozen securely in heavy-duty foil or commercial freezer paper. And the most boring reminder of all, both label and date packages.

Keep freezer at zero degrees. You will read that lamb and beef roasts can be kept frozen for a year. This drops to three months for ground meat, chicken livers and gizzards. I prefer a six-month turnover for all other frozen food. Never defrost frozen food at room temperature. Either do so overnight in refrigerator on in the microwave oven.

If you plan to buy shrimp and freeze them, check with your market. Much of the shrimp that comes in has been frozen and then defrosted by the market. You certainly don't want to refreeze previously frozen shrimp without first cooking them. Much of the shrimp that comes in has been frozen and then defrosted by the market. While raw tomatoes do not freeze well, it can be done if you plan to use them in cooked dishes such as soups or sauces, not for salads, as follows: Freeze good, ripe summer tomatoes on freezer plate, bag and store in freezer. When ready to use, frozen skins will slip off easily.

When planning to serve so-called one-pot dishes such as soups, stews, gumbos, get into the habit of doubling amounts and freezing balance-short term. These are of course nice to have on hand for guests, expected or unexpected or perhaps for nights when you do not feel like cooking. I consider the curried lamb stew, pork and curried lamb stew, pork and bread stew, vegetable soups and of course gumbo, (all of which see) suitable for company dinners.

Storage Tips

Canned goods, such as fruits, vegetables and meat have a shelf life of varying estimates, depending on acidity and how they were stored. I like to keep mine for a year only, not that they will necessarily spoil but that their taste will disintegrate. Bulging cans spell danger; always discard them.

Briefly, both granulated sugar and semi-sweet chocolate bits are our most enduring staples, good for two years, a little less time for unsweetened chocolate. Both brown and confectioners' sugar has a shelf life of only four months. All flours are good for a year. I prefer to keep rye, whole wheat and, by all means, water or stoneground cornmeal in the refrigerator.

Pantry Shelves

Well-stocked pantry shelves are indeed an asset, as are refrigerator, freezer and vegetable bin. Seasonings, which, of course should be included, are gone into under that heading. This basic list (no frills) should take you a long way.

Baking needs: both all-purpose and cake flour, stone-ground cornmeal, cornstarch, a vegetable shortening, such as Crisco, yeast, baking soda, cream of tartar, and baking powder.

Sweet: various sugars, granulated and brown (keep brown refrigerated), Vermont maple syrup, honey, corn syrup, chocolate, various nuts (you can go a long way with pecans and almonds; refrigerate the shelled), various dried fruits, gelatin.

Canned goods: imported Italian plum tomatoes, tomato paste (plus sun-dried tomatoes), anchovies (plus the paste), artichoke hearts, baby clams, hearts of palm tuna, both beef and chicken broth (for when you run out of your own stock), red kidney beans (for a fast soup), coffee, tea and buttermilk powder. Bottled goods: tomato juice, clam juice, olives, olive oil, a vegetable oil, if you fry, various vinegar, perhaps white and red wine, the Spanish sherry wine vinegar, mayonnaise. Packaged: rice, pasta, couscous, grits, dried beans, cereals, crackers and cheeses. Keep the latter in warmest part of the refrigerator.

How to Chop Potatoes

A food processor takes care of chopping, slicing, and shredding. Unless many vegetables are involved or it is a matter of slicing potatoes paper-thin or slicing cabbage, say for coleslaw, I will do them by hand. It is faster than assembling processor and subsequent clean up; a mandolin can also be used for this. The cheaper plastic is perfectly acceptable. For pureeing certain vegetables such as those to be used in gazpacho, I prefer the vegetable mill, as it does not turn them into a mish-mash. To peel, cut off thin slice from bottom and place on board, cut-side down. Holding vegetable with one hand, fingertips curled under, make thin, successive, vertical cuts across vegetable from front to back with the other hand.

Onions

A fast way to chop onions is as follows:

1. Peel onion, leaving root end intact. Cut in half through root and stem end. Lay one half on board, cut-side down, root end away from you.

2. Make thin successive downward cuts across face of onion from one side to the other, stopping short of the root end but going all the way through to the board.

3. Holding knife horizontally, slice horizontally from top to bottom, still stopping short of root end.

4. Repeat step two, again, cutting vertical slices from one side to the other. Onion will now be properly chopped. Repeat with other half.

Cutting into Julienne Strips

To cut into julienne is to cut food into thin, matchstick-sized strips. Carrots, potatoes and chicken breasts come to mind.

The carrot serves as a perfect example. Not only does cutting into julienne improve its appearance but somehow seems to make it taste better. To this end, first scrape carrot, cutting off ends. Cut off thin strips from one side so that it can lie flat on board. Make long, thin vertical cuts from top to bottom. Mound two of these slices on top of one another and slice, again from top to bottom, into 1/8 inch thick strips. Repeat. Strips can now be cut into any length you wish.

Garlic and Mushrooms

As a garlic lover, I prefer the texture of the chopped to that which has been through garlic press. First of all, with a number of garlic cloves to be peeled, blanch by first dropping them into a pan of boiling water to cover for a good minute. Drain, refresh under cold running water and slip off skins. If only a few to peel, give each a whack with bottom of skillet. Skins will break and can be removed. To chop, mound peeled cloves together on cutting board and sprinkle   with good pinch of salt. Hold sharp heavy knife over them. With one hand, hold tip of blade down to the board. With the other, grasp handle of knife and move blade back and forth over garlic in a fanlike motion, tip of blade still held down. You will have to stop now and then to scrape scattered garlic pieces together. Continue this fanning motion until garlic is thoroughly chopped. Mushrooms are chopped in the same way but are not first peeled.

Herbs

Herbs, stems removed, can be chopped on board with sharp knife. Leaves of the leafy, basil, for example, can be rolled up and chopped, known as a chiffonade. However I find it easier to cut herbs directly into dish with kitchen scissors. One final note, emulate Chinese cooks and chop or slice vegetables into neat slices of approximately the same size. This will certainly improve the appearance of your dish and they will cook at the same speed.

How to make herb butter
Herb Butter

1 stick or ½ cup unsalted butter, softened

¼ cup chopped parsley
1 tsp. dried or fresh thyme
1 ½ tbsp. lemon juice
1 small minced garlic clove
½ tsp. salt and twisting of black pepper

Mix butter, garlic, and parsley together until well blended. Add salt and pepper and mix. Using plastic wrap, roll herb butter into a tight cylinder, (about the size of a quarter)) and refrigerate until firm. This will keep for a week or a month if frozen.

Measures

Unlike the professional baker who will weigh rather than measure ingredients, I weigh both flour and sugar only in cake making, having learned from past experiences. Measuring equipment, other than scales, consists of measuring spoons and metal (rather than plastic) measuring cups in the proper 1, 1/3, ½ and ¼ cups sizes. Measuring level should be at top of cup, that is, no overhang.

To measure flour, first stir it up in bag or canister with fork, for aerating purposes. If, for example, 1 cup is called for, measure by scooping flour gently from container with 1 cup measure, or spoon gently into cup, no pressing down, leveling off surface with back of knife. Do not shake cup nor tamp down flour. Granulated sugar can be measured in the same way while brown sugar can be tamped down into cup.

I sift only when recipe so directs or when making cakes and when baking powder is to be added to flour. Biscuits are an example in which case, scoop out flour as above, add baking powder and sift into mixing bowl.

Save time by learning to measure small amounts of dry ingredients, such as sugar, flour and salt, in the palm of your hand. However, this does not apply to either baking powder or soda, which should be measured accurately. For years I have been thickening gravies by scooping flour from bag with my fingertips (see gravy).

Dry measurements
3 teaspoons = 1 tablespoon
4 tablespoons = ¼ cup or 3 ounces
5 tablespoons plus 1 teaspoon = 1/3 cup

8 tablespoons = ½ cup or 4 ounces
10 tablespoons plus 2 teaspoons = 2/3 cup
16 tablespoons = I cup or 8 ounces.
Liquid Measurements
1 cup liquid= ½ pint or 32 oz.
2 cups liquid=1 pint or 16 0z.
4 cups liquid=1 qt. or 32 oz.
1/2 pint=1 cup or 8 oz.
2 pints or 1 quart. =32 oz.
4 quarts = I gallon or 64 oz.

Butter

At the risk of sounding like an idiot, myself that 1 pound of butter, I still have to remind: 4 sticks - equals 2 cups, 32 tablespoons, 16 ounces and even more taxing, that 1 stick is the equivalent of ½ cup, 4 ounces, or 8 tablespoons.

Miscellaneous Equivalents

Apples

1 apple, sliced (3 medium) yield 3 cups.

Beans, Dried

2 cups dried white beans (1) yields 6 cups cooked.

Breadcrumbs

2-1/2 slices of bread, crusts removed, processed, yield 1 cup.

Cabbage

You can get more mileage out of this vegetable than almost any other can.
3 cups shredded = ½ cup

Carrots

1 medium carrot weighs 2- ½ to 3 ounces and 1, sliced, 3 ½ to 4 cups.

Cheese

1/2 cups grated = 2 ounces.

Cream, (heavy)

1 cup yields 2 cups whipped.

Eggs

Using large eggs, 1 white weighs 1   ounce or 2   1 large yolk, ½ ounce or 8 to 11 whites will fill one cup.

Onions, Shallots

One medium onion weighs 2-1 /2 to 3 ounces. 1, sliced, yields 3- ½ to 4 cups.

Potatoes, (sweet)

3 medium or 1, yields 3 cups.

Potatoes, (white)

3 medium potatoes equal 3 cups or 1 sliced.

Rice

1 cup of raw rice, when boiled or steamed, equals 3 cups.

Tomatoes

1 tomato will weigh from 4 to 5 oz.
1 lb. of fresh, peeled, chopped yields 1-1/2 cups.
A drained, 28-ounce can of plum tomatoes yields 3 cups.

The Well-Equipped Kitchen

It was not always this way. I started out in a cramped kitchen, almost no counter space, unreliable equipment. All entertaining took place in the living room, which meant my rushing back and forth in order not to miss the living room cocktail talk.

Through the years, there have been changes. My present kitchen has turned into a family room, a repository for friends, grandchildren and dogs alike, the cocktail talk transferred to the kitchen. So keep your priorities in mind and decide what you want of a kitchen.

While the number of skillets and saucepans can be reduced if cooking for yourself alone, basic requirements are pretty much the same whether for few or many. If you have been cooking for a while, some of the following equipment has no doubt seeped in. If not, buy it as you need it, your golden opportunity to start out with the best. Expensive, yes; but with proper care, it should last a cooking lifetime.

Saucepans

Forget the lightweight aluminum saucepans which tend to stick and scorch in favor of heavy, sturdy, cast-aluminum, lined with stainless steel, or stainless steel with copper bottoms.

Ideally, you will need: a small pan of 3 or 4 cup capacity, if only for melting butter or heating up a cup of liquid, a general purpose of 2 quarts, 4-quart for vegetables and soups and if into large amounts of stock or pasta, some 9 or 10 quarts, all with lids. I find the old-fashioned double boiler essential if only for certain custards (the Spanish flan comes to mind), or for melting chocolate. Steaming? Both steamers and/or steaming racks which fit into saucepan are available.

Skillets

The above-mentioned materials, cast-aluminum lined with stainless steel and the stainless steel with copper bottoms can be recommended. However, my top favorite is the cast-iron and I know of no better material for the sauté. You will need three skillets, material of your choice, a 5, 7 and 10 inches in diameter measured across the bottom, also with lids. You will hear that the addition of an acid, wine or vinegar to an iron pan will cause a sauce to discolor; I continue to make brown sauces in mine and have done so for years. As for the non-stick skillets, I use so little fat in the sauté pan that I forego them. I use my seasoned cast iron pots in lieu of the nonstick, cooking both steaks and lamb chops in a hot dry skillet without any fat at all.

Oven Cookware

Take good care of them. Some come with directions for first conditioning or seasoning, a simple matter of heating up oil in them. Some clean theirs by scouring with kosher salt. I wash mine in soap and water (never in dishwater) and am careful when it comes to drying, doing so by setting pan over lowest of stove-top heat, then rubbing with a few drops of oil. Never run water over a hot skillet as it will crack.

For roasting, you want a sturdy roaster- with rack, preferably enamel-over-iron of some 17 by 12 inches in length. Casseroles of the same material, which can be used both in oven and on stove-top, are recommended and are nice enough to bring straight to the table, a real plus. Add oval gratin dish (same material), say for scalloped potatoes, small metal baking pan or two and porcelain soufflé dish, which can also be used for puddings

Beating and Chopping Tools

For beating in general, eggs, cream and the like, my preference is the hand-held electric beater or, for adding or blending one substance into another, the wire whisks. Unless very much into cakes, I see no particular need for a heavy-duty electric mixer nor even a blender. A small food processor, yes. To reiterate, certain vegetables are better pureed in food mill than in processor used primarily for pureeing. I also use a small vegetable or food mill for this purpose as it not only does so less thoroughly but strains as well, good for gazpacho.

Of course, a processor can be used to knead bread, mix a pie dough and for chopping or slicing vegetables. A mandolin is a handy gadget for slicing vegetables paper-thin.

Knives

You want knives of professional quality even if you have to go to a restaurant supply store to achieve this. Both carbon and stainless steel can be recommended. My preference is the stainless steel, as it does not stain as does the carbon steel.

You will need a so-called chef 's knife, a utility knife of 6 inches, a good paring knife, serrated bread knife, a carving knife, plus sharpening steel, and, of course, a cutting board, preferably of wood or plastic.

Treat knives well, that is, use a knife rack rather than letting them rattle around in drawer, never put them in dishwasher, wash and dry right after using and no cutting on a surface harder than wood. Keep them sharp with the steel and an occasional professional sharpening. Consult your butcher.

Miscellaneous Equipment

I recently came across a pre-Revolutionary will in which cups and saucers were considered valuable enough to be listed. It would be interesting to know how an early settler would have regarded the following rather extensive list. In addition to the above knives, your cutlery needs should include vegetable peeler, measuring spoons, a wooden spoon or two, ladle, both long-handled spoon and fork, wire whisk, metal and rubber spatula, the latter for folding beaten egg whites into a substance, skimmer for removing scrum from a stock.

And what about an apple corer, coffee and tea pot, lemon zester, fruit reamer, coffee and spice grinder (if you grind your own), poultry shears, kitchen scissors, mortar and pestle, tongs, potato ricer, pepper mill, nutmeg grater, can and bottle opener, corkscrew, large and small sieve, colander, four-sided box grater, sharp biscuit cutter, cheesecloth for making bags for the herb bouquet, not to mention mixing bowls and measuring cups? As for the garlic press, I feel it so intensifies the flavor that I would say forget it.

While I could conceivably live without the apple corer and lemon zester, I am not sure that I could cook without an instant read meat thermometer, candy thermometer for syrups and custards, mortar and pestle, the above mentioned vegetable mill, plastic gravy deglazing pitcher, sometimes called a gravy separator (see deglazing) and, of course, a salad spinner, a pure gadget but a great help when it comes to drying salad greens.

To go a few steps further, could you make cakes without cake pans, small scale for weighing flour and sugar, pies without rolling pin and tins, cookies without cookie sheets, breads without bread stone and lastly, muffins without tins? At the risk of being called microwave illiterate, I use my microwave (a gift) for three reasons: defrosting (very effective), heating up a cold cup of coffee and cooking bacon (the best way).

3

STOCKS

If I seem carried away on the subject, it is because I firmly believe that if there is a secret to good cooking, homemade stock could very well be it. Taste and flavor are essentially what we are after and there is no better way to get it.

Define stock as a concentrated broth, made by covering chunks of beef, veal, fowl or fish, flavorings and aromatic vegetables with water. Simmer together for several hours or until the flavor exchange has taken place, that is, when vegetables and meat flavors have been extracted into the liquid.

How is it used? It adds a great deal of flavor to stews, braised dishes, sauces and is the prime ingredient in soups. Your alternatives are a good grade of canned beef or chicken broth (broth, not bouillon nor consommé') or plain water. I will use the canned if out of my own stock but I draw the line when it comes to using the canned in soups. There is a discernible taste difference, no excess salt, sugar, fat nor additives. While stock requires no particular culinary skill, it does take time, even though the time is largely unsupervised, a good job for a rainy Sunday. As it freezes well, it is not something that has to be done on demand.

The following directives appear to the point of tedium and should be kept in mind.

Simple or White Stock

Here are some guidelines:

1. Always simmer a stock, pan partially covered, never letting it boil. If pan is left uncovered, stock can reduce to the point of nothing while if tightly covered, it can sour.

While recipes will call for boiling down a weak stock to concentrate the flavor, this is not done until stock is made and degreased.

2. As even a gentle reduction can intensify the natural salt content of the meat, salt lightly during the last hour of cooking, again at the end.

3. Never cover a hot stock as it comes to room temperature (nor any other hot food, for that matter).

4. As stock cooks, remove surface froth with spoon or spatula to ensure a clear stock.

5. Chill finished stock overnight (this time covered) or long enough for fat to congeal on surface for easy removal.

6. And last of all, always bring a frozen stock to the boil before using.

The two types of meat stock are the simple or white and the brown. The simple is made as defined above, simmering chunks of meat and vegetables in water. Ingredients for the brown are first browned, followed by simmering for several hours.

Chicken Stock (2   quarts)

As all the following simple stocks follow the same procedure, chicken stock will serve as an example. A good habit to get into is to save and freeze chicken bones and carcasses. These can be added to the supermarket chicken but be sure to defrost the frozen bones before adding. You will need:

3 supermarket chickens, backs and wings
1 spring fresh thyme
3 stems parsley
1 onion, unpeeled, studded with 2 clove nails
1 bay leaf
1 carrot, scraped, sliced
1 celery rib, sliced
6 peppercorns
2 garlic cloves, peeled

Rinse off chicken parts and place in large soup kettle. Cover with cold water by some 3 inches. Bring slowly to the simmer. Be prepared to skim off any rising froth. Add balance of ingredients. Partially cover pan, leaving inch or so exposed.

Keep at a gentle simmer for 2 hours or more. The longer the simmering, the richer the stock but the lower the yield. Add boiling water if liquid level drops appreciably. Salt lightly during last hour of simmering, and to taste at end of cooking.

Strain through colander, pressing down on solids which will be discarded. Bring to room temperature (uncovered) and refrigerate overnight (this time covered) or as long as it takes for fat to congeal. Remove fat. Taste and if it seems weak put back on stove and boil down or reduce to strengthen flavor.

After fat has been removed, stock can be kept in refrigerator only a week and has to be brought to the boil every three days, but if fat has not been removed, stock can be kept a week as is until used.

Use or freeze in small manageable amounts. I find large muffin tins convenient for this purpose.

Double Chicken Stock

This is my favorite because of its strong flavor. Try it in the fast chicken soup (which see). Proceed as for chicken stock but instead of covering chicken pieces with water, cover with your own chicken stock, recently made or frozen and defrosted. An hour or more of simmering should take care of this.

Better yet, poach a small whole chicken in your own stock (see poached chicken). Remove chicken when fork-tender, some minutes later for 3-pound chicken. You not only have a wonderful broth but chicken for a meal, perhaps chicken pie, salad or hash.

Turkey Stock

This too, is made like the chicken stock, substituting roasted turkey carcass for the chicken pieces, simmering for several hours, chilling and degreasing. Rice cooked in this stock makes a great turkey soup.

Fish Stock (2 quarts)

Simplest and fastest of all, this is nice to have in your freezer for possible fish soup, fish-poaching liquid or for gumbo. Ask your fish dealer for

3 lbs. of fish scraps, bones, heads and (no gills) from lean, white-fleshed fish
6 cups of water
1 cup of dry white wine
1 slice of lemon
1 sprig of rosemary
4 peppercorns
several small strips lemon peel
3 sprigs fresh thyme
1 bay leaf
6 parsley sprigs
3 carrots, sliced
3 celery ribs, sliced
1 onion, unpeeled, studded with 3 clove nails
He will give them to you free of charge but you may have to order them a day ahead. It's a good idea to save and freeze your shrimp shells; they will give additional flavor if added to this stock. Rinse off scraps and cover with 6 cups water. Add white wine, slices of lemon, sprigs of fresh rosemary, thyme, bay leaf, parsley, 4 peppercorns, sliced carrot and celery rib, 3 clove nails inserted into small unpeeled onion.

Bring to a slow simmer; turn down heat, this time pan uncovered. Barely simmer for 30 minutes. Taste for salt at the midway mark and again at end. Strain and chill. I have not gone into Court Bullion or Vegetable stock, as it is made in the exactly same fashion as the above fish stock, minus the fish bones and the addition of a few more spices.

Simple Beef or Veal Stock (2 ½ quarts)

Other than substituting 3 lbs. each beef bones and chunked beef for the chicken and letting it simmer for 3 or 4 hours, the procedure is the same as for the simple chicken. I do not make this stock, preferring the chicken for soups.

Brown Chicken Stock

This can be done in the oven exactly as below in brown beef stock. This also can be done in the sauté pan but the oven is easier.

Brown Beef Stock

While this can certainly be used to advantage in beef stews, I find that its strong flavor masks that of the vegetables in vegetable soup. It is indispensable in making the classic brown sauces but be forewarned, there is still another step before the sauce is made, demi-glace (see brown sauces).

Meat, bones and vegetables for this stock are first browned in a hot oven, followed by several hours of simmering. Preheat oven to 450 degrees. You will need:

3 lbs. meaty beef bones
2 carrots, scraped
2 celery ribs with leaves
3 lbs. cubed beef from the tough, inexpensive shank
1 bay leaf
1 sprig fresh thyme or rosemary
1 onion, peeled
1 whole head garlic, unseparated, unpeeled
2 celery ribs
6 parsley stems
10 peppercorns

6 qts. water
Meat and bones go into large, shallow, lightly greased roasting pan in one layer. Place this in preheated oven. The idea is to turn ingredients a rich brown. Roast for 15 minutes (total roasting time will be 50 minutes)

Now add onion, carrots, celery and continue to roast for an additional 10 minutes At this point, turn meat and vegetables over to brown on other sides. Allow some 25 minutes more.

Now with the aid of tongs, remove ingredients to large soup kettle.

Deglaze roaster by setting it momentarily over high heat. Add 1 cup of hot water and scrape up and dissolve brown bits of food on pan bottom. Do not be concerned about fat in roaster as stock will later be chilled and degreased. Pour contents of roaster into the soup kettle. Add garlic, herb bouquet, parsley, and peppercorns and water to cover by 2 inches. From now on, the procedure is the same as for simple stock. Bring to the simmer and continue to do so, gently, partially covered, for 3 or 4 hours. Salt lightly when halfway through cooking and again at end. Strain, chill and degrease.

Glacé de Viande or Meat Glaze

Should you care to proceed further, you can make what is called Glaze de viande, in which case the beef stock is reduced to a jelly. It is then cut into cubes and added to make a wonderful brown stock. If you were to reduce half the yield of the above brown stock, you would end up with about a cup of the glaze. This is not as discouraging as it sounds when you consider that this will give you 2 quarts of reconstituted stock at the rate of 1 per cup of hot water. A small dab will do wonders for a sauce or gravy and it is most certainly a space saver.

Proceed as follows: put the amount of stock, chilled and degreased, in a smallish saucepan and bring it to just under the boil and turn down to the merest simmer, pan uncovered. This takes time and it will have to be carefully watched. As stock reduces, move it to a smaller saucepan. It will visibly start to form a syrupy mass, which will coat the back of a metal spoon. Immediately take off heat. As it cools, it will harden into something resembling a hard jelly. Cut into cubes and freeze.

Jus Lié (Quick Brown Stock)

2 cups stock
2 cups coarsely chopped mushrooms
2 tbsp. arrowroot
3 cups water

Heat stock with mushrooms. Bring liquid to boil and simmer uncovered for 15 minutes. Dissolve arrowroot in water and stir to dissolve. Simmer 5 or 6 minutes and strain.

4

SOUPS

For purposes of flavor, countless dishes start with directions to soften aromatic vegetables - leeks, onions, carrots, celery and the like - in a little hot oil.

There are also countless ways to make a soup. Add more vegetables plus stock and you end up with minestrone (see below), broccoli, a broccoli soup, squash, a squash soup and so on ad infinitum. You can thicken with beans, pasta or rice. You can puree or not puree. Be careful if you puree in blender. They have been known to erupt hot soup over the user. Keep covered, if only with a dish towel.

Neither kind nor proportion of vegetables is especially important. Make use of those you have on hand and be sure that you have plenty of them. This is only one of many kinds of minestrone. It is elastic.

For thickening purposes you can puree half the soup and return it the balance or add a can of pinto beans, rice or pasta. I prefer soup crammed with vegetables. If you think to soak beans overnight, you can add fresh beans, and much better, but remember it will take them 2 hours to cook.

If you have a large enamel-over-iron casserole, you can soften your vegetables in it and add the boiling liquid. If not, after sautéing, vegetables can be added to the boiling stock and cooking continued.

Meat soup

A more American vegetable soup consists of covering meat soup bones with water and simmering several hours. Strain, reserving meat. Chill, degrease. Add the following:

2 tsp. tomato purée
2 cups tomato juice
1 diced potato
1 diced tomato
½ cup barley
several broccoli flowerets
¼ cup corn kernels

During the last few minutes, add broccoli flowerets and corn.
Fish soup

There are many ways to make a fish soup. Like vegetable soup, neither propositions nor ingredients are particularly important. You can substitute at will. Flavor is what you are after. As the soup is hearty, try it for a winter Sunday dish. With it you will only have to serve a green salad, a good loaf of bread and a bottle of wine.

If you have fish broth in your freezer, it becomes easy as you can prepare the vegetables ahead and freeze them also. As a matter of fact, you can freeze them both together but do not cook seafood until ready to serve. At serving time, all you have to do is defrost and cook the seafood –a matter of minutes. As I have always said, if having guests, do everything you can possibly do ahead of time. If a new cook, guests can be frightening and even old hands have to give it a little thought.

3 tbsp. oil
½ cup each finely chopped onion, leeks (white part), carrots, celery
2 cloves garlic, finely chopped
2 cups peeled, diced tomatoes or 2 cups canned Italian plum
¼ tsp. each salt and pepper

pinch each ground cumin and allspice
6 parsley stems, tied together
4 cups fish broth
1 lb. white-fleshed fish cut into bite sized pieces
½ lb small shrimp, shelled
½ lb bay scallops
2 chopped fresh herbs
Chopped parsley

Heat up empty skilled over low heat. When warm, add the oil and when it heats up, add the vegetables except for the garlic. Cover skillet and cook over low hear for some 15 minutes. Add garlic and cook 1 more minute. Add tomatoes, salt, pepper to taste, the ground spices and parsley stems. Uncover and simmer for 10 to 15 minutes or until vegetables are soft. Remove parsley stems. Add this vegetable mixture to the 4 cups fish stock and bring to the simmer. Drop in fish pieces and simmer for 1 minute. Add shrimp and herbs and cook two minutes more. Add scallops and cook for an additional minute or so. Season to taste and serve.

You can now do one or two things. If you like a thick soup, you can puree the vegetables or leave them as they are. Once again, a food mill is preferable of you have the time and who does? So if you process, do so very briefly. If the soup is too thick, thin it out with a little hot milk or more stock. Remove bay leaf and parsley stems if you haven't pureed. In any event, bring the 4 cups of stock to the simmer and add the vegetables. Drop in fish pieces and simmer 1 minute before adding cleaned shrimp and herbs. Give them 2 minutes. Add scallops, which should be done in a minute or so. Season to taste and serve.

Irish chowder

After sautéing vegetables (no tomatoes used) purée and add ½ cup mashed tomatoes to thicken. Then also cook a piece of mackerel in reserved broth. Remove bones and puree what is left.

Vegetable Soup

2 medium potatoes
2 small young turnips

half a butternut squash, deseeded
2 small parsnips
1 carrot
1 celery rib
1 medium onion, chopped
3 tbsp. glacé de viande
salt and pepper to taste
6 parsley stems
sprig rosemary
1 unpeeled onion, studded with several cloves
1 whole garlic head, unseparated
chicken   stock, in water or simple beef stock.
1 pinch each ground allspice cumin and anise seed
2 or 3 tbs. olive oil
1 ½ cups Italian plum tomatoes
1 ½ cups shredded cabbage
1 ½ cups zucchini, unpeeled, cut into thin slices
16 oz. can pinto beans
1 cup broccoli flowerets, stems removed, divided into flowerets
2 cups corn kernels, fresh or frozen fresh herbs

Peel and chop potatoes, turnips, squash, parsnips and carrot. Dice celery. Tie piece of string around parsley stems for easy later removal. Put all of these in a 3-quart saucepan.

Dissolve glacé de viande in small amount of boiling water. Add this to saucepan with 6 cups of cold water.

Add the salt, pepper to taste. Bring to boil and partially cover with lid. Immediately turn down heat and allow soup to barely simmer for an hour. If the liquid reduces appreciably, add a little boiling water.

The next step is to soften the onion. Soften might be a better term than sauté as the onion must not brown. Place empty skillet over low heat for five minutes or so. When warm, add fat, only enough to film bottom of skillet. Add chopped onion and cloves garlic. Cover pan and cook over low heat for 10 minutes or until onion softens. Even though the heat is low, at has a way of heating up, so if it starts to sizzle, be prepared to take pan off heat momentarily.

Raise heat just a bit and add tomatoes. Cook, this time uncovered, for an additional 10 or 15 minutes, mashing them down with fork now and then, assuming that the soup has simmered for its allotted hour, season tomatoes and onion and turn contents of skillet into the soup. Continue to simmer partially covered, for 40 minutes. Soup will have simmered for a total of an hour and 40 minutes before green vegetables are added.If you do not with to use any fat at all, there is a way out. Instead of softening onion in fat, simmer them in a small amount of water, add tomatoes and proceed as above.

Prepare green vegetables. Shred cabbage finely. Cut and add zucchini, broccoli flowerets, fresh or frozen (easier) corn. The timing for the vegetables is as follows: cabbage will take 10 minutes. Add pintos at the same time. The zucchini will take 5 minutes, the broccoli, herbs and corn, 2 or 3. Remove garlic head, parsley stems and clove-studded onion before serving.

Easy Vegetable Soup

2 onions, peeled, chopped
3 garlic cloves
1 celery rib, chopped
2 leeks, peeled, chopped
2 cups tomato juice
2 zucchini, sliced, not peeled
¼ tsp salt and pepper
2 carrots, sliced, peeled
1 tbsp. chopped parsley for garnish
1 bouquet garni (4 parsley stems, bay leaf, sprig rosemary)
4 rounds lightly toasted bread topped with olive oil and
15 oz. can tomatoes
While the customary

way is to first sauté your vegetables and then   add to your stock, this is quicker and easier. Wash and chop vegetables. Bring the stock and juice the liquid to the boil and add the vegetables, herb bouquet and garlic. Reduce heat and cook uncovered 30 or 35 minutes. Puree with care as blenders have been known to overflow. Do a small amount at a time, covering blender bowl with towel. It has been suggested that you will have better luck if you add the soup with the machine running. Pour into serving bowls topped with bread rounds.

Minestrone

The secret to this is more vegetables than you think you will need.

1 chunk salt pork, rind removed, blanched in boiling water for ten minutes, rinsed, drained and cut into small pieces
1 sliced onion
1 garlic clove, mashed
2 diced tomatoes
12 cups stock
3 sliced celery stalks
1 shredded lettuce
3 sliced carrots
1 cup shredded cabbage
1 ½ cups or lbs of green vegetables such as peas, green beans, etc.
1 drained can pinto beans
½ cup grated parmesan cheese
3 fresh basil leaves
½ cup broccoli flowerets
½ cup corn.

Sauté salt pork gently in just enough oil to keep it from sticking. When crisp, add onions and cook very slowly until soft but not brown, during last 5 minutes or so add garlic. Add this to the 12 cups stock with the tomatoes and the potatoes. I was once told by a vegetarian woman in Rome that potatoes keep the color of the other vegetables.

Simmer this for an hour or so, partially covered, having added the lettuce, carrots and celery. 20 minutes before serving, add green vegetables and 10 minutes before, sprinkle with cheese and slivered basil leaves.

Sometimes when making a small amount of soup, say with 3 cups of stock and fewer vegetables, I will add two cups hot milk during the last 10 minutes of cooking and pour the soup over a buttered slice of bread in each soup plate.

If you really want taste, add this to simmering soup: make a paste of a small piece of salt pork, parsley, very small onion, small piece of carrot, celery and a good squirt of anchovy paste, garlic clove. Sauté lightly and add to simmering soup.

A more American vegetable soup might consist of covering meaty soup bones with water and simmering several hours. Strain, reserving meat. Chill, degrease. Add:

2 tbsp. tomato puree
2 cups tomato juice
1 diced potato
1 diced tomato
1 handful of barley

During the last few minutes, add broccoli flowerets and corn.

Carrot Soup

1 carrot, thinly sliced
1 tbsp. each butter and olive oil
1 large onion finely chopped
3 garlic cloves, minced.
3 cups chicken stock
½ tsp. nutmeg
½ tsp. each anise seed and cayenne

Steam carrots until tender, about 10 minutes. Reserve steaming water. Soften the fat. Add garlic at the last minute, and there is nothing worse than browned garlic. Puree onion and carrots in the steaming liquid, put these in a saucepan. Add chicken stock and seasoning. Heat through and season to taste.

Cakik

This is another cold soup for a hot day. I have heard its origin described variously as Armenian, Bulgarian and Turkish. Mix and chill for an hour or two:

1 tsp. salt
1 small cucumber, peeled, minced
1 cup plain yoghurt
1 cup chicken stock
2 minced garlic cloves

1 tbsp. lemon juice
1 tbsp. oil
½ cup chopped walnuts
2 tsp. each chopped parsley and dill
¼ tsp. pepper

Salt minced sliced cucumber and let sit for 20 minutes. Drain and rinse.

Mix 2 cups each yoghourt and, chicken stock, add garlic lemon and oil. Add cloves, minced garlic and chopped walnuts.

Garnish with pepper, parsley and dill.

Fast Chicken Soup

This soup can be put on the table in a matter of minutes. Use your strongest chicken stock, preferably double chicken stock (which see). Toast one slice of bread per serving lightly in oven. Butter bread and spread heavily with grated cheese. Place 1 slice in each serving bowl. Pour over boiling stock and sprinkle with parsley. Season to taste.

Bread and Tomato Soup

This soup is so good that I find myself freezing tomatoes in mid summer in order that I may have this in the winter months. In-season tomatoes can be frozen on freezer plate and used for soups and sauces, not for salads. If your tomatoes are not the best, substitute tomato juice for some of the water.

1 medium onion, chopped
¼ cup olive oil
2 cups tomatoes, peeled and seeded
1 tsp. tomato paste
7 cups water
5 slices or Italian bread
10 basil leaves, chopped
4 garlic cloves, peeled

Soften medium onion chopped in the olive oil, until soft. Now add peeled, seeded and quartered tomatoes and tomato paste for color.

48

Simmer together for 15 minutes. While tomatoes are simmering, heat up water and add slices of   Italian bread, a good handful chopped basil leaves and peeled garlic cloves. Cook and stir until mixture becomes quite mushy. Add the tomato mixture. Taste for seasoning, mix well.

Gazpacho

Your gazpacho will only be as good as your tomatoes. Do not use the above frozen tomatoes for this.

Friends in Seville assure me that this is the "true" gazpacho, but this might not hold true in, say, Malaga or Cordoba. The abandon with which a Spanish housewife uses olive oil never ceases to amaze me. They also thin out soup with water. I prefer a thicker soup so I will leave this to your discretion.

This can be accomplished in two ways. You can first process sliced not peeled vegetables and then put them through a food mill, which takes forever. I prefer to peel and slice the vegetables and process in a blender or processor but not too thoroughly, that is, not to a mish-mash. You will need:

2 slices French type bread
2 lbs. red ripe tomatoes
1 large cucumber
1 large green pepper
3 garlic cloves
1 medium sweet onion, diced
¼ cup good olive oil
4 tbsp. vinegar
¼ cup cold water

Begin by soaking the bread in water just to cover while you cut up the vegetables. Put these into the blender and purée, in which order is not important, just as long as you process the bread, the soaking water, oil and garlic together. Add oil drop by drop as if for mayonnaise, beating with fork or in blender. Stir in vinegar, salt and water. Season to taste and chill for several hours or if time is short, add ice cubes.

White Gazpacho or Sopa de Ajo Blanco

This is great cold soup for a hot day but is forewarned. The flavor of garlic is pervasive even though I have reduced the amount in a Spanish friend's recipe from 5 to 3 cloves. You will need:

1 cup blanched almonds, white or slivered
1 small bunch Thompson's seedless grapes
3 cloves garlic
4 tbsp olive oil
3 thin slices or Italian type bread
4 tbsp. vinegar
½ tsp salt
1 diced hard-boiled egg
Soak almonds in water just to cover in refrigerator overnight. Process or blend almonds, their soaking water; add garlic and grapes to the soaking water. Remove mixture to bowl. Add salt, bread and 2 cups water including soaking water. Again process briefly, grapes included. Beat in oil. Stir vinegar into mixture and chill.

The grapes are optional, but they add an interesting flavor. Garnish the soup with sautéed croutons or sieved hard-boiled egg yolks, one per serving, or even a few grapes.

Claiborne's Buttermilk Soup

1 ½ cups cooked, chopped shrimp
½ cup sliced cucumber
4 cups buttermilk
1 tsp. dill
1 tsp. salt
1 tbsp. sugar

Another good, cold soup. Add all ingredients to the chilled buttermilk and serve.

Onion Soup

3 cups onions, sliced

1 tbsp. sugar
½ tsp. salt & pepper to taste
3 tbsp. butter
1 heaping tbsp. flour
1 cup dry white wine
1 quart boiling beef or chicken stock
2 tbsp. oil
¼ cup dry sherry
3 rounds of hard toasted good bread
1 cup grated Swiss cheese
Turn down heat and cook covered for 15 minutes. Add salt and sugar, turn up heat and cook until onion caramelized to deep brown, an important step.

Add flour and stir for some 3 minutes. Off heat add the wine, boil down a bit, add the stock and simmer partially covered for 30-40 minutes. Add sherry. Toast bread in 350-degree oven until brown.

Soup can go into ovenproof bowl or casserole or, if you happen to have earthenware soup cups, by all means uses them. Top with bread, sprinkle with cheese, and bake 15 minutes or so until golden.

This makes a great luncheon dish accompanied by a salad.

McCall's Lentil Soup

1 cup dried lentils, rinsed, picked over and soaked in 4 qts. water for one hour

1 tsp. salt
¼ each dried thyme and marjoram
4 minced large onions
4 sliced carrots
½ cup olive oil
2 fresh or canned tomatoes (peeled and chopped if fresh)
¼ cup chopped parsley
2 tbsp. dry sherry
2 tbsp. grated Swiss cheese or gruyere

Add salt, thyme and marjoram to soaking lentils. Bring to boil, reduce to a simmer, cover and cook for an hour.

Heat up oil in skillet over moderate high heat. Reduce heat, add onions and carrots and cook slowly for 10 to 15 minutes until vegetables are tender. Pour skillet contents into lentils. Add parsley, tomatoes and sherry. Cover and simmer another hour or until lentils are tender and most of the liquid is absorbed.

Pour in heated tureen and sprinkle over cheese.

Spanish Garlic Soup

This is another Spanish specialty often made with water. I say use chicken stock.

½ loaf of stale bread broken into walnut-sized pieces.
4 garlic cloves, peeled and chopped
3 tbsp. olive oil
1 tsp. paprika
¼ tsp. ground cumin
salt to taste
4 cups chicken stock

Heat up oil over moderate heat. Add garlic pieces and cook slowly for a minute or two. So not let them brown. Remove garlic with spatula and set aside.

Add bread to the oil and let pieces brown slightly. Take skillet off heat for a few minutes before adding paprika, cumin, the reserved garlic and the chicken broth. Simmer gently until bread softens. Do not let it disintegrate.

Another Garlic Soup

1 cup minced onions, chopped
1 clove garlic, minced
2 tbsp. butter
2 tbsp. mushrooms, minced
1 diced celery rib

1 parsnip, diced, peeled
1 tbsp. flour
1 qt. chicken stock
¼ tsp. each white pepper and salt
2 cups light cream
½ sliced mushrooms
2 egg yolks
2 chopped chives
Soften onions in butter. Add ½ lb. of the mushrooms and cook until they release their juices. Now add the other ½ and cook 3 more. Add flour and cook for 2 min. Add stock, season and cook for 20 minutes. Add cream. In separate bowl, beat yolks with 1 cup of the hot stock. Put   this back in soup, stirring. Do not let it boil. Add chives.

Garlic Soup (still another version)

1 ½ heads garlic, separated
3 medium onions, chopped
1 ½ tbsp olive oil
1 ½ cans tomatoes
3 cups beef broth
1 ½ cups water
salt and pepper   taste
4 ½ slices bread
1 cup croutons of toasted bread

Drop   garlic into boiling water to cover for 1 minute. Rinse under cold water and slip off skins. Thinly slice onions and lightly sauté for 6 minutes. If you are going to use canned tomatoes, use 1 ½ cans and process them. Leave in work bowl and pulse chop of slice garlic into the tomatoes. Put all of this in saucepan and bring to boil. Simmer, covered for 40

Toast cubed bread in 350 degree oven for 10 min.   Process.   Ladle soup into bowl and sprinkle with   croutons.

Inquirer's Cream of Mushroom Soup

1 cup minced onions, chopped
½ cup mushrooms, sliced

½ mushrooms, minced
1 ½ tbsp. flour
1 clove garlic, minced
1 parsnip, diced, peeled
1 diced celery rib
2 tbsp. butter
1 qt. chicken stock
¼ each white pepper and salt
2 cups light cream
2 egg yolks
3 chopped chives

Soften onions in butter. Add ½ of the mushroom and cook until they release their juices. Now add the other ½ and cook 3 minutes more. Add flour and cook for another 3 minutes. Add stock, season and cook for 20 minutes. Add cream. In separate bowl, beat yolks with 1 cup of the hot stock. Put this back in soup, stirring. Do not let it boil. Add chives.

Fish Fumet and Soup

A fish can be poached in salted water, a mixture of bottled clam juice and dry white wine of a fish stock or more properly, fish fumet. There is nothing wrong with salted water unless you wish to boil it down to make a sauce. There is also nothing wrong with the clam juice and wine mixture which either can be boiled or a sauce base or reduced to a syrup glaze.

5

SAUCES

The idea behind a sauce is to enhance a fine dish, not as some will tell you, to cover up an inferior one. The rich, classic sauces are certainly not designed for everyday use the pan sauces will take care of that. Reserve the classic for special occasions. If you are interested in cooking, my feeling is that you should know how these sauces work, part of one's culinary training.

With Gaelic logic, they have divided the more than 200 sauces into 6 families or groups. They are: white, brown, tomato, emulsified, (hollandaise and béarnaise) mayonnaise and vinaigrette. There are also pan, dessert and butter sauces. These groups or families are headed by so-called mother sauces. Like a genealogical chart, each mother has her own sauce descendants based on her characteristics.

White Sauces

I find these sauces boring but as they turn up all the time, such as in the soufflé base, they are almost impossible to avoid. White sauces have two mothers, Béchamel and Velouté. The difference between the two is that the B6chamel is made with milk, the Velouté with chicken stock. These two have numerous sauce descendants. To name a few, add cream to a Béchamel and it becomes a sauce crème, cream to a Volute and you have a sauce supreme, both eggs and cream, a sauce parisienne. Cheese added to either produces a sauce mornay, tomatoes, a sauce aurore. Both white and brown sauces are based on what is known as a roux, a mixture of butter and flour cooked together to a paste. A liquid is then added. The roux will thicken the liquid which will constitute your sauce. A so-called white roux is used for the white sauces, one in which the flour/butter mixture has not been allowed to color while the roux destined for a brown sauce is first browned before liquid is added. Both Béchamel and Velouté come in 3 thicknesses. The thickness is determined by the ratio of flour to the liquid, not by the amount of fat. The thinnest, used for cream soups calls for 1 tbsp. of flour, 1 tbsp. butter to 1 cup liquid, The medium thick, general purpose, for 1-½ tbsp. flour, 1 to 1 cup liquid and the thickest, the soufflé base, for 3 tbsp. flour, 1 of butter, and 1 cup liquid. Thick or thin, the procedure is the same. Melt butter over moderate heat in heavy-bottomed saucepan and let it sizzle briefly. Add flour and stir for several minutes with wooden spoon. Scald milk or stock. Take saucepan momentarily off heat; let it sit for a minute. Add half the hot liquid. Whisk well and pour in the balance. Set saucepan over moderately high heat, stirring constantly as it comes to the boil. Turn down to the simmer and stir for some 5 minutes. Visiting men have been known to refer to an improperly cooked roux as library paste.

Other Sauce Thickeners: Slurry and Beurre Manié

There are several ways of thickening sauces made from simmering or braising meat. If one cup of liquid is to be thickened, mix one of arrowroot or cornstarch in an equal amount of cold water, or if you wish sherry or liqueur. This can be added to the hot liquid and stirred until thickened. This is known as slurry. And then there is the beurre manié, which consists of equal amounts of butter and flour mixed with fingers until thoroughly amalgamated. One of each will thicken one cup of liquid. I find it easier to mix the butter and flour together in a bowl, add a little of the hot stock, mix thoroughly and pour back into saucepan. Simmer briefly until properly thickens.

Brown Sauce

Brown sauces descend from what is known as demi-glace, a long-simmered, thickened, flavored brown beef stock (see below). You have all manners of sauce descendants. Add Madeira to the demi-glace and you have a sauce madère, mushrooms, a sauce duxelles, white wine and pepper, a sauce diable, white wine and mustard, a sauce robert. Top a meat dish, say a fine steak or broiled chicken with any of them and you will have produced something special.

Demi-glace

The true demi-glace on which the brown sauces are based is so complicated and time-consuming, requiring a day or two of simmering, reducing, re-simmering, and straining that I do not think you will find it short of our best restaurants. The following is considered an acceptable shortcut, should you wish to try it. But be forewarned. Not only do you have to start with brown beef stock, (liquid or the meat glaze, hopefully stored in your freezer) but you must then make the demi-glace and after that the sauce, the easiest and fastest part. Is it worth the effort? Try it once. You may become a convert.

For the demi-glace, you will need:

3 tsp. butter
I tbsp. oil
small celery rib
1 chopped onion
1 carrot, finely minced
4 cups strong beef stock
4 tbsp. flour
2 tsp. tomato paste
1 clove mashed garlic
herb bouquet
salt and pepper to taste

Begin with a brown roux. Heat up butter and oil in heavy skillet and slowly soften onions, carrots and celery for some 10 minutes. In this instance, you can let them color slightly. Add flour, stirring constantly until it turns a golden brown. Do not let it burn. In another saucepan, bring the stock almost to the boil. Take skillet momentarily off heat and whisk in half the stock, followed by the other half.

Back on low heat, add tomato paste, garlic and herb bouquet.

Cover partially and simmer very slowly for some 2 hours. When ready, it will just coat back of spoon. Tilt pan and skim off any fat. Strain, pressing down on solids and season to taste. If you feel that it is too thick, thin out with a little hot stock. Remove herb bouquet. Yield will be around 2 cups. Keep in mind that very small amounts of the finished sauce are required for topping a dish but it is difficult to make the demi-glace in small amounts as it reduces by half. While you can increase ingredients, it can be frozen only for two weeks. You are now in a position to make all manners of sauces.

They generally finish their sauces with what is known as a butter enrichment which might seem excessive in this fat conscious age. Should you wish to do so, cut tablespoon of soft butter into   pieces.   Take finished sauce off heat and drop in one of these pieces. Shake and swirl pan until butter has been incorporated. Repeat this operation, one piece at a time until all butter has been added and absorbed. You will see that butter has definite thickening properties.

Sauce Duxelles or Mushroom Sauce

Consider this a representative brown sauce and one of the better. Begin by snapping off stems of ¼ mushrooms. Quickly rinse off caps under running water and dry thoroughly with paper, towels. It is important that they be dry. Those who suggest simply wiping off mushrooms with a damp cloth are obviously not familiar with the pervasive odor that emanates from mushroom soil.

Mince caps and 2 tbsp. of shallots. Over moderately high heat, saut6 them in 2 tbsp. of butter and 1 of oil, stirring and shaking pan. After 5 or 6 minutes, mushrooms will have begun to brown and lose their juices. Add ¾ cup of dry white wine and boil down to a tablespoon or two. Add cup of demi-glace, tsp. tomato paste, tbsp. finely chopped herbs and simmer for 5 minutes. Season and pour sauce over meat, chicken, fish or whatever.

Deglazing or Pan Sauces

These sauces are made from the pan drippings after meat, fish or fowl have been sautéed and removed from skillet. They are delicious and unlike- the classic sauces can be used on a routine basis. They are not particularly rich unless you do as the French, enriching with a final pat of butter. Remove sautéed food to warm platter and skim off most of the fat from skillet, leaving a tablespoon or two and the brown bits of meat in the bottom of the skillet. Deglaze with ¼ cup of red or white wine, reduce it and add perhaps ½ cup of stock and reduce again. Season and pour over food.

To reiterate, you must be very careful when adding an alcoholic beverage to a hot sauce or a hot skillet. To avoid flaming, take skillet temporarily off heat, and add beverage. You have many options. You might begin by sautéing of chopped garlic or one tablespoon chopped shallots for 1 minute before adding the liquid. You can deglaze with wine only and season with lemon juice, capers or Dijon mustard. And best of all you can first soften shallots and then add, say, a half cup of mushrooms and brown lightly; then add and reduce dry wine or sherry, and follow with stock as above. If you sauté steaks and lamb chops in a dry skillet as I do, you can remove them from skillet when done, add a pat of butter, heat it up and proceed as above.

Gravies

Pan gravy has been thoroughly gone into in the chapter on beef. Briefly, cooked roast is removed from roaster. Pan juices and fat are poured into what is called a deglazing pitcher or gravy separator, (plastic cup with long, samovar-like spout) in which fat will rise to the top, pan juices remaining on bottom. A little fat is poured back in heated up roaster, flour and subsequently pan drippings and a liquid are added all of which will constitute your gravy. Giblet gravy can be found in the chapter on chicken.

Mushroom Sauce Duxelles

¼ lb. diced mushrooms
2 minced shallots

2 tbsp. butter
½ tbsp. oil
½ cup of dry white wine
1 ½ cups brown sauce
1 ½ tsp. tomato paste

Mix mushrooms, minced shallots and sauté in half the butter and oil for 4 or 5 minutes. Add dry white wine and reduce to almost nothing. Stir in brown sauce and tomato paste and cook for 5 minutes. Season to taste and off heat, beat in softened butter, parsley and herbs.

A Lesser Duxelles

This is more of a flavoring than a sauce. It is quick, easy, keeps in the refrigerator for a week or two and is delicious as a fish stuffing or coating. It is made exactly as the first duxelles up to a point. Mushrooms and shallots are sautéed, the wine added and boiled down as above. It is now ready for stuffing or coating. Due to salmonella, recipes for the egg yolk sauces, béarnaise, hollandaise and mayonnaise will have to wait. You might experiment with a commercial egg substitutes

½ lb. finely minced mushrooms
2 chopped shallots
2 chopped garlic cloves
4 tbsp. butter
¼ cup dry white wine.
1 sprig parsley
1 sprig thyme
1 tbsp. lemon juice
¼ cup cream

Sauté finely minced mushrooms, shallots, garlic in butter, med. high for 2 minutes. Increase heat and cook 5 minutes. Add dry white wine. Reduce by half. Add parsley, thyme, lemon juice. Simmer 5 minutes. Add cream and thicken for 30 seconds.

Tomato Sauce

If good local tomatoes are not available, use the canned Italian plum tomatoes. Remember that tomato sauce freezes beautifully.

½ small chopped onion
2 tbsp. oil
2 chopped garlic cloves
3 lbs. chopped tomatoes
¼ tsp. each salt and pepper

Soften onion in oil for 10 minutes. Add garlic cloves and cook 1 more minute. Now add tomatoes. Add salt, pepper to taste and cook uncovered for 20 minutes. Put through food mill. Back on low heat, check seasonings again and add a handful of finely chopped basil leaves and cook a few minutes more.

Bologna Meat Sauce (3 cups)

1 tbsp. olive oil
3 tbsp. butter
1 chopped yellow onion
1 chopped celery stalk
1 chopped carrot
1 tsp. salt
¾ lb. ground lean chuck
1 cup dry white wine
½ cup milk
¼ tsp. nutmeg
2 cups canned tomatoes with juice

Sauté onion in oil and butter   until just translucent.   Add celery and carrot. Cook for 2 or 3 minutes before crumbling meat into skillet. Stir in salt and cook only until meat just loses its raw look.

Turn heat down to medium, add milk and nutmeg, cooking until milk has evaporated, stirring. Add tomatoes, continuing to stir.

When tomatoes start to bubble, turn down heat to merest simmer for minimum of 4 hours.

Galangal from Café De Paris in Geneva

1 piece galangal, a type of blue ginger root

½ tsp. each curry and paprika
½ dl. of cognac
1 garlic clove
juice of 1 lemon
50 grams shallots
¼ tsp. salt
¼ tsp. thyme
¼ tsp. tarragon
¼ tbsp. parsley
¼   tsp. cayenne

Mix dry ingredients in mortar. Add lemon to make paste. Dilute with cognac. Serve over fish or eggs

Salsa Picante Catalana

3 pinches saffron
2 garlic cloves
½ oz. each almonds and hazelnuts, minced and toasted
½ tsp. of cayenne pepper
1 sprig parsley
¼ cup sherry
1 cup stock

Pound dry ingredients in mortar. Add sherry and a little water to make paste. Dilute with stock. Serve with fish, meat or fowl.

Red Sauce

1 large pepper
¼ tsp. each paprika and salt
1 garlic clove
1 hard boiled egg yolk
1/3 cup olive oil
½ lemon juice or ½ cup wine vinegar

Pound dry ingredients in mortar. Add egg yolk and lemon or vinegar to make paste. Dilute with olive oil.

Blender Hollandaise

large yolks
¼ tsp. cayenne
4 or 5 tsp. lemon juice
2 sticks butter, melted and cooled
½ tsp salt
Put yolks, salt, pepper and lemon juice in food processor. Turn on and then immediately off. With motor running, add butter in steady stream. Can be kept warm in top of double boiler, covered, over warm, not hot water.

Blender Béarnaise

2 tbsp. minced shallots
3 large egg yolks
¼ salt
2 sticks melted and then cooled butter
¼ tsp. white pepper
1 fresh or ½ tsp. dried tarragon

Salt, pepper, tarragon and vinegar go in saucepan. Over moderately high heat, reduce to 1 tbsp. Add eggs and briefly turn on machine, on and off. Machine back on, add butter in steady stream.

Mayonnaise

This recipe will make 1 ½ cups mayonnaise. Unlike commercial mayonnaise, there are no preservatives, so I make it in small quantities. Here are a few admonitions:

1.Egg yolks should be at room temperature; the beating bowl rinsed out with hot water and thoroughly dried.
2. As egg yolks can absorb just so much oil at a time, add oil slowly.
3. Once you start beating egg yolks, do not stop until eggs start to thicken.

1 egg yolk
1 tbsp. lemon juice or vinegar
¼ each salt and pepper

½ cup each good olive oil and salad oil

Beat egg yolks with salt and pepper a minute or so. Start adding the oil almost by droplets. You can relax and start adding it by tablespoons as soon as it starts to thicken. Add lemon juice or vinegar and at the very end and a tbsp. of boiling water. Chill.

Sauces to Try

Curry

Heat up 2 tbsp. butter. Add 2 shallots, 1 tbsp. curry. Cook 1 minute and add chopped golden delicious apple, ½ cup stock, 1 tsp. tomato paste. Cook over moderately high heat for 3 minutes or until reduced to ½ cup.

Add ¼ cup heavy cream and cook 2 minutes. Spoon over and sprinkle with almonds.

Pesto

Process 3 oz. and set aside. Put 2 garlic cloves in work bowl, plus 3 tbsp. pine nuts and ¾ tsp. salt. Gradually add ½ cup oil, motor running. Add 4 basil leaves, 1 cup firmly packed parsley, tarragon and process about 30 seconds or to a paste. Add cheese and process for 5 seconds.

Wolferth

Mix 4 tbsp. parsley, good squirt of anchovy paste, 1 crushed, drained and rinsed capers, chopped garlic clove. Add vinegar and beat in 6 oz. oil.

Horseradish Sauce for Cold Meat

Mix bottled horseradish, prepared mustard, few drops of vinegar and fold into whipped or sour cream - all to taste.

Wine and Cream

In saucepan cook together 2 garlic cloves, 2 shallots, ½ cup dry white wine. When reduced by half, add chives, parsley, 2 tbsp. lemon juice, and ½ cup cream and simmer a few minutes. Cream can be omitted.

Pine Nut Sauce for Roast Chicken

½ tsp. cumin seeds, crushed
3 oz. pine nuts
½ liter chicken stock
1 garlic clove
1 hard boiled egg yolk

Crush cumin seeds, garlic, and add to pine nuts. Add 1 hard boiled egg yolk and make a paste with a little chicken stock. Put in saucepan, add rest of chicken stock, simmer 10 minutes.

6

Salads

When I was a child, green salads tossed with vinaigrette did not enter into it. They were either considered "rabbit food" or part of the mystique, only to be tossed at the restaurant table by a somewhat intimidating waiter. How food habits have changed.

Whether you serve them as a first course, with or after the main course, the precepts are the same. As with all simple dishes, every step of a salad counts. Clean, crisp greens, a good olive oil and good vinegar are musts. My preferences are the expensive, so-called extra-virgin (first pressing) olive oil and the superb Spanish sherry vinegar, both to be used exclusively for salads and sauces. Without either, I would settle for fruity Spanish oil, available in our supermarkets and good wine vinegar.

The three grades of olive oil are extra virgin, virgin and pure olive oil. Other than the expensive balsamic and the fine Spanish sherry vinegar, it is a good idea to experiment until you find a wine vinegar to your taste. Apple cider vinegar is used in my kitchen only for potato salad.

My limited personal lettuce preferences run to the tender Bibb or Boston but do not let this deter you from trying them all. For a salad, you will need 2 cups of torn-apart greens per person, less if other ingredients are involved.

Place lettuce head or heads, tough portions discarded, in a big bowl of lukewarm water, plunging them up and down with your hands. Again with your hands, (your best tool) transfer them to a colander. Rinse out bowl, refill it with water and return lettuce leaves to bowl. Repeat this procedure, plunging and draining until there is no grit in bottom of bowl.

A salad spinner for drying lettuce is a gadget worth owning. Otherwise you will have to pat leaves dry thoroughly in a succession of paper towels. The leaves are then torn into serving pieces, rolled in fresh paper towels, enclosed in a dish towel and chilled until ready to use. This can be done a day ahead if having a party but vinaigrette is better made and the salad tossed just before serving. Remove lettuce from refrigerator just long enough to take off chill. Add vinaigrette and toss with your hands.

Caesar Salad

This is a rich and gala salad, one that lends itself to tossing at the dining room table, all ingredients having been assembled beforehand. I prefer to toss mine in the kitchen, leaving the culinary flourishes to the restaurants.

Serve it before, with or after the main course or do as I do and make it the main focus of a luncheon or light supper, serving it with a loaf of bread, preceded by a soup, followed by dessert. As romaine is not one of my favorite, I will often substitute Bibb lettuce, 2 heads. Of course, if it matters to you, you no longer have a traditional Caesar salad.

1 large head romaine lettuce
7 tbsp. good olive oil
1 egg
2 tbsp. bacon, diced
2 tbsp. grated cheese
1 tsp. minced garlic
1 ½ slices bread
2 tbsp. lemon juice
2 tsp. vinegar
¼ tsp. salt
¼ tsp. pepper
½ tsp. Worcestershire sauce
1 tsp. Dijon mustard
4 anchovy fillets or anchovy paste

Begin by washing, drying and tearing lettuce into bite-sized pieces. Chill. Heat oil in a small saucepan with the minced garlic over lowest possible heat. When warm to the touch, take pan off heat and let it steep or at least 30 minutes, longer if you have the time. Coddle egg. Drop it in boiling water to cover. Take pan off head and let egg stay in water for exactly 4 minutes. Set aside. Sauté bacon until crisp. Drain on paper towels. Grate cheese. Remove 1 tbsp. of the garlic flowered oil and rub over the bread slices. Cut into ½ inch pieces. These go into preheated 350 degree oven and should be lightly toasted in about 8 to 10 minutes.

The dressing is made as follows: Mix in mortar (or process in food processor) the lemon juice, vinegar, salt and pepper, Worcestershire and mustard. Mash in anchovies or 2 good squirts of anchovy paste. Slowly whisk in oil almost drop my drop. Pour over greens in salad bows with the grated cheese and toss lightly with your hands. Sprinkle over croutons and crumbled bacon.

Picadillo

This simple salad is common place in Southern Spain and is not to be confused with the Latin American dish of the same name.

Arrange thinly sliced peeled tomatoes, strips of skinned green bell peppers (see below) and thin slices of red onion on a pretty platter. Pour over vinaigrette. You might add crushed cumin seed, if you wish. Enclose in Saran wrap and chill for several hours.

How to skin bell peppers; put whole peppers under a hot broiler for 8 minutes or until charred. Turn at intervals to make sure that they char evenly. Remove from oven and put the hot peppers in a paper bag. Close bag and let steam for 10 minutes. If skins do not pull off easily, run under cold water. Marinated strips are very good on a vegetable hors d'oeuvre platter.

Vinaigrette

The French call this mixture of oil and vinegar (or sometimes lemon juice), vinaigrette, while we often refer to it as dressing. Proportion of vinegar to oil varies according to taste. The most generally used is three parts of oil to one of vinegar. 6 tbsp. of oil to 2 of vinegar (½ cup in all) which should take care of 4 salads. You want only enough to moisten greens, not to drown them.

¼ clove of peeled garlic
½ tsp. salt
¼ tsp. pepper
½ tsp. anchovy paste
2 tbsp. wine vinegar or lemon juice
6 tbsp. oil

Mash clove of peeled garlic, salt and pepper, almost to a paste in mortar. Stir in a small squirt of anchovy paste, wine vinegar or lemon juice. Beat in oil with fork, almost by droplets. This can be done in the food processor in the same sequence but the amount-- is so small and the time involved so short, that it hardly seems worth while.

Fruit Salad Dressing

¾ cup olive oil
1/8 cup each wine vinegar and lemon juice
1 tsp. salt
½ each dry mustard and paprika
1 tsp. Worcestershire sauce
1/8 tsp. catsup
1 grated onion
1 tsp. horseradish
2 tsp. sugar
1 clove garlic

Mix olive oil, wine vinegar and lemon juice, salt, mustard and paprika, Worcestershire, catsup, grated onion, horseradish, sugar and clove garlic. Remove garlic before serving.

Greek Salad

Toss lettuce, raw vegetables, Mediterranean adornments such as the black olives, capers in a vinaigrette, sprinkle with Feta cheese and call it a Greek salad.

½ cup vinaigrette

1 small zucchini, sliced
1 head Boston, washed
6 radishes, sliced
1 head lettuce torn into small pieces
2 scallions, finely minced
1 small red onion, thinly sliced
8 minced tomatoes
1 tbsp. drained capers
3 tbs. fresh basil chopped
10 black olives, sliced
1 green pepper, cut into rings
¼ tsp. each salt, pepper
½ cup crumbled Feta cheese

Toss the above vegetables with the vinaigrette. Scatter over crumbled cheese.

Spinach and Mushroom Salad
1 ½ pounds of tender young spinach
¼   cup small mushrooms
½ cup vinaigrette
1 ½ tsp. prepared Dijon mustard
2 slices bacon, cooked, crumbled

Wash spinach (see lettuce above). Dry well.   Strip off stems and tear leaves into bite-sized pieces. Rinse mushrooms briefly. Dry. Slice thinly. Combine the two. Season. Toss with the vinaigrette. For a spicier effect, after mashing garlic for dressing, add prepared Dijon mustard. You might sprinkle with a few slices of cooked, crumbled, crisp bacon.

Chicken Salad

The chicken flavor in this recipe predominates, no added pineapple   nor sour cream. You can poach a chicken breast for this recipe but a 3 ½ to 4 lb. chicken will yield roughly 1 quart of meat plus a good strong stock.

3 ½ to 4 lb. chicken

2 cups chicken stock
2 tbsp. chopped parsley
bay   leaf

1 tsp. each fresh basil or thyme
1 tbsp. lemon juice
1 grated onion
2 cups of finely chopped celery
1 tbsp. capers, rinsed and drained
½ cup chopped walnuts
2/3 cup of mayonnaise
4 to 6 lettuce leaves
2 hard-boiled eggs
4 to 6 tomato wedges
salt and pepper to taste

Place chicken in sauce pan and cover with cold water. If you plan to turn the cooking liquid into a chicken stock, add various aromatics, such as peppercorns, salt, parsley, bay, onion, carrots, celery, fresh herbs, basil or thyme and garlic. If you do not want to bother with the chicken stock, you can get away with the salt, peppercorns and the clove-studded onion, although the chicken will not be as flavored.

As pointed elsewhere in this book, boiling and poaching are   not   the same thing. Bring chicken to just under the boil and immediately turn down heat to the merest simmer, uncovered. That is to say that there is only an occasional bubble breaking on the surface. Chicken should be fork-tender in about 45 minutes. Take pan off heat and let chicken cool in liquid. The chicken is now usable but the stock should be refrigerated overnight o long enough for the fat to rise to the surface. Remove bones and thrown them in the stockpot.To process with the stock, remove and discard fat. As there is now no fat to become incorporated in the stock, it can be boiled down to strengthen the flavor after which, it should be strained, re-chilled and frozen. The stock will not be very strong to begin with but it certainly will be suitable for soup.

My chicken salad is as simple as can be as I believe in letting the chicken flavor predominate. Shred meat with your fingers or cut into pieces with scissors. Season to taste with salt and pepper. Sprinkle over lemon juice and a good grating of onion. (Use grating side of 4-sided grater.) Add chopped celery, rinsed-off capers, and chopped walnuts.   Fold in mayonnaise or enough to moisten. Chill covered for an hour or two. Serve on a bed of lettuce leaves, garnished, if you wish, with hard-boiled eggs halved, or perhaps tomato wedges.

Cuisinart Creamy Garlic Dressing

1 garlic clove
6 tbsp. oil
1 tbsp. light cream
2 tbsp. vinegar
1 egg
¼ tsp. pepper and mustard to taste

Process garlic oil, light cream, vinegar, egg, pepper and mustard to taste.

Potato Salad

I learned to make this form an old German woman who was famous for her potato salad in her town. There is a secret; it is in slicing the potatoes thinly, not dicing nor chopping them and serving the salad warm.

6 potatoes, scrubbed
1 sliced small onion
2 chopped celery ribs
¼ cup water
¼ cup cider vinegar
1 tbsp. olive oil
2 tbsp. mayonnaise
½ cup chopped parsley

Cover potatoes with cold water and bring to the boil. Turn down heat, cover and simmer until just fork-tender. Do not let them overcook. Drain and allow to stand for 20 minutes or until cool enough to handle. If too warm, they will crumble when sliced. Peel and slice on the large slicer of a 4-sided grater. Do the same with a smallish, peeled onion. Add chopped celery ribs.

Bring water and cider vinegar with 2 tsp. salt to the boil in saucepan. When it reaches the boil, pour over potatoes. If there is an excess of liquid in bottom of bowl, pour it out. Add olive oil followed by mayonnaise. Fold in chopped parsley.

Be sure to serve warm.

Cole Slaw

This is a very simple recipe and like the potato salad, the taste is dependent on how the vegetable, in this case, of course cabbage, is cut up. The slicing disk of a food processor is perfect for this job.

1 cup of cabbage
¼ tsp. celery salt and celery seed
1 onion, small
2 tsp. dried dill weed
2/3 cup or more of mayonnaise

First remove any wilted outer cabbage leaves, leaving as much green as possible. Remove core and cut into lengthwise quarters. Rinse off well under running water and pat dry. A salad spinner will take care of this chore. Slice or process with small onion. Season   to   taste with both celery salt and celery seed. Add dried dill weed. Fold in mayonnaise. Cover and chill for an hour.

Waldorf Salad

This is an old fashioned salad.   My apple choices for salads are Gravenstein,   Golden or Red Delicious as they do not discolor.

2 cups apples, peeled and diced
½ cup lemon juice
2 cups celery, finely minced
1 cup chopped walnut
1 ¼ cups mayonnaise

Sprinkle diced apples with juice of a lemon.   Combine with minced celery, chopped walnut and just enough mayonnaise to make a creamy mixture. Taste for any necessary salt. Cover and chill for an hour or so. Serve in individual bowls on chilled lettuce leaves.

Shredded Carrot Salad

A fast salad can be made in this fashion:
2 cups carrots, shredded

½ cup vinaigrette
½ tsp. Dijon mustard
¼ tsp. cumin
4 lettuce leaves

Shred carrots on box grater; dress with vinaigrette to which you have added Dijon mustard and cumin. Serve on lettuce leaves.

Tabouleh

1 cup couscous
½ cup parsley
1/3 cup mint, minced (or 1 of dried)
½ cucumber, peeled, seeded, chopped
½ cup each minced green pepper and minced scallions, tops included
2 large tomatoes, peeled, seeded, juiced
1/3 cup each lemon juice
¼ tsp. each salt and pepper
¼ cup olive oil
2 heads of romaine

This is an Arab salad made with kasha, or Sarasin wheat, moistened with vinaigrette, lots or parsley, lemon juice, onions and the like. The whole-grain type had to be cooked with an egg. I use the package directions. Soak couscous cup in cold water to cover for 30 minutes. Squeeze out water by handfuls and put in bowl. Add chopped parsley, cup minced fresh mint (or tbsp. of dried) cucumber, green pepper, scallions, and large, peeled, seeded, juiced tomatoes.

In another bowl, mix dressing: lemon juice and oil, salt and pepper to taste. Pour over vegetables. Cover and chill for at least an hour. Garnish with cherry tomatoes and leaves from heads of romaine.

Other directions say to omit chopped tomato and not to toss until the last minute.

Frozen Fruit Salad

This is still served in the South but regarded as ladies' luncheon fare in the North.

1 3 oz. package cream cheese, softened
1 ½ cup mayo
2 tsp. lemon juice
2 tsp. lemon extract
8 oz. can of crushed pineapple
½ cup each pecans and maraschino cherries
2 cups sliced bananas
4 cups chopped apples
2 cups minced celery
1 cup each chopped walnuts and raisins

Mix all ingredients, bananas go in at the end.

Heat lemon juice, apples (see apples for proper variety), celery, and walnuts and raisins.

Rice Salad

1 cup of freshly boiled rice
4 strands saffron
1 garlic clove
½ tbsp. spicy vinaigrette
1 onion, chopped
1 cup parsley, chopped
Cook rice with saffron and garlic clove, later to be removed. While still warm, pour over cup of spicy vinaigrette – as much rice as will absorb. When cool, add chopped onion. Why not grated onion and lots of chopped parsley?

Hearts of Palm

2 coarsely chopped avocadoes
4 tsp. lemon juice
1 14 -oz. can each hearts of palm, sliced, and artichoke hearts
2 skinned, chopped tomatoes
2 sliced cucumbers
½ cup oil
¼ cup vinegar

Mix ingredients. Chill and dress at the last minute.

Macaroni Salad

3 cups cooked elbow macaroni
1 cup sliced celery
¼ cup each chopped peppers, sweet pickle and green onion
1 tbsp. lemon juice
½ cup mayonnaise
¼ each salt and pepper
Mix and chill several hours ahead.
Blue Cheese or Roquefort
1 cup Blue cheese or Roquefort
1 cup yoghurt or sour cream
1 tbsp. olive oil
½ tsp lemon juice

Crumble cup one of the above. Mash lightly, leaving cheese in fairly large pieces.   Beat in olive oil and lemon juice.   Refrigerate and cover for several hours.

Avocado Dressing

1 tbsp. chopped parsley
1 tbsp. chopped chives or scallions
1 tsp. each lemon juice and Dijon
½ cup oil
2 ripe mashed avocadoes

Mix and pour over salad.

Cheese Dressing

1 ½ oz. cheese
1 tbsp. vinegar
5 tbsp. heavy cream
1 tbsp. chives

Mash cheese. Beat in vinegar, heavy cream, chives.

Cucumber Mayonnaise

1 cup   mayonnaise
3 tsp. lemon juice
¼ tsp. Tabasco
¼ tsp. curry
½ cup chopped cucumbers.

Mix ingredients.

Fruit Salad

6 tbsp. oil
1 tbsp. each oil and vinegar
½ tsp. mustard
½ tsp. salt
¼ tsp. pepper
1 tsp. sugar
1 tbsp. Worcestershire
2 tbsp. catsup
1 tbsp. grated onion
dollop mango chutney.
Blend everything but oil. Add to salad, separately.
Sherry Vinegar
1 ½ qts. white wine vinegar
¾ cup dry sherry
2 ½ cups peeled, halved shallots

Put in sterilized qt. jar.   Seal.   Room temperature for at least 3 weeks.
Fine sieve into 2-cup sterilized Mason jar. Seal and discard shallots.

7

FISH

This is nowhere near a complete treatise on fish. Let us just say that if you are unfamiliar with the subject and interested, it is a start, perhaps more "about" than "how to". When a prominent Philadelphia seafood restaurateur was quoted as saying that he buys the freshest fish he can find and then does as little as possible to them, he said it all. His fish are cooked to a moist perfection. The only adornments are melted butter and lemon juice. With their penchant for fish sauces, the might take exception to this rather Spartan approach.

Distinctions

There are various fish classifications: fresh water, salt water, shellfish and finfish. Finfish are divided into round fish and flat fish. Round fish refers to any fish that has eyes on both sides of the head, and swims in a vertical position, such as sardines or snapper. Round fish are not necessarily round; they might also be oval or compressed. Flat fish have flat bodies, for they swim, not in a vertical, but in a horizontal position, with both eyes on one side of the head. The flat fish category includes sole, flounder, plaice and halibut. Bone structure determines how the fish is cut up.

It is important to know whether the fish is lean or fatty as this largely determines the cooking method. Lean fish, usually white in color and low in calories, are best poached, sautéed or fried (moist heat processes). Fatty fish bake and broil beautifully, but tend to fall apart in a sauté pan or a poaching liquid.

While these are not ironclad rules and there are exceptions, keep them in mind. It is not a good idea to poach a fatty fish. One can bake a lean fillet if it has been well coated with a fish topping. An exception to the rule is the versatile catfish to which you can do almost anything.

Lean Fish

Bass
Catfish
Cod
Flounder, sole
Grouper
Haddock
Hake
Halibut
Mackerel, king
Red snapper
Orange roughy
Salmon, chum
Swordfish
Tilapia
Trout, rainbow and brook
Tuna, big eye, blue fin, skipjack and yellowfin

Fatty Fish

Bluefish
Shad, king
Mackerel, Atlantic and Spanish

Pompano
Salmon, Atlantic and Coho
Trout, lake
Tuna, albacore and bonito

Buying Fish

To clear up any confusion, what we call sole in this country is actually flounder. Sole is a European fish, not native to our waters. What we refer to as sole, gray sole, plaice or fluke, are all members of the flounder family. This misnomer is a common mistake. Forget supermarket fish counters in favor of a good fish store, one specializing in fresh fish and nothing but fish, delivered to them daily. Other than a slight smell of the sea, fresh fish has no odor whatsoever. Your eye as well as your nose can tell you a lot about a whole fish. Their eyes should be bright and protruding, never sunken or dull, scales should be moist and shiny, gills pink or red. While fillets should also appear moist and shiny, their freshness is more difficult to judge; another reason to patronize a good fish store.

You can buy a whole fish, gutted and scaled, head and tail intact which, incidentally, adds a good deal to the flavor. This fish is 45 percent edible. Then there are the pan-dressed, also scaled and gutted, head and tail removed; these are 67 percent edible. Fillets cut from the sides along the backbone are 100 percent edible. The thicker steaks are cross-sections from larger fish. Medallions (small slices) and large split fish are suitable for broiling. A whole fish is about half bone, so allow roughly 12 to 16 oz. per person, about eight oz. if pan-dressed; a six-or seven-oz. fillet or steak, an adequate portion for one serving. As yields vary with the type of fish, consult your dealer.

Fish is extremely perishable. Bring it straight home from the market, no sitting around in a hot car unless it is packed in ice or stored in a cooler. Once home, feel for and pull out any pin bones (small upright bones sometimes found running through the flesh) with tweezers. Rinse off under cool running water and pat dry with paper towels. Place in a plastic bag over a bowl of ice and refrigerate. Plan to use it that day if at all possible. Keep in mind the old Irish adage as to what happens to guests and fish after three days.

Marinating

A marinade not only keeps a fish from drying out but also adds flavor, particularly to the lean, white-fleshed fish generally lacking in it. However, marinating fish in the customary lemon juice or in an acidic such as vinegar for more than 15 or 20 minutes will partially "cook" your fish and throw off your timing. The South American appetizer, ceviche, is a case in point. Raw fish refrigerated overnight in a lime or lemon juice marinade is edible the next day. The FDA, right or wrong, says not to make it unless your fish is absolutely fresh.

2 tsp. lemon or lime juice
2 tbsp. olive oil
2 tbsp. chopped fresh basil or thyme
1 grated yellow onion
¼ tsp. salt

Add all the ingredients to the fish in plastic bag. Let it stand at room temperature for 20 minutes or so. Always bring the fish to room temperature before cooking.

Timing

Fish is much too easy to overcook or, equally bad, to undercook, a matter of only a minute or so in either direction. Unlike four-footed animals, their muscles have not been toughened by any exercise more strenuous than swimming; the point in cooking fish is not to tenderize, but to heat it through and bring out the flavor.

Some time back, the Canadian Department of Fisheries came up with the following well-publicized rule, applicable to all fish-cooking methods: measure the thickness of the fish (whole or filleted), at its thickest point and cook it for 10 minutes per measured inch. (It is now suggested that a poached fish should be cooked for only seven minutes per inch.) If the fish measures two inches at its thickest point, cook it for 20 minutes, if it's ½-inch, five minutes, etc. There are too many variables to give an exact to-the-minute-timing, but the above rule certainly gives you approximate times and when to start checking for doneness. However, baked fish, casseroles, oven-steamed fillets wrapped in foil and baked fish slathered with a topping will take a few minutes longer.

An experienced cook will not only go by approximate times, but also will check with both hand and eye. The flesh of a raw fish is translucent. As it cooks, it becomes an opaque white. Prod it gently with a fork. If it is cooked, the flesh is should be opaque all the way through and it should separate easily (separate, not flake, which means it is overcooked). Touch with your finger. A properly cooked fish is springy rather than soft to the touch. An old-fashioned grandmother's way of testing is to insert a knife into the thickest part of the fish and then gingerly put it between your lips; if the knife is hot the fish should be done.An alternative method for baking fish, which I recently came across in Pat Jester's The Complete Cook, involves the following: bring to room temperature one-quarter to one-half inch thick fillets. Place in a baking dish. Paint the fillets with a mixture of melted butter and lemon juice. Add a little white wine to the pan. Place in cold oven. Turn oven to 350 degrees and bake for 19-20 minutes. In this chapter recipes are given for baking, oven steaming, sautéing, poaching, or broiling.

Baked Fish
Baked Fatty Fillets

Fatty fish has somewhat darker flesh because of the fat it contains. The fat content can range from 5 to 35% according to the type. Baking,   rather than frying, suits it better.

6 (6-to 7- ounce) fillets salmon or other fatty fish
2 tsp. olive oil
½ cup dry white wine
2 tsp. lemon juice
2 tbsp. finely chopped parsley
¼ tsp. minced clove garlic

Preheat oven to 425 degrees. Season fish and marinate in plastic bag at room temperature for about 15 minutes before cooking. Arrange the fillets, skin side down, or if skinned, former skin or milk white side down, in one layer, in a greased, shallow, metal baking pan. Pour over a dry white wine to the depth of 1/8 inch and top with a mixture of equal parts of lemon juice and finely chopped parsley with garlic. Bake according to thickness: five minutes for a ½-inch thick fillet, up to 20 minutes for a two-inch steak.   Remove cooked fish to warm platter. Reduce juices to syrup and pour over fish. Serves   6.

Baked Lean Fillets

Should you elect to bake a lean fillet, the procedure is the same as for a fatty fish. However, a lean fish should always be coated with a topping before baking, to keep it from drying out in the oven.

Marinade (see recipe below)

6 marinated fish fillets
½ cup dry white wine
3 cups topping (see list below)

Preheat oven to 400 degrees. Place marinated fish in greased, shallow, metal baking pan and pour over a dry white wine to the depth of 1/8 inch. Cover the surface of the fillet with a coating of your choice and bake using the Canadian guidelines under Timing above, not forgetting that an extra minute or two must be added to a coated fish. Serves   6.

Toppings

There are numerous toppings:

Buttered breadcrumbs
Mayonnaise mixed with garlic and lemon juice
A semi-soft cheese
Simple tomato sauce
Duxelles sauce
Marinade

This marinade gives flavor to otherwise bland fish:

2 tsp. lemon or lime juice
2 tbsp. olive oil
chopped fresh basil or thyme
1 grated yellow onion
salt   to taste

Add all the ingredients to the fish in plastic bag. Let it stand at room temperature for 20 minutes or so. Always bring the fish to room temperature before cooking.

Oven-Steamed Fish

Baking a Fish in a Bag

You can buy special cooking bags at the grocery stores. Fish and ingredients are baked together.

6- or 7-ounce bluefish fillet
2 tbsp. melted unsalted butter
2 freshly squeezed lemons
1 Lipton's Onion Soup Mix

Preheat oven to 425 degrees. Each fillet will be baked in an individual aluminum foil package. Begin by cutting the foil into roughly 12-inch squares, large enough to completely enclose one fillet. And lay each fillet in the center of its foil square. Season with salt and pepper and douse each fish portion liberally with melted butter and lemon juice. Scatter over each with 1 tbsp. of Lipton's Onion Soup Mix. This packaged mix has raised the eyebrows of cooking friends, but in this instance I have no apologies.

Foil packages should be as airtight as possible; to ensure this, with the fillet lying vertically in front of you, fold topside of foil down, bottom side up. Fold in the two long sides of foil, roll edges together and crimp. Place on baking sheet, sealed side down and let stand at room temperature for 15 minutes. Place the baking sheet into a preheated oven. Theoretically, the foil packages should swell when fish is done. If this does not happen, bake for 20 minutes. Serve in the packages.

Baking a Whole Stuffed Fish

Keep the fish from drying out by basting it with oil or butter or else topping it with other ingredients such as chopped onions shallots and parsley.

3 lb. fish, such as sea trout or weakfish
3 tbsp. chopped green peppers
3 tbsp. chopped mushrooms
3 tbsp. chopped zucchini
3 slices fresh tomatoes

2 tbsp. lemon juice
2 tbsp. unsalted butter

Rinse and pat the fish dry. Fish is stuffed with vegetables and placed in a roasting bag (a grocery store paper bag) found in supermarkets, placed in a cold oven. The cavity can be stuffed with a small amount of green pepper, mushrooms and zucchini. Top fish with tomato. Douse fish with a mixture of the melted butter and lemon juice, make a few slits in the bag, fasten with a tie and put in a cold oven. Turn oven to 350 degrees. For 2 to 2½ inch small fish, bake for 45 to 50 minutes. Check tenderness by inserting a fork through the slit. Serves 4.

Variation:

1 cup fresh breadcrumbs
2 tbsp. whole milk
2 tbsp. olive oil
1 clove mashed garlic
2 tsp. oregano
2 tbsp. chopped parsley

Sautéed Fish

You will have better luck with fish from the lean, white-fleshed category than with fatty fish. Both flounder and sole, in particular, are excellent choices. Whether or not the fish is dipped in a coating (more interesting), the procedure and also the admonitions are the same.

Marinate fish at room temperature; unless coated, pat dry with paper towels; damp fish will not brown.

Heat skillet over low heat; when hot, heat mixture of butter and olive oil just enough to coat pan bottom by 1/8 inch. Heat butter/oil mixture to a sizzle. When sizzling subsides, immediately drop in fillets. Allow one to two per person. Lower heat. Sauté for a minute or two. Repeat on other side.

Set aside fillets; wipe out skillet, melt and brown with ½ tsp. butter. Add capers, olives, and lemon juice. Sauté two minutes. Pour over fillets. Serve immediately.

Sole à l'Anglaise

As I said before, true sole we see in the United States is imported, such as Dover sole that is flown in from England.

1 ½ pounds of sole or flounder
2 tbsp. water
1 egg
all-purpose flour for dredging
2 beaten egg yolks
seasoned breadcrumbs (garlic and parsley)
4 tbsp. unsalted butter

Few drops freshly squeezed lemon juice

Dip sole or flounder in egg beaten with water; dip in flour, egg yolks, and then in seasoned breadcrumbs. Heat skillet and melt 2 tbsp. butter to sizzling. Add coated fish and sauté one minute per side. Wipe pan clean, and add remaining butter and a few drops of lemon juice; pour over fish.

Sautéed Trout Amandine

1 small trout, seasoned with salt and pepper
2 tbsp. butter
1 tbsp. olive oil
½ cup chopped almonds
1 tbsp. chopped parsley

Heat the butter/oil mixture and place the trout fillet in a warm 12-inch skillet. Sprinkle with chopped almonds. Brown on underside only. Cover tightly with lid, lower heat and sauté slowly for 10 minutes. Arrange the almonds around the fish in a deep dish.

Poached Fish

As explained in the beginning of the chapter, the lean white-fleshed fish are much more suitable for poaching than the dark-fleshed oily varieties. The exceptions are salmon, rainbow trout and catfish. Although fatty, they are firm enough not to fall apart as would a bluefish. Flounder, cod, red snapper and sea bass are all good poaching candidates.

If there is a secret to poaching, it is in remembering that poaching and boiling are not synonymous. A poaching liquid should never boil. In fact the liquid should never get above the merest summer with only a barely perceptible movement.

What liquid do you use? You have several options. If not making a sauce, you can get away with salted water plus a little lemon or vinegar. If you want a liquid that can be boiled down and poured over the fish or used as a basis for a sauce, try a fish broth or fumet (which see). Other possibilities are dry white wine or a mixture of bottled clam juice and dry vermouth. I specify dry vermouth as if the wine is even slightly sweet, the mixture becomes unpalatable. You might find this last too assertive for any but the blandest of fish such as sole or flounder.

The size of your pan and the material of which it is made are important. If poaching a large whole dish, I would suggest a fish poacher. I solve this problem by baking them in a roasting bag. The poaching dish should be just large enough to hold the fillets comfortably in one layer. If using wine of vinegar, the dish should be nonreactive, that is lined, enamel or stainless steel. Many enamel-over-iron dishes are nice enough to be brought to the table.

If fillets are thin, sole or flounder for example, make two or three cuts along each side (on skin or darker side) to keep them from curling. Grease pan well and scatter in a few chopped herbs and a (2 tbsp. in all) finely minced shallots or scallions. Lay seasoned fillets on top in slightly overlapping layers. Add a few more chopped herbs, the rest of the shallows and dot with butter or margarine. Pour over cold or tepid liquid barely to cover fish. Bring to just under the simmer. I prefer the latter method as heat is sometimes difficult to control on an electric stove and your filled are boiling before you know it. There is an exception. Thin fillets, sole and flounder again, can be started as above on top o the stove. When just under simmer, cover with the buttered paper plus lid. Take pan off heat and let sit for exactly eight minutes. It's a breeze.

The next step depends on what poaching liquid you have used and whether you want a sauce. Carefully transfer fillets to a warm plate and cover with a piece of foil. If you have used salted water, you can do as little as giving fillets a good squirt of lemon juice. It that seems a bit sparse, top each fillet with a dab of herbed butter of margarine (see butter). If you have used the wine, fumet or clam juice mixture, boil down to a syrupy glaze and pour over fish. You will not need more than a few Or you might boil it down, not as extensively as above, take pan off heat and drop in a 2 or 3 tbsp. of butter or margarine, one at a time, swirling pan around and not adding another until previous tablespoon has been thoroughly incorporated into liquid.

Broiled Fish

Fatty fish are more suitable to broiling than the lean. Broiled sole is often featured on restaurant menus but the restaurant broiler isn't the same as the home variety, which can dry out a fish before it is even done. Preheat broiler to its maximum, some 30 minutes in advance, but do not heat up the pan in which fish will be cooked. Use a metal baking pan rather than the slotted broiling pan so that the hot metal will cook the underside of the fish.

Broiled Shad

You broil fish in the oven, generally fatty fish.

4 (6 to 8 ounces) fillet of a fatty fish, such as shad
3 ¼ tsp. melted butter
juice from 2 freshly squeezed lemons
½ cup dry breadcrumbs
2 tsp. grated lemon rind
1 tsp. lemon rind
2 chopped garlic cloves
For the sauce:
4 chopped mushrooms
2 chopped shallots
2 tbsp. unsalted butter
½ cup dry white wine

Place fish three to six inches from heating source depending on thickness. The thinner fillets can go three inches from the element; the thicker fish, six inches. Drizzle the fillets or steaks with 2 tbsp. melted butter and lemon juice. Sprinkle fish with breadcrumbs. Broil 8 minutes; add a little lemon rind, a small, peeled garlic clove and one of   melted butter; continue broiling two more minutes. Monitor carefully.

Sauté mushrooms and shallots briefly in butter. Add juices, if any, from broiling pan. Add dry white wine; reduce to light syrup and pour over fish.

Broiled Bluefish with Sherry Vinegar

It is customary to broil flat fillets three inches away from the heat source. Broiling is one of the best cooking methods; it is chancy and time-consuming in that it requires constant checking. This method where the fish is broiled at the lowest oven level is one of the best. Dip any fish to be broiled or baked in this unusual mixture of a ½ cup of milk with sherry vinegar added. Braised pork can also be improved by dipping it in this same mixture.

2 (6- to 8- ounce) fish fillets
½ cup whole milk
¼ cup sherry vinegar
seasoned bread crumbs

Preheat broiler. Place fillets in a metal baking pan at lowest oven level. Combine milk and a tablespoon of vinegar to the depth of ¼ inch. Sprinkle with seasoned breadcrumbs. Broil   for 15 minutes   on lowest rack or until done.

Shellfish

Outside of live crabs, fresh crabmeat can be bought frozen or canned. The best grades of fresh crabmeat are lump, back fin, flake and claw, all pasteurized and packed in containers refrigerated until use.

Crab Cakes

Crab cakes are nice for a company dish as they can be assembled in the morning and refrigerated until ready to sauté. Preheat oven to 375 degrees. During preparation, handle crabmeat as little as possible.
3 tsp. mayonnaise to bind crab cakes

1 egg, slightly beaten
1 tbsp. chopped parsley
2 tbsp. minced onions
2 tbsp. minced celery
4 tsp. Worcestershire sauce
1 tbsp. freshly squeezed lemon juice
1 tsp. salt
¼ tsp. pepper
2 tsp. prepared mustard
1 4 oz. can crabmeat, picked over for any shell fragments
½ cup fresh bread crumbs for coating
1 tsp. each butter and olive oil for sautéing

In a bowl, combine mayonnaise, parsley, onions, celery, egg, Worcestershire, lemon juice, salt, and pepper and mustard. Pour this over crabmeat and mix as gently as possible. Shape into cakes. Chill in refrigerator for at least an hour.

Coat crab cakes lightly in breadcrumbs. Melt butter and olive oil over moderate heat. When hot, drop in cakes and sauté about four minutes per side or until golden or put in the oven at 375 degrees for 10 or 15 minutes until cooked through. While tartar sauce is generally served with this, cole slaw makes an excellent alternative. Makes 6 cakes.

Oysters

There is no comparison in taste between oysters opened by you and those sold in the supermarkets, labeled "stewing oysters". It is not hard to open an oyster, but it may take you a few tries to become adept. Ask your dealer to give you a demonstration. Do not open oysters on the half shell unless you have opened them yourself. This applies to scalloped and broiled oysters. You can get away with "stewing oysters" for frying or stewing.

An oyster in its shell is still alive. Make sure that they are still alive by discarding any with broken shells or even partially open. The FDA no longer recommends serving raw oysters, a shame for they make wonderful hors d'oeuvres. Fortunately, there are other great ways of serving oysters, cooked in casseroles or stews, or fried.

Sautéed Oysters

Pat oysters as dry as possible; dip them in a cup of milk into which egg has been beaten, the dipped in bread crumbs. Sauté   until brown and crisp. Do not overcook, as oysters will become tough and rubbery.

24 very small oysters
2 red hot pepper sauce
4 minced shallots
1 tsp. salt
¼ tsp. pepper
1 cup half-and-half
2 tbsp. dry sherry
2 tbsp. minced parsley
4 tbsp. butter

Shuck oysters over bowl to catch juices.   Reserve.   Heat half and half until   hot but not boiling. Set aside, covered. Heat butter in large soup kettle. Lightly brown   shallots over moderate heat, stirring.   Add oysters and cook until edges curl,   1 or 2 minutes.

Add sherry and reserved oyster juices, straining it in through damp cheesecloth or coffee filter. Adjust seasonings and heat through, Garnish with parsley. The usual alternative is to first heat oysters in milk, add in other ingredients.

Oyster Soufflé

24 oysters, shucked
1 cup milk
3 eggs, separated
3 tbsp. dry white wine
3 tsp. each butter and oil
1½ tsp. salt
1 tbsp. flour
1/8 tsp. cayenne

When you shuck oysters, do so over strainer and bowl and reserve juices. Poach oysters briefly in this liquid for about 2 or 3 minutes, keeping liquid just below the simmer. Reserve   this liquid.   Add milk to this to make 1 cup. Make roux,   add wine, salt and pepper. Beat yolks and beat the hot sauce into them. Cook until it just reaches the boil. Add oysters. Fold in egg whites and bake. Is this worth trying? Bake at 375 degrees for 35 minutes. I would say that the eggs should be on the top, oysters below.Proportions to try: for 8 cup mold. Roux of 3 tbsp. flour and 1 cup milk. 11 cups oysters. 6 yolks, 7 whites.

Curried Shrimp Creole

This party dish is a basic recipe. It is indigenous to New Orleans.

6 strips bacon
2 ¼ tbsp. unsalted butter
1 tbsp. oil
1 ½ cups chopped onion
1 ½ cups chopped celery
½ cups minced green pepper
1 clove minced garlic
3 cups undrained Italian plum tomatoes
Bouquet garni (3 or 4 sprig fresh thyme, or ½ tsp. dried)
1 bay leaf
½ cup chopped parsley
salt and pepper to taste
2 small, shelled, de-veined shrimp, butterflied (see note)
2 ¼ tbsp. flour
1 ½ tsp. curry powder
1 cup light cream or fish stock (see Taking Stock)
¼ tsp. paprika
dash nutmeg
1 tsp. lemon juice

Cook bacon until it is rendered. Heat butter and oil. Now do onions, celery, peppers and garlic; cook five minutes more. Wilt. Add tomatoes with juice and the bouquet garni and cook 15 minutes. Season with salt and pepper. Add shrimp (Freeze shrimp shells for fish stock). To de-vein, remove dark vein, which runs from top to bottom with fingertips or tip of knife. Stir flour and curry powder into the vegetables; stir thoroughly before adding cream, paprika and nutmeg. If the sauce seems unduly thick, fish stock may be substituted. Cook another five minutes. Add shrimp and lemon juice and heat from five to ten minutes over a lowered flame, or until shrimp is pink. Remove herb bouquet, season to taste and serve over boiled rice sprinkled with grated orange rind if desired. To butterfly   a shrimp. First peel and de-vain it, and then make a lengthwise cut down the back, splitting it open so that it lies flat.

Broiled Scallops

1   lb. scallops
¼ tsp. salt
¼ tsp. pepper
¼ tsp. paprika
1 tbsp. butter
4 scallop shells
4 tsp. lemon juice
1 lemon, sliced
1 sprig parsley

Preheat broiler. Spread scallops in shallow baking dish and   sprinkle with salt, pepper, paprika, dot with butter. Broil three inches from heating element about five minutes, or until very lightly browned and opaque. Serve in scallop shells, which, oddly enough, are sold in hardware stores, as well as supermarkets, gourmet and specialty shops. Sprinkle with fresh lemon juice. Garnish   with lemon slices and parsley.

Crab Cakes with Tartar Sauce Gourmet

For the sauce:

2 cups mayonnaise
¼ cup lemon juice
¼ cup minced onion
2 tbsp. drained, minced capers
4 dill pickles, chopped
2 fresh jalapeños, peeled, minced (wear rubber gloves)
2 tomatoes, peeled and minced.

Whisk all the above together and chill for at least an hour or overnight.

For the Crab Cakes:

¼ stick butter
¼ cup flour

2 cups milk
1 can crab meat, picked over
½ cup each minced red, green and yellow bell peppers
½ cup minced scallions
1/8 tsp. cayenne
3 cups fine fresh bread crumbs
¼ cup clarified butter
lemon wedges for garnish

Make roux by melting the butter over moderate-low heat. Add flour and stir for 3 minutes. Whisk in milk in a stream. Season.   Continue to simmer for 10 minutes, stirring. Set aside.

Mix crabmeat, peppers, scallions, cayenne, salt and pepper to taste and when well mixed, the white sauce. Let mixture cool a bit. Add 1 cup of the crumbs and shape mixture into cakes, using ¼ cup measure. Coat with remaining bread crumbs.

In skillet, heat up some of the clarified butter over mod. high   heat until hot but not smoking. Do cakes in batches, adding rest of the clarified butter when necessary, 5   to 6 min. per   side until just golden. Drain on paper towels.

Serve with tartar sauce and lemon wedges. Makes   about 20 cakes.

Crab Imperial

5 tbsp. butter
¼ tsp pepper
1 ½ tbsp. flour
1/8 tsp nutmeg
1 cup half-in-half, hot
1 lump crabmeat
¼ cup snipped fresh chives
1 cup coarse saltine crumbs
2 tbsp. lemon juice
2 tbsp butter
2 tsp. prepared mustard
1 tsp. salt
¼ tsp. pepper
1/8 tsp. nutmeg

1 lb. lump crabmeat
1 cup coarse saltine crumbs
2 tbsp. butter

Preheat oven to 350 degrees. Melt 3 tbsp. of the butter in small saucepan over medium heat. Whisk in flour and whisk constantly for 2 minutes. Whisk in hot half-and-half and whisk until it just comes to the boil, about 3 min.

Take off heat and beat ¼ of this sauce into the egg. Now whisk this back into the sauce. Cook whisking constantly until it thickens and boils, about 3 min. Whisk in chives, mustard, salt, pepper and nutmeg. Fold in crab and pour into 1-quart soufflé dish.

Sauté crumbs in the remaining 2 tbsp. of butter until golden, about 3 min. Top soufflé with crumbs and bake at 350 degrees. Dip oysters, as dry as possible, in cup of milk into which egg has been beater, then in crumbs. Sauté.

Shrimp Mousse

1 ½ tbsp. unflavored gelatin
½ cup cold water
4 cups shrimp
1 bay leaf
1 inch piece of lemon rind
1 sprig of parsley
½ tsp. dried thyme
In small bowl, sprinkle gelatin over cold water and let soften.

Drop shrimp into saucepan of boiling water which has been seasoned with bay, lemon rind, sprig of parsley and dried thyme. Return water to the boil and when it reaches it, drain shrimp in colander. Run cold water over them, shell, devein and mince.

Scalloped Oysters

½ cup shallots
2 tbsp. butter

½ lightly pressed down fresh breadcrumbs
1 ½ tsp. minced parsley

6 to 7 large oysters

Soften shallots in butter. Add lightly pressed down fresh crumbs and brown lightly. Season and fold in parsley. Spread half of this in baking dish large enough to hold oysters in one layer. Top with rest of crumbs. 8 to 10 in middle level of 450 degree oven. Dot with more butter if you wish. I would process crumbs, garlic and parsley.

New Orleans Oysters

2 dozen oysters
2 large onions
1/8 tsp. Tabasco
1 tbsp. Worcestershire
2 celery ribs
1 clove garlic
1 cup butter
1 cup oil

Pour this over oysters: blend onions, Tabasco, tbsp. Worcestershire, celery ribs, garlic, and add cup each butter and oil (excessive). Bake at 350 degrees until oysters turn white.

In regard to the proceeding 2 recipes, try processing crumbs, parsley, garlic, onions, Tabasco plus butter and pour it under and over oysters, baking at 450 degrees.

Crab Mousse Gourmet

2 envelopes gelatin
1/3 cup water
½ cup mayonnaise at room temperature
¼ cup each lemon and lime juice
tsp. each minced parsley and chives
tsp. Dijon mustard
¼ tsp. each salt and pepper
1½ cups heavy cream

2 cups crab meat
3 peeled, quartered tomatoes
3 tbsp. vinaigrette dressing (see vinaigrette)

Soften gelatin in ovenproof bowl, in 1/3 cup water and stir to dissolve. Set in pan of lightly simmering water to further dissolve. In another bowl, add room temperature mayo, lemon and lime juice, minced parsley, chives and Dijon mustard, salt and pepper, the gelatin, heavy cream, crab meat. Stir into 1 ½ qt. ring mold. Cover loosely with plastic and chill for at least 2 hours or up to 24. Invert and surround with tomatoes and 3 tbsp. vinaigrette.

Julia Childs does it differently. Chicken and/or fish are processed. For her chicken mousse, sauté tbsp. minced onion or shallots in tbsp. butter only until soft, a minute or so. Add 2 cups chicken stock and the gel mixture (2 envelopes softened in ¼ cup dry white wine). Blend or process 2 tightly packed cups of cooked fowl plus ½ cup lightly sautéed chicken livers. Beat in 3 tbsp. cognac or Madeira, salt, pepper, nutmeg. Over season a bit. Cover and chill until almost set.

Large Print Crab Mousse

Beat ½ cup chilled heavy cream in chilled bowl until it holds its shape softly. Fold into chilled chicken mixture

2 envelopes gelatin
2 tbsp. sherry
1 cup of boiling chicken stock
2 egg yolks
1 cup heavy cream
3 tbsp. lemon juice
5 drops Tabasco
1 ½ to 2 cups picked-over crab meat
2 small celery ribs
2 scallions, chopped
1 parsley sprig
½ tbsp. each marjoram, thyme
½ cup mayonnaise

Process gelatin, sherry. Add cup of boiling chicken stock and process 10 sec. Add and process until well mixed; yolks, heavy cream, lemon juice. Tabasco, crab meat, celery ribs, scallions, parsley sprig, marjoram, thyme. Fold in mayonnaise.

Curried Shrimp Creole

This party dish is a basic recipe. Many others in this book are based on the same method.

6 strips bacon
2 tbsp. unsalted butter
1 tbsp. oil
2 cups each chopped onions and celery
1 cup minced green peppers
1 clove minced garlic
bouquet garni: 1 sprig fresh thyme, or ¼ dried, 1 bay leaf, ½ cup parsley
5 tsp. chili sauce
6 cups canned Italian plum tomatoes
¼ tsp. salt
¼ tsp pepper
2 tsp. curry powder
1 cup cream cheese
2 tbsp. gelatin
2 lbs. shrimp, cleaned
1 cup mayo
2 tbsp. gelatin
¼ cup minced scallion
1 tbsp. lemon juice
½ tsp. Worcestershire
salt and pepper to taste
cayenne to taste

Cook bacon until it is rendered. Now do half of onions, peppers, celery and garlic. Wilt. Add all else but shrimp, cook 30 minutes.

In saucepan, combine cream cheese, cut into bits and softened and chili sauce. Heat over moderately low heat until smooth and heated through. Add gelatin and cook, stirring, until gel dissolves. Transfer to bowl and let cool. Add shrimp, mayo, celery, minced scallions, lemon juice, Worcestershire, salt, pepper and cayenne to taste. Mix well.

Rinse 1-qt. decorative mold with cold water. Do not dry. Pour in shrimp mixture. Chill, loosely covered for at least 2 hours. Run knife around edge of mold. Dip bottom of mold in hot water and invert on serving platter. If served as hors d'ouevre, this will take care of 10 to 12.

More on Shrimp Creole

¼ cup butter
2 tbsp. flour
2 tbsp. curry
½ tsp. salt
¼ paprika
1/8 tsp. nutmeg
2 cups light cream
3 cups or 1 ½ lbs. shrimp in shell, cleaned, cooked, split
1 tsp. each lemon juice, candied ginger
1/8 tsp. Worcestershire
½ tbsp. onion juice

Broiled Shad

Melt butter. Blend in flour, up to 2 tbsp, curry, salt, paprika, nutmeg. Stir in light cream why not sour cream -and cook until bubbly. Add shrimp, lemon juice, candied ginger, dash Worcestershire, and onion juice. Heat through and season to taste. Small   individual casseroles, makes 2 cups in all. Cook at 350 degrees, 10 to 12 minutes.

Orange rice:
¾ cup rice
1/3   cup orange juice
1 ¼   cup water
2 tsp. grated orange peel
¾   tsp. salt

To serve with orange rice, cook cup rice, orange juice, 1 cup water, grated orange peel, salt. Scatter with salted peanuts, flaked coconut and pack into 6-cup mold, lightly oiled.

If using salmon, use 2 1/3 cups of canned or cooked and substitute white wine stock for the chicken stock.

If you want a ham mousse, use 2 1/3 cups of cooked ham.

McCall's Salmon Mousse

1 envelope gelatin
¼ cup dry white wine
½ cup boiling water
½ cup mayonnaise
1 tsp. each grated onion and lemon juice
½ tsp. each paprika and Tabasco
1 tsp. salt
2 cups cooked salmon or 2 6 ½ oz. cans, drained
½ cup of heavy cream
½ cup cream
2 tsp. dill
2 medium cucumbers, unpared

Sprinkle envelope gelatin over dry white wine and stir to dissolve. Add boiling water. Stir and when completely dissolved, set aside to cool, at which point, add mayonnaise, grated onion and lemon juice, paprika, Tabasco and salt.

The next step is to set this bowl over larger bowl of ice cubes. Stir occasionally until it reaches the consistency of unbeaten whites. Lightly oil 4-cup mold.   Remove all skin and bones of cooked salmon or cans, drained. Process with heavy cream. Beat remaining ½ cup cream to soft peak stage. With whisk, fold in salmon purge, whipped cream and dill into the slightly thickened gelatin mix. Cover and chill for at least 2 hours.Meanwhile thinly slice cucumbers, and marinate in vinaigrette. Chill, wrapped, and surround unmolded mousse with them. It might be simpler to dissolve gelatin in the wine and bring just under the simmer with half the cream or would this curdle and if so, substitute stock for the wine. Purge salmon, all seasonings and gelatin mix. Flavor with sherry and over season a bit. Pack in mold and when almost set, fold in cream.

Scallops with Orange Zest and Scallions

3 tsp. orange zest
2 tsp. orange juice

2 scallions, chopped, including tops
3 tsp. parsley, chopped
1½ lbs. bay scallops
1/3 cup white wine
¾ cup clam juice
¼ of butter

Remove zest from orange and shred. Squeeze out 2 tbsp of the juice and reserve. Cook zest in small pan of boiling water to cover for about 3 minutes. This removes bitterness. Drain and set aside.

Chop scallions, included tops and parsley. Set aside. Scallops, the reserved orange juice, 1/3 cup white wine, scallions, go in skillet. Add enough clam juice to just cover (about ¾ cup). Bring just to boil, lower heat and simmer, covered for 2 minutes. Remove to warm serving platter with slotted spoon. Cook liquid over high heat to reduce to 2 tbsp. Swirl in butter in the usual way. It should be creamy, not melted. They say over the lowest possible heat. I say swirl it in, bit by bit, off heat. Stir in zest and parsley. I will try lemon instead of the orange.

Seafood Pudding

2 ½ lbs. halibut
½ cup cream
1 ½ tsp. pepper
¼ tsp. cardamom
¼ tsp. cayenne
2 eggs, separated

Process halibut. Beat in cream, pepper, cardamom, cayenne. Separate eggs and beat whites until stiff and fold into processed fish. Buttered 8-cup mold, 1 hour at 350 degrees, cover, and in a double boiler.

Sauce

3 tbsp. butter
1 cup shiitake mushrooms
3 tbsp. flour
½ cup of the fish juice
¾ cup cream

½ tsp. salt, pepper
3 egg yolks

Melt butter and stew shiitake mushrooms in it. Add flour, bit by bit. Add fish juice plus cream. Add salt, pepper. Beat egg yolks into this.

Broiling

Always   preheat broiler even though it may have to be turned down when fish goes in. The larger the fish, the further it goes from broiling element. 4 inches for a fillet, if crumbed, 5 inches the same for a steak, 6 inches for a whole fish. Whole fish and steak are turned midway. As salt burns under broiler, do not salt until fish is done. Always grease broiler rack.

Basic Broiling

Dip fish in melted butter. If crumbed, process crumbs with lemon rind, garlic. Or you might marinate with pat of flavored butter or cover with mayo or aioli. As fillets are not in the oven for any length of time, they don't exude much if any juices. Rectify this by making an instant sauce while fish cooks. Sauté a few chopped mushrooms and chopped shallots lightly in butter. When fish is done, pour in pan juices and cup dry white wine or vermouth. Reduce for a couple of minutes.

Broiled Scallops

Spread 1 lb. in shallow dish and sprinkle with salt, pepper, paprika, dot with butter. Broil 3   inches from element, 6 -9 min., or until very lightly browned.

Baked Cod

4 tbsp. butter
1 tsp. salt
1 tbsp. Worcestershire
 sprinkling paprika

4 cod steaks, 1   inch thick
1 cup seasoned flour
¼ cup oil
1 large onion, sliced thinly
3 minced garlic cloves
½ tsp. ground ginger
1 tsp. ground hot pepper flakes
½ cup fresh minced coriander

Mix seasonings and pour butter, salt, and Worcestershire over the fish. Sprinkle with paprika.

Dredge steaks in the seasoned flour. Heat up half the oil until hot but not smoking over mod. Heat.   Sauté steaks for 1 min. or until lightly browned, turning once. Remove fish. Add rest of oil and cook onions moderately but in this instance, until golden. Add garlic, spices, pepper flakes and cook for minute. Off heat, stir in yoghurt and blend in processor.

Put steaks back, cover and cook at the barest simmer for 6 min.   Sprinkle over coriander.

Cod Sautéed in Yoghourt

4 ½ inch-thick cod steaks
seasoned flour for dredging
½ cup oil
2 large onions, thinly sliced
3 minced garlic cloves
¼ tsp. ground ginger
½ tsp. ground hot pepper flakes
¼ cup fresh minced coriander

Dredge steaks in the seasoned flour. Heat up half the oil until hot, but not smoking, over moderate heat. Sauté steaks for   2 min.   or until lightly brown, turning once. Remove fish. Add rest of oil and cook onions moderately but, in this instance, until golden. Add garlic, spices, pepper flakes and cook for minute. Off heat,   stir in yoghourt and blend in processor.   Put steaks back, cover and cook at the bared simmer for 6. Sprinkle coriander over the dish.

Another Cod Sautéed in Garlic Sauce

4 large   lemon sole fillets, (6 to 8   oz. each)
3 tbsp. vinegar
1 cup oil
4 garlic cloves, minced
1 slice homemade-type bread, crusts removed
½ cup blanched almonds, seasoned
1 cup flour for dredging steaks
2 tbsp. oil
2 minced parsley

In blender, blend vinegar, garlic, 1/4 cup of the oil, bread, almonds, and cup water, salt until smooth. Rinse, dry and lightly salt sole fillets. Preheat oven to 350 degrees and spray an 11 x 7 inch baking dish with Pam.

Heat up the rest of the oil and sauté steaks for 8 min.,   turning   once. Transfer cod and thin sauce with a little hot water. Sprinkle with the parsley.

Baked Cod with Vegetables - Cuisinart

1 ½ slices of bread
2 tbsp. butter
¾ medium onion, sliced
1   medium carrot cut in strips
¾   tsp. salt
1 tsp. pepper
1 ½   medium baking potatoes, julienned and dropped in the boiling water for 5 minutes
1   lb. of cod fillets
3 oz. mushrooms, sliced
1 garlic glove, peeled and processed
1/3 cups   parsley and buttered bread, dry white wine.

Grease baking dish and turn over to 350 degrees. Bring pot of water to boil.   Butter   1   slice   of   bread   with   tbsp. butter. Process butter, onion, carrot, salt and pepper. Blanch potatoes.

Arrange onions on bottom of 9 by 9 inch baking pan. Add carrots, the blanched potatoes, pepper and half the salt, dotting with remaining butter. Now add mushrooms, the garlic, parsley, garlic mixture. Bake for 35 or 40 minutes.

Stuffed Baked Lemon Sole

6 sprigs parsley
1 small onion, peeled and quartered
1 small apple, peeled and quartered
2 tbsp. white seedless raisins
2 tbsp. oil
1/3 cup soft bread crumbs
½ cup egg substitute
¼ tsp. pepper
¼ tsp. dried thyme
½ tsp. salt
2 tbsp. lemon juice
1 lb. flounder fillets
½ cup sour cream
1 tsp. paprika

With metal blade, process parsley for 15 sec. or until chopped. Add onion and small apple, the quartered apple and raisins. Pulse, chop about 10 times. Heat up oil in medium saucepan. Add onion mixture and cook slowly, covered, until onion is soft, 8 minutes.

Put this mixture into small bowl and add bread crumbs, egg substitute, pepper, dried thyme, salt. Mix. Spread this filling on each fillet and starting at narrow end, roll up fillets and place them, seam side, in prepared pan. Squeeze over lemon juice and bake for about 45 minutes.

Line bottom of shallow baking dish with thin slices of

lightly sautéed onions. Top with lightly seasoned flounder fillets. Slather with sour cream and redden with paprika.

Broiled Salmon

6 salmon steaks, ¾ inches thick

¼ cup butter
1 tbsp. chopped parsley
1 tbsp. fresh chopped herbs ¼ tsp fines herbs
1 sliced garlic clove

Lay on greased grill and brush with the following sauce. Turn at midpoint, basting. They say broil 3 inches from element for 12 minutes. I say 8 at the most. Basting sauce: combine butter, parsley, chopped herbs or fines herbs, sliced garlic clove and let stand 15 minutes.

Salmon Sautéed Followed by Baking Sauce

1 small onion, minced
12 brine-cured black olives Kalamata or Gaeta, pitted and chopped
3 garlic cloves, minced Kalamata or Gaeta
1   lb. Italian plum tomatoes-about 6
¼ cup dry red wine
2 tbsp. balsamic vinegar
¼ tsp. salt
1/8 tsp. pepper
4 1-inch thick salmon steaks
3 tbsp. olive oil
Preheat oven to 375 degrees, middle position.

Mince onions, garlic, peel, chop tomatoes, pit and chop olives coarsely, chop anchovies. Sauté fish in hot oil until lightly colored on one side, then on the other. Remove to plate. Add onion and garlic and sauté until soft, about 3 min. Add tomatoes and cook 2 more. Add wine and vinegar and bring just to boil. Return salmon to skillet, cover and bake 8 to 10 minutes. Remove salmon to serving dish and cover to keep warm.

Return skillet and sauce to stove top. Bring to boil, lower heat until it thickens slightly –I would say about 1 minute. Now add capers, olives and simmer until heated through - 1 min. or so. Season and serve.

Basic Grilled Fish

2   tsp. fresh thyme
¼ small garlic clove.
5 tbsp. olive oil

Process thyme, garlic clove. Stir into olive oil.

Pesto for Grilled Fish

10 basil leaves
¼ tsp. each kosher salt and black peppercorns
1 small garlic clove
5 tbsp. oil
Try coating a fish with this. Process basil leaves, kosher salt and black peppercorns, small garlic clove. Stir into oil.
A l'anglaise for Franey's Grilled Fish
8 fillets or 1 large fish
1 egg
2 tbsp. water

Dredge fillets in flour, shaking off excess. Dip in egg beaten with 2 tbsp. water. Broil and sauté.

Chris does it like this: butter bread and process with garlic and parsley. Heat up 2 tsp. butter and sauté 1 per side. Wipe out pan and add 2 tsp. butter.

Can also be first dipped in milk and then flour.

Sole Poached in Tomato Sauce

½ cup chopped onions
1 tsp. minced garlic
2 tbsp. butter
½ cup dry white
1 tbsp. each dried basil marjoram
3 cups fixed, or canned, tomatoes

Soften onions, minced garlic in butter. Add dry white, tsp dried basil and marjoram. Simmer until liquid almost has evaporated. Add fixed tomatoes and cook 3 min. Add sole fillets. When done, remove and add juice of lemon.

A Baked Fillet

1 cup mayonnaise
1 tsp. each lemon juice and horseradish
½ cup green pepper, chopped
½ cup onions, chopped

Place in shallow baking dish and slather with 1 cup mayo, lemon juice and horseradish. Top with cup each green pepper, chopped and chopped onions. They say 400 degrees for 10 minutes. I say this is not too long and would suggest pre sautéing vegetables, as there is not time enough to cook them.

Red Snapper

Marinate. I do it know why recipe specifies skin left on. Marinate for an hour in equal parts of oil and lemon juice plus salt, pepper, grated onion and chopped herbs at room temp. Top with sliced tomatoes and bake.

Fillets Dipped In Sesame Seeds

Dip fillets in lightly beaten egg white to which drops of   soy sauce have been added. Dredge in mixture of cup sesame seeds, ¼ tsp. cornstarch plus ¼ tsp. cayenne.

Pompano en Papillote

4 cleaned pompano fillets
1 tsp. minced chervil
1 tbsp. butter
8 cleaned and peeled baby shrimp
2 tbsp. dry white wine

Can be tried in foil or parchment paper. Wrap each of 4 cleaned pompano in parchment adding (presumably for each) butter, baby shrimp, minced chervil or tarragon, dry white wine. Bake on steel   pan   in 350 degree oven for 20 to 25 minutes or until parchment is   browned and puffed. Slit parchment and slide parsley out. Lemon   wedge   garnish.

Porgies Sautéed with Sesame Seeds

8 4-oz. porgy fillets
1 egg white, beaten
1 tbsp. soy sauce
¼ cup of sesame seeds
3 tbsp. cup cornstarch
1/8 tsp. cayenne
2 tbsp. peanut oil
1 tbsp. sesame oil
1 scallion, minced
½ cup lemon juice

Brush porgy fillets with egg white beaten with soy. Dredge in cup of sesame seeds which have been mixed with cornstarch plus cayenne. Sauté in peanut and sesame oil until brown. Garnish with minced scallion and pour over juice of lemon.

Sole à la Meunière

4 sole fillets
2 cups milk
2 cups seasoned flour
2 tbsp. butter
2 lemon juice

Marinate fillets in milk for 20 minutes. Dredge on seasoned flour and shake off excess. Heat up mixture of oil and butter, half oil and half butter. So t hat you want more than the usual ¼ inch deep. Failures are due to not having fat hot enough, fish will stick to pan and necessary crust will not form. Fat will be just short of smoking. After adding fillets, be sure to regulate heat so that they do not burn. Brown quickly on each side and remove to warm platter. Add lump of fresh butter, after wiping out pan with paper towel. When butter turns a light brown, pour over fish with seasonings and a few drops of lemon juice with a noisette of butter.

Baked Salmon

4 salmon fillets

4 tbsp. butter
2 green peppercorns
dash cinnamon

Rub salmon with mixture of butter, green peppercorns, and cinnamon. Use brine or natural packed peppercorns. Save remainder in plastic in refrigerator for 3 weeks or freeze.

Broiled Salmon Steaks

½ cup olive oil, margarine or butter
¼ cup dry white wine
1 chopped parsley
1 tsp. chopped fresh herbs or ¼ teaspoon dried
1 clove garlic, slice
6 salmon steaks, ¾ inch-thick (2)
1 tsp. salt

Combine fat of your choice, wine parsley, herbs and melt over low heat. When fat is melted, take off heat and let stand 15 minutes.

Sprinkle salt over salmon and place in greased broiler pan. Pour the above sauce over fish and broil 3 inches away from heating element. Broil about 4 minutes, basting now and then. Turn steaks and broil 4 minutes more. Find out if broiler is preheated.

Salmon Steaks- Pierre Steaks

4 salmon or tuna steaks, 1 inch thick
1 tsp. salt
3 tbsp. olive oil
2 tsp. Dijon-style mustard
1 tbsp. mustard seed
1 tsp. ground cumin
¼ teaspoon red pepper
1 tsp. lemon juice
1 tbsp. grated orange rind
3 tbsp. melted butter
3 tbsp. chopped parsley

Rub steaks with the salt. Put oil in a flat dish. Add mustard, mustard seed, cumin, pepper flakes, orange rind hand beat with fork until blended. Put steaks in this marinade, coating well on both sides. Marinate for 30 minutes, covered with plastic in cool place -not in refrigerator.

Remove fish from marinade. Broil on greased rack 3 inches from heating element and broil about 5 minutes per side. Remove salmon and put it back in the kept-warm marinate and turn to coat in marinade. Sprinkle with the parsley.

Poached Sea Bass Fillets

¾ cup chopped onions
2 tbsp. oil
2 minced garlic cloves
1 28 oz. can drained or fresh tomatoes, 1 1/2 lbs. fixed
4 anchovy fillets, chopped
4 sea bass fillets, at least ½ inch thick
½ tsp. red pepper flakes
1 tsp. dried thyme
¾ cup chopped Nicoise olives
1 tbsp. drained capers
¼ tsp. salt and pepper

Sauté ¾ cup chopped onions slowly in oil, add garlic cloves and cook some 30 seconds more. Add drained tomatoes, plus chopped anchovy fillets. Cook over moderate, high heat for 5 min., stirring. Add seasonings: red pepper flakes, dried thyme. Recipe says to bring to boil, reduce to simmer and add bass fillets. I would suggest letting tomato sauce cool to room temperature. Be sure to season bass.

Cook 3 or 4 min, per side, cover. Boil down sauce until thick. Add chopped Nicoise olives, capers, salt and pepper and simmer for 2 to 3 minutes. Drain bass if necessary and spoon over.

Fluke Fillets Andalouse

½ cup chopped onions
1 tsp. chopped garlic
1 cup green and red peppers (mixed), chopped

1/3 cup carrots, chopped
1 tsp. saffron
2 tbsp. oil
½ cup dry white wine
3 cups fixed tomatoes
4 fluke fillets - 5 to 6 oz. each
½ cup lemon juice

Soften cup chopped onions, garlic, chopped green and red peppers (mixed) chopped carrots and saffron in oil. Add cup dry white wine and simmer until nearly evaporated. Add fixed tomatoes and simmer 5 minutes. Top with fluke fillets. Cover and cook gently for 4 minutes. Remove fish and add juice of half a lemon.

Sea Bass with Caper Sauce

They say that you can use any filletable fish, even bluefish, which I do not go along with.

4 boneless fillets, skinned or is it unskinned?
½ cup milk
2 tbsp. vegetable oil
½ cup flour
2 tbsp. butter, melted
1/3 cup drained capers
sprinkling pepper

The usual milk, flour. Use vegetable oil. Fish go in skin side down so they are unskinned. They are cooked as above but they specify 3 or 4 min. per side, so they are probably thicker than sole. Transfer -rest of recipe lost. I gather that pan is wiped out and butter melted. Add drained capers and swirl around

Sole Steamed with Lime and Chives

4 skinned 5 to 6 oz. sole
2 tbsp. walnut oil
2 tbsp. lime juice
2 gratings nutmeg
1/3 cup chopped chives

1/3 cup chives
1 lime wedge

Arrange 4 skinned fish top side down on 14 inch heat-safe plate and sprinkle with tbsp. walnut oil, lime juice, gratings of nutmeg and chopped chives. Cover with foil and place over a 12- inch skillet of simmering water. Steam 8 to 10 minutes or until fish is opaque. Uncover and garnish each fillet with chives and lime wedge.

Broiled Swordfish with Mignonette Sauce

2 chopped shallots
1 tsp. crushed pepper
1/3 cup of red wine vinegar and tbsp water
4 steaks, 1 inch thick

Mince shallots and mix with crushed pepper, red wine vinegar and water. Rub 4 steaks 4 inches away from boiler, 4 minutes per side. Splash with sauce.

Pan Fried Trout with Tapenade Relish

1 cup of black olives -finely chopped and oil-cured
1 tsp. minced clove garlic
½ cup virgin olive oil
4 cleaned 8-oz. brook trout
1 cup milk
1 cup bread crumbs
¼ cup oil

Toss cup of black olives -finely chopped and oil-cured with minced garlic and   virgin olive oil. Dip brook trout in cup milk and then in same of seasoned bread crumbs. Pan   fry in oil until skin is crisp, about 3 minutes per side. Serve with the pan drippings.

Bluefish Baked in Mustard Sauce

2 tbsp. chopped onions
1 tbsp. minced garlic

3 tbsp. butter
1/3 cup white wine
1 ½ lb. bluefish fillets in 1 layer
3 tbsp. Dijon mustard
2/3 cups sour cream or yoghurt

Place bluefish fillets in one layer. Bake at 375 degrees for 12 to 15 minutes. Mix mustard with sour cream or yogurt. When fish is done, remove and add mustard juices to hot pan juices. Heat up but do not boil.

Shrimp and Sausage Bisque

4 tbsp. flour
¾ cup   oil
2 chopped onions
½ chopped   bell pepper
¼ cup parsley, chopped
1 tbsp. garlic, chopped
1 cup tomatoes
1 lb. andouille sausage
2 cups water
1   qt. seafood stock
4   lbs. shrimp
additional 2 cups water
1 1b. crab claws
¼ lb. oysters
¼ lb. scallops
3   oz. brandy
16   oz. heavy cream

Seasonings

3 whole bay leaves, crushed
4 tsp. lemon juice
1 tsp. dried thyme
½ tsp. whole allspice berries
¼   cup fresh parsley
6 whole cloves
5 tsp. salt

1 ½ tsp. pepper
¼ tsp. cayenne

Make brown roux by heating up oil over moderate heat. Add cup flour, a bit at a time, stirring to incorporate. Turn heat down to low and stirring constantly; cook until roux has turned the color of a pecan shell. This might take as long as 30 minutes. Now add onions, green pepper, scallion tops, parsley and garlic. Cook 10 minutes, stirring constantly until these vegetables are lightly browned. Add tomatoes, sausage, 2 qts. water, the above seasonings and half the above amount of shrimp, reserving other half to be added at the last minute. Add oysters and scallops, bringing mixture to the boil, turn heat to low and just simmer for an hour.

Add additional 2 cups water and allow to sit until room temperature is reached. Scrape meat from crab claws, if you have used them and discard claws. When ready to serve, add reserved shrimp, bring to boil, turn down heat and simmer for 5 minutes. At this point, add scallops and oysters and simmer an additional 5 minutes, at which point, shrimp should be pink. Again take pan off heat, cover and let sit for 10 minutes. Serve in soup bowls over boiled rice.

Some Sauces
Provencal

2 cups chopped onions
2 chopped garlic cloves
2 tbsp. soft butter
1 can undrained tomatoes
1 tbsp. sugar
3   oz. or ¼ cup tomato paste
1 tsp. thyme

Sauté chopped onions, garlic cloves in butter until soft. Add undrained tomatoes, sugar, tomato paste, thyme. Simmer 20 minutes.

Perrier's Stuffed, Sauced Sole

Perrier, the chef of Le Bec Fin, in Philadelphia, processes in a blender cut-up cold sole and with motor running, 2 or 3 eggs plus ½ cup cream.

Put sole fillets - how many? Sprinkle over chopped shallots and pipe on mousse. Probable fillets should be folded over. Half cover with mixture of fumet and dry white wine. Heat in oven at 350 degrees for 20 minutes. For sauce, reduce fumet and add chopped shallot, 3 oz. each dry white wine and vermouth, another cup fumet and juices from cooked mushrooms. Reduce and add cup cream. Strain and add pat butter.

Another Franey Marinade

1 inch-thick tuna fish steaks
1 ½ inch piece fresh ginger
4 sprigs thyme, fresh or dried
2 tsp. dark soy sauce
1 tsp. lemon juice
2 tbsp. oil
1 medium, peeled, diced tomato
2 tbsp. red wine vinegar
¼ cup each chopped scallions and olive oil
2 tsp. mince garlic cloves
¼ cup minced basil leaves

For tuna steaks, Franey says 3 minutes per side, 4 inches away from heat source. He marinates (cover with plastic for an hour out of the fridge with fresh ginger, thyme, 2 tsp. soy sauce, lemon juice, oil. He serves this fish in this case, tuna) with a vinaigrette on the side with medium tomato, vinegar, chopped scallions, olive oil, minced garlic and chopped basil leaves.

Sea Bass Sauce

Rub fillets with soft butter and smear with mixture of minced parsley, mince onion, garlic, finely minced, a little minced green pepper. Dot with butter and baste frequently. Pour cup or so canned tomatoes around it. A whole sea bass is called for in which case, I would put it in a roasting bag.

8

BREADS

All flour used in recipes in this book is all-purpose unless otherwise specified. I only sift when baking powder or soda is added. Do not use flour made from soft wheat, such as those available in the South, like Martha White, used for biscuit dough, when making bread. Use all-purpose flour, which is made from hard, or winter, wheat.

Flour

Measure flour by scooping it out of the bag or canister with a cup and leveling off with the back of a knife, being careful not to tamp or shake the cup. In this book sifting flour, unless the recipe calls for it or baking powder or baking soda have been added to the flour, is unnecessary.

Breadcrumbs

Your own breadcrumbs are far superior to what you can buy in the supermarket.

If possible, use your own homemade bread. If not, supermarket or bakery bread will do. If the recipe calls for fresh crumbs, remove crusts, tear bread into pieces, remove crusts and process in food processor. One slice should yield roughly half a cup. If dried breadcrumbs are called for, bread can be hardened or dried in a 250 degree oven. If you are topping food that is to be cooked or baked with crumbs, add crumbs to a little hot melted butter, plus a little parsley.

Bread

It seems that there is no food more appreciated than a loaf of homemade bread. Excellent as it is, this bread would not have been acceptable for dinner in the transplanted Southern household in which I grew up. It would have had to have been baking powder biscuits or cornbread. For best results, the bread should be made in small one-lb. batches (3 ½ or so cups flour): that two rises are as effective as the customary three. It is really a simple process, using the simplest of ingredients plus a bread stone, two pastry cloths, and a rubber bulb atomizer available in houseware stores. Bread is a time-consuming task It is difficult to be specific to the exact timing as it depends on the weather and the temperature of your kitchen. If the kitchen is cold, it will take longer for the bread to rise; if weather is humid, less water is required. Getting the feel of the dough comes with experience. Bread making is time consuming; perhaps four hours from start to finish. But the time is largely unsupervised; that is to say, there is nothing to prevent you from leaving the house while the dough is rising.

1 envelope dry active yeast
1/3 cup lukewarm water for the yeast
1 1/3 cups tepid water
2 ½ tsp. salt
4 level cups all-purpose unbleached flour

Mixing Dough

Check expiration date on yeast package. Drop yeast into 1/3 cup of lukewarm water, between 105 and 120 degrees. Stir well and allow to dissolve thoroughly for 5 or 10 minutes. Measure   lour into a fairly large mixing bowl. Scoop out flour from the bag or a canister with a measuring cup; leveling off in each instance with back of a knife. Add salt and combine thoroughly. Give yeast a final stir and pour into flour. Add the rest of the tepid water, using the cup in which yeast was dissolved so as to utilize any leftover bits of yeast. Mix with your hands, adding more of the water. The dough should be slightly sticky but certainly not firm. If necessary, more flour or water can be added.

Kneading

Kneading can be done in a heavy-duty mixer or processor, but many people prefer kneading by hand rather than assembling and cleaning a processor or mixer. Form the dough into a ball and turn out on lightly floured board. Kneading consists of turning the dough over on itself and pressing down with the heel of hand, turning the dough as you do so, slapping the dough down occasionally. Continue kneading for three or four minutes, sprinkling with a little flour if the dough gets too sticky.

Put the dough back in the bowl, cover the bowl with a towel and let rest for about 25 minutes. At the end of this time, the dough goes back on the board and is kneaded again for some three minutes more.

First Rise

Dough is returned to a clean bowl and again covered with a towel. (Always cover bowl with a towel). Rising temperatures should be generally within the 70 degrees to 75 degrees. In the summer, let the dough rise on a kitchen counter. In the winter, place the bowl in a kitchen cabinet, closing the door. If the kitchen is very cold, preheat the electric oven for one minute; turn off the oven and open the door for five to ten minutes to air oven out. When it is cool, place the bowl of dough inside of the oven, closing the door.

This only applies to the first rise and will not work if you have a gas stove. Ideally, dough should double in bulk in two hours. If it has not doubled, be patient.

Second Rise

Begin by heating oven to 400 degrees; insert a bread stone in upper third of oven if oven will accommodate both bread and bread stone. If not, bake bread in the middle portion of the oven.

Punch to deflate risen dough and turn out on a lightly floured board. With knife, cut dough into two equal portions. One portion stays on the board; the other goes back in the bowl, both covered by a towel for five minutes. Meanwhile, flour the two pastry cloths by thoroughly rubbing a handful or so of flour into each, shaking off excess.

Gently press one portion of dough on the board into a rough rectangle. Fold one long end over to the center. Do the same thing with the other long end and then fold each short side in to the middle. Turn dough over and repeat this process. To form this into a loaf, pat dough into a rectangle roughly nine inches in length. With side of hand, make a trench lengthwise down the center of dough from one end to the other. Fold one side of dough over to the trench. Do the same with other side and seal the two ends together with your fingertips.

Lay one of the floured pantry cloths on counter and place loaf in center, seal side up. Hold the two ends of cloth together and insert them in an open kitchen drawer. Close drawer and let loaf hang suspended. Go through the same process with the remaining ball of dough.

Final Rise

Bread should take roughly an hour to rise; it should be swollen and heavy.

Baking

Lightly flour cutting board. Gently and carefully, unroll each loaf onto board, seal side down. Do not let the two loaves touch. Working fast (or the dough will stick to board), with a sharp knife or a razor blade, make three long, shallow, diagonal slices down the length of each loaf. If you have a rubber atomizer, spray dough with water. If not, dip your fingers in cold water and sprinkle over dough. This, incidentally, should be done two more times during the baking process, once after bread has been in the oven for three minutes, and again after three more minutes.

Place board as far back in the oven as possible, directly over stone. Give board a jerk or two towards you; loaves will slide off onto the baking stone. Bake for 30 to 35 minutes, or until a light golden, not dark, brown. Tapping the bottom should yield a hollow sound. An instant thermometer inserted in bottom should read 200 degrees. Turn off the oven, open the door and let bread dry for three minutes. Remove loaves to rack and let cool. The longer the bread cools, the more intense the flavor.

Storage

This bread is good only for a day or two at the most. Wrap well in foil and store in the refrigerator or freezer. Defrost by unwrapping and placing in a cold oven. Heat the oven to 400 degrees and remove after 20 minutes.

Focaccia

1 envelope dry active yeast
1/3 cup lukewarm water for the yeast
1 1/3 cups tepid water
2 ½ tsp. salt
4 level cups all-purpose unbleached flour
3 ¼ tbsp. olive oil
4 oil-packed sun-dried tomatoes
1 tsp. capers
1 grating of garlic
3 tbsp. grated cheese

My own non-Italian version, delicious as an hors d'oeuvre. Focaccia is made exactly like the recipe for bread, but an 8"x8" baking pan substituted for the bread stone. Preheat oven to 375 degrees. Duplicate the French recipe before and after the first rise. Pat dough into rectangle, folding in the two ends exactly like above. Repeat this step and now pat dough into a rectangle the size of baking pan. Place dough in lightly greased pan. Drizzle over a little oil ad cover with oil-packed sundried tomatoes, a few capers, a grating of garlic, and, lastly, grated parmesan cheese.

Bake at 375 degrees in the lowest oven level for 35 minutes.

Cornbread (known in Tennessee as "egg bread")

A word on the subject of bacon fat, buttermilk and cornmeal. Bacon fat can always be found in Southern refrigerators. If you have to cook a slice or two of bacon to achieve this, crumble up the slices and add to cornmeal mixture. Use the powdered buttermilk if necessary; lastly, if Southern stone ground cornmeal is unavailable, my suggestion is to wait until you can find it.

3 tbsp. bacon fat
1 cup buttermilk or powdered buttermilk
1 ½ cups yellow, stone-ground cornmeal
2 eggs
½ tsp. salt
1 tsp. double-acting baking powder
1 tsp. baking soda

Preheat oven to 450 degrees. Some 10 min. or so in advance, add bacon fat to a 6 ½ inch skillet; it should be very hot, but short of smoking.

Break 2 eggs in bowl. Beat eggs lightly, adding baking powder, salt, buttermilk and one cup water, mixing well. Set skillet in oven. Batter will later be added to this skillet; it should be very hot, but short of smoking. Pour the mixture into the cornmeal, stirring only enough to mix. It should have the consistency of waffle batter. If too thick, stir in hot water.

Pour this mixture into the hot skillet and bake for 10 minutes; lower heat to 375 degrees and continue to cook for some 15 until browned and puffy.

Hoe Cake

Hoecake is said to have been the bread made by Confederate soldiers in the field on their shovels over an open fire.

1 cup buttermilk
½ tsp. baking soda
1 ½ cups stone-ground cornmeal
¼ tsp. salt

Mix together as in the previous recipe for cornbread. Pour half of the batter onto a hot, greased skillet, flip over and cook until brown. Repeat with the other half of the batter. Slice and serve.

If using powdered buttermilk, see above. Combine ingredients, adding enough boiling water to make a waffle batter consistency. Cook on greased, hot griddle, turning once.

Southern Biscuits

Southern custom requires that biscuits not be removed from the oven until they are ready to be served, one biscuit at a time. The purist will tell you that for true Southern biscuits you must purchase Southern flour and true Southern lard, rarely available in the North, and make your own baking powder with equal amounts of cream of tartar and baking soda. My family has made this word-of-mouth recipe for many years, for both breakfast and dinner. Here transcribed, the method is a little different in that, after the vegetable   shortening is added to the flour, enough milk is added so that the dough is soft, but workable. If the dough is too soft, add a little flour. This step makes better biscuits.   In addition to the ingredients listed below, you will need a flour sifter, baking sheet and a sharp biscuit cutter; a dull one will toughen the biscuits. If lucky, you may be able to find Southern soft wheat flour. Place:

a heaping cup of all-purpose flour, or Southern soft wheat
2 tbsp. double-acting baking powder
¼ tsp. salt
3 good tbsp. of cold vegetable shortening
½ cup of whole milk
¼ cup buttermilk

Preheat oven to 350 degrees. Aerate flour with fork, into a sifter. Scoop lightly into a one-cup and then a ½ cup measure; place the flour in sifter with the baking powder and salt and sift all into large bowl. Break the shortening into small bits and lightly work into flour mixture. Add all but two tbsp. of the buttermilk and mix into the dough with hands until it is of a workable consistency. If too hard, add the additional two tbsp. of milk; if too soft, add the same amount of flour. Knead no more than 8 or 9 times and turn onto lightly floured breadboard. On the board, pat dough out with your hands into a circle roughly ½ inch thick. Pour the melted butter over the dough and flick one half of the dough over the other. Press the two layers together lightly. Cut out biscuits with sharp cutter by pressing hard straight down. Do not twist. With a light hand, place in non-touching layer on baking sheet. Bake for 20 minute or until light golden.

Onion Bread

1 envelope yeast
½ cup water
4 cups flour
1 ½ tsp. salt
½ cup milk
¼ cup soft butter
½ cup hot water.
1 egg
1 cup chopped onion
1 tsp. poppy seeds
1 tsp. garlic powder
1 tsp. paprika

Dissolve envelope yeast in water. Add 2 cups flour, salt, milk, soft butter, and hot water. Add egg and beat for 2 min. Stir in rest of flour and kneed until smooth and elastic. Cover and let double – about an hour. Knead until no longer sticky and roll into 2 rectangles of 9 by 12 inches. Mix butter and onion, poppy seeds and, garlic powder and paprika. Spread on edges of dough. Cut rectangles into 3 equal strips and roll up from long side. Seal edges and braid. Brush with egg wash just before baking and sprinkle with poppy seeds.

Put on greased sheet and let rise 45 to 60 minutes. Makes two loaves. Bake at 350 degrees, 25 to 30 minutes.

Angel Biscuits with Food Processor

1 envelope yeast
¼ cup cake flour plus 2 ¼ cups all-purpose flour
1 ½ tbsp. sugar
1 tbsp. baking powder
½ tsp. salt
¾ cup shortening
2/3 cup buttermilk

Dissolve yeast in ¼ cup flour. Process dry ingredients for 30 seconds. Add yeast mixture and buttermilk with motor running but process only until mixed. Roll into ½ inch rectangles and bake on greased baking sheet for 15 minutes.

Latest Bread

6 cups flour
2 tsp. salt
1 envelope yeast dissolved in ½ cup water
2 cups water

First rise should double about 1 ½ hours; second, 45 minutes. After shaping, allow half hour. This was designed for four baguettes, 450 degrees for 20 minutes.

Food Processor Bread dough

30 seconds for yeast dough. Can do one at a time which is about 1 loaf (3 ½ cups). 10 seconds equals 30 seconds of kneading. Process dissolved yeast into dry ingredients, motor running, through feed tube.

Food Processor Pie dough

Pulse flour and butter until butter disappears. Add water and pulse until dough begins to mass or crumble. Do not let it go so long that it forms a ball. If using egg, first pulse egg and butter until you have a sticky mixture. Then pulse in dry ingredients until it clumps.

Frances Roth first processes yeast and water, then adds dry ingredients and processes 5 seconds. Add water, salt and process until smooth. Do this 20 seconds, processing, not pulsing. Scraped down and add dry ingredients, processing 10 seconds.

9

MEAT

Beef

As we are a nation of beefeaters, it is to our advantage to learn all we can about the various cuts, and where they come from on the animal, because this determines not only the tenderness but the cooking method as well. Tender cuts call for roasting, broiling or sautéing; the tough cuts require the tenderizing effects of long, slow stewing or braising. If you know your cuts, you will avoid the classic error made by inexperienced cooks of buying a nice-looking steak, ignoring the label and broiling it, only to find it unchewable.

Broiling a flank steak produces a meal consistent with shoe leather. Do not make the mistake of braising or stewing a tender cut; the meat will simply fall apart.

Grading

The mandatory federal and state inspection of and stamps on meat attest to the health of the animal. This is not to be confused with the USDA grading of meat for quality. This grading system is not compulsory and, while generally subscribed to by the meat industry; it is up to the individual packer or supermarket chain as to whether or not to use it. Some stores have their own ratings.

The grades (for quality), which concern us, are the highest four categories: top, prime, followed by choice and select. The age of the animal and the appearance of the meat are taken into account. In the past, the main criteria for quality and tenderness was the amount of internal fat or marbling; the more marbling, the higher the grade. In the mid-seventies, the USDA, bowing perhaps to consumer pressure, revised their policies on marbling, modifying the required amounts.

As a result, today's beef is much leaner, for better or worse, depending on how you look at it. Some feel that all grades have moved up a notch; that is, what used to be classified as choice is now considered prime.

It is preferable to spend more at a good butcher shop where prime or choice are available, or even order from one of the Western mail order houses specializing in prime beef.

Keep in mind that a good cut of beef should be firm, well marbled with white bones or blotched with red

Cuts of Beef

The tender cuts, those that can be broiled, roasted or sautéed (dry heat) come from the non-working, unexercised parts of the animal. This is the midsection along the backbone, namely the rib, loin and, to a lesser degree, the sirloin. Cuts from the other sections have been toughened by exercise and should be cooked by moist heat methods, such as braising or stewing. Visualize the back of a steer from shoulder to tail. Start with the chuck or shoulder, followed by the rib and loin sections, the sirloin and the rump.

Shoulder

The chuck or shoulder is tough, a good source of stewing meat and hamburger. It also yields the blade roast, arm cut and cross rib pot roasts, sometimes cut into steaks, which should be braised.

Rib Section

Next comes the rib section which runs from the shoulder to the loin. It provides the fine standing rib roasts and rib steaks. The farther away you get from the chuck, the more tender the cut.

Loin

The loin follows the rib section and yields the finest cuts, T-bone, fillet, shell and porterhouse steaks. The tenderloin or fillet can be removed, cooked whole or cut into fillets, Chateaubriand, fillet mignon or tournedos.

Sirloin

While the term "tenderloin" is synonymous with tenderness, it is the best part of the animal, inferior to the loin. Part of the "working" flesh of the animal, the most familiar and most tender steak is the pin bone, that can be either broiled or sautéed.

The flat and the wedge bone steaks are less desirable.

Round

This section starts in back of the hipbone and goes from the leg to the ankle. It consists of the top sirloin, the rump, the eye roast, the bottom and the top round, plus shin or shank, generally used for soup or stock. These cuts are great for braising.

Flank and Plate

These two cuts are located on the underside of the animal, beneath the loin and rib sections. Flank steaks can be stuffed, rolled up and braised. London broil is made from cuts in this section. The plate is next to the flank section and below the rib. This yields the so-called skirt steak, similar to the flank.

Brisket

This is next to the plate. The entire brisket makes a good pot roast that is usually cut into two or three smaller roasts, good for braising, boiling, and corned beef. A favorite is the standing rib roast. It has flavor, tenderness and, unlike the fillet roast, texture. The two ribs next to the chuck are too tough and are not included in a roast. If the roast is halved, the small end nearest to the loin, known as a first cut, is more desirable. If you buy your roast from a good butcher, you can rest assured that all the necessary trimming will have been done, backbone removed or broken for easier carving. On the other hand, the supermarket does little other than package theirs. A minimum of three ribs, which could weigh from six to eight pounds, is recommended.

Among food writers, there is a surprising variance not only with regard to serving portions but as to roasting temperatures. Suggested serving portions can range from 10 to 12 ounces to two ribs per person, but 10 ounces is, in my opinion, perfectly adequate.

Standing Rib Roasts, Prime or Choice

My favorite is the standing rib roast. It has flavor, tenderness and unlike the fillet roast, texture. The roast can be large, comprising all 7 ribs and I say the bigger, the better. It is often halved. The desirable half is the small end next to the loin, known as the first cut. Count on close to 12 oz. per person.

If you have a well-insulated oven, try the high temperature method of roasting. If you time it to the minute, your roast will be unfailingly brown on the outside, rare in the middle. Preheat oven to a hot 500 degrees. Bring roast to room temperature by taking it out of the refrigerator an hour before roasting. Rub it with a cut clove of garlic and a little seasoned flour.

The Beef Roast goes into shallow roasting pan, rib side down and into oven. Roast for exactly 5 minutes per pound. At the end of this time, turn oven off and without once opening door, let roast stay in the oven for 2 hours. Remove from oven and give it a 20 minute rest before carving. Make gravy (see gravy).

Should you use the moderate temperature method, preheat oven to 450 degrees, season roast and bring to room temperature as above. Roast for 15 minutes, rib side down. Turn heat down to 325 degrees and cook until roast is done. A small 4-lb. roast should take a total of an hour and a quarter while a larger roast of say, 11 lbs., will take 2 hours, 45 minutes or a meat thermometer reading of 125 degrees to 130 degrees, rare.

Timing

It is difficult to give precise cooking times due to differences in the shape of the roast, the individual oven and how much initial chill has been taken off roast. For this reason, an instant-read meat thermometer is indispensable. Check by inserting thermometer in the thickest part of the meat near the end of cooking. A rare roast will register at 120 degrees, medium will read 125 degrees and well-done will read 140 degrees. Remove thermometer immediately.

Gravy

One food writer has written that the sophisticated avoid flour when making a gravy. Not all would agree with this notion. If you are among them, then the following gravy is for you. Whether beef, lamb, chicken, or any other kind, all gravies begin in the same way, that is, by degreasing the roasting pan. This is a lot easier if you have a plastic, long-spouted, deglazing pitcher, or a so-called gravy separator. If so, pour contents of roaster into the pitcher.

Fat will rise to the top and the pan juices will remain on the bottom. (Five minutes in the freezer will help congeal the fat. If you use the cup, fat will have to be spooned off in order to get to the pan drippings underneath). Reserve 2 tbsp. of fat: skim off remaining fat from drippings.

Do not wash the roaster out. Place the reserved fat into the roasting pan. Heat roaster   over moderately high heat. When hot, add 2 tbsp. all-purpose flour (unscientifically, a handful). Turn down heat and stir until flour is thoroughly incorporated (properly done, this will ensure that you will never have to strain gravy). Pour pan drippings through spout of pitcher into roaster, stirring well.

Add approximately one cup of beef stock, or half dry wine and half stock or plain water, a little at a time, stirring constantly. Continue to add liquid until proper gravy consistency is reached, adding more if necessary. Simmer for a minute or two, season and serve immediately in gravy boat. If allowed to stay in pan over even the lowest heat, flour will soak up liquid and more will have to be added.

There is waste in a standing rib roast, which can be turned into stock. Place carcass and any bones in kettle with the appropriate aromatic vegetables (see stocks) and cover with cold water; add appropriate aromatic vegetables.   Partially cover pan and simmer very slowly for several hours. Strain and chill for degreasing purposes.

Remaining Roast Beef (Boeuf en Miroton)

If this dish were not so elegant, you might use an old-fashioned Southern term, "a made dish," or as we would call it, a hash leftover. This is a way of dealing with slices of remaining roast beef other than in sandwiches or pot roast.

2 thinly sliced onions
1 chopped carrot
2 chopped celery ribs
5 tbsp. unsalted butter
2 tbsp. all-purpose flour
1 cup stock or gravy from previous roast
1 tbsp. tomato paste
1 minced garlic clove
1 tbsp. red wine vinegar
½ lb. sliced mushrooms
¼ tsp. each salt and pepper
1 bouquet garni
1 tbsp. chopped, drained capers
1 ½ to 2 lbs. reserved sliced beef

1/3   cup dry bread crumbs
1 tbsp. melted unsalted butter

Preheat oven to 350 degrees. Soften vegetables, remove from pan, blend in flour and stock. Then return vegetables to pan. Add tomato paste, garlic, vinegar, mushrooms, reserved gravy, bouquet garni, salt and pepper to taste. Simmer slowly for 10 minutes to make a velouté.

In a 1½-quart greased baking or gratin dish, layer five or six slices of the cooked beef on the bottom of dish. Pour the resulting velouté over the beef; sprinkle with breadcrumbs to which a little melted butter and capers have been added. Bake in for 25 minutes or until golden and bubbly.

Steaks

We all have our favorite cuts. Mine happens to be the T-bone, cut about 3/4 inch thick. Why not the fillet? It is a tradeoff. The fillet is wonderfully tender but lacks the flavor and the chewiness of the T-bone. My butcher tells me that it is a waste of time to marinate his meat. I compromise by rubbing steak with a cut clove of garlic and a few drops of oil per side.

Bring the meat to room temperature for 30 minutes, pat dry, season and rub with a cut clove of garlic and a few drops of oil. Rather than using fat, dry cook in a heavy skillet, preferably cast-iron. When good and hot, hot enough to make a drop of water sizzle. Drop in steaks, regulating heat so that they do not burn in non-touching layer, reducing heat so that meat browns but does not burn, 3 or 4 minutes per side, turning and cooking additional minute on the other side. (A ¾-inch thick steak will take four minutes on one side, two on the other.) Steaks are ready when small beads of moisture appear on the surface which will be springy to the touch as opposed to soft. Season.

Rather than using fat, dry cook in a heavy skillet, preferably cast-iron. When skillet is hot enough to make a drop of water sizzle,

When steaks are ready, small beads of moisture will appear on the surface and meat is springy to the touch. If steak   is   one inch thick or more, it is preferable to broil and season.

A simple pan sauce
1 tbsp. unsalted butter

1 chopped shallot or green onion
½ tsp. minced garlic
½ cup dry white or red wine
½ cup beef or chicken stock
1 tbsp. tomato paste
salt and pepper to taste

Melt butter in a skillet. Over medium low heat, add shallot or onion and garlic; sauté one minute. Pour in dry red or white wine; slowly reduce to almost nothing. Add stock and tomato paste. Reduce to slightly less than ½ cup. Season to taste and pour over steak.

Hamburger

Buy ground beef marked lean rather than super lean, from the chuck or round. When ready to form into cakes, handle meat as little and as lightly as possible in order not to toughen it, even to the extent of not bearing down on patty with spatula when cooking.

1 lb. lean hamburger from chuck or round
½ tsp. salt`
¼ tsp. pepper
1 tbsp. chopped parsley
½ tsp. Worcestershire sauce

Season meat with salt, pepper, parsley and Worcestershire sauce. One lb. will yield three five-ounce patties. Patties should be on the thin rather than the thick side. Heat an ungreased skillet, preferably cast-iron, until very hot. Sprinkle salt on skillet bottom and cook patties, cooking roughly three minutes per side.

Boeuf à la Bourguignonne

This fancy beef stew differs from others in that the wine is not added until toward the middle of the cooking time. The mushrooms are first sautéed, and the onions browned and cooked in stock before adding them to the stew at the last minute.

3 lbs. boneless beef, rump or chuck, cut into 1 ½- inch cubes
2 tbsp. olive oil

¼ tsp. each of ground cumin and allspice
squirt of anchovy paste
2 tbsp. all-purpose flour
¼ tsp. white or black pepper
3 cups beef stock
3 cloves garlic, peeled and mashed
1 bouquet garni (bay leaf, 1 sprig dried thyme, parsley)
2 or more cups dry red wine
1 tbsp. tomato paste
1 tbsp. unsalted butter
8 blanched, stemmed and peeled pearl onions
½ cup chicken stock
1 cup sliced mushrooms
1 ½ tsp. salt
1 tbsp. olive oil

Pat dry beef cubes with paper towels. Heat up enough oil to film bottom of large skillet by 1/4 inch. Stir in cumin, allspice and anchovy paste. Place beef in one layer. If pan is too small, brown in batches. When well browned on all sides, season with salt and pepper. Gradually add the flour, mixing well. Heat up beef stock and add to skillet; add the garlic, herb bouquet and tomato paste. Bring to boil, immediately reduce heat to a simmer for one hour. Add wine and continue simmering for another hour and a half or until beef is tender. Meanwhile, prepare the pearl onions. Cut a cross in bottom of onions and blanch onions in pan of boiling water to cover, for exactly one minute. Slip off stems and peel. Add enough oil to film bottom of another skillet. Heat over moderately low heat, add onions and brown lightly, turning often: season and add chicken stock. Bring to the boil, reduce heat, cover and simmer slowly for about 25 minutes, or until onions are tender. Set aside.

Slice mushrooms. Heat up oil and butter in skillet over moderately high heat and add mushrooms, shaking pan. Brown for another minute or so; set aside. When stew is cooked, add mushrooms and onions to the beef mixture, and warm briefly.

Beef In General

When Europeans criticize our food, a proper retort would be that our beef is second to none. Nowhere in Europe can you walk into a supermarket and find the well marbled steak that we take for granted.

The most important thing to know about beef is where it comes from on the animal, as this is what determines the cooking method. The tender cuts, those that can be roasted, broiled or sautéed, come from the least exercised part, the mid section, along the backbone, namely the rib, loin and to a lesser degree, the sirloin. Cuts from the other section, the shoulder, leg, rump, etc., have been toughened by exercise and should be cooked by moist heat methods, such as braising or stewing.

Most beef is federally inspected for quality. The top grade is Prime, followed by Choice. The 3 lesser grades, Good, Standard and Commercial do not concern us. As Prime beef is difficult to find unless you have a specialty butcher shop in your neighborhood (I do not), my observations will be based on Choice, readily available at the supermarket, a bit less tender than prime, less marbled with fat but perfectly acceptable.

The chart below should help you place these cuts. Try perusing the meat bin in your supermarket. It will help you avoid the classic error made by all beginning cooks - including this one of bringing home a handsome steak and broiling it. After it has been proved inedible or uncutable, you look at it. Yes, it is a steak alright but an unbroilable one, perhaps a blade or flank steak.

Terrine De Boeuf

1 lb. of thinly sliced precooked beef
10 oz. each cooked ham and bacon
1 tbs. parsley
1/8 tsp. allspice
2 cloves minced garlic
2 tbsp. brandy
2 cup beef stock

This is a cold version of leftover cooked beef. Layer 1   lb. of thinly sliced precooked beef in greased casserole, 10 oz. each cooked ham and bacon, starting with bacon strips, ending up with beef. Use very little salt. Sprinkle over chopped parsley, allspice, minced garlic, brandy and stock. Cover tightly and place casserole in bain marie. Bake at 350 degrees for 1 ½ hours. Chill for 3 days. Slice with care.

Roast Beef Hash

1 tbsp. oil
½ cup chopped onion
1 minced garlic clove
1 tsp. dried tarragon
½ tsp. dried basil
½ cup each dry white and sherry
2 tsp. curry
½ tsp. salt
2 tbsp. cider vinegar
¼ tsp. pepper
1 tsp. Worcestershire
4 cups cooked beef, sliced
1 tsp. each butter and flour or breadcrumbs
1 cup beef stock or breadcrumbs sautéed in butter

Sauté onions lightly over moderate heat for 5 or 10 minutes. Add garlic and cook 1 minute more. Add rest of ingredients and bring to boil. Add beef to this plus 1 cup stock. Simmer covered for 20 minutes. If not thick enough, thicken with beurre manié (butter and flour) or sautéed bread crumbs.

Steaks with Herb Butter

1 tbsp. herb butter
1 tbsp. finely chopped shallots or onions
½ tsp. finely minced garlic
½ cup dry red wine
1 tbsp. tomato paste
2 tbsp. brandy
1 cup créme fraîche

You could now drop a pat of seasoned (see herb butter) on each steak or you could go a step further and make a fast pan or deglazing sauce (see). As you will have sautéed steak in dry skillet, drop small pat of butter into steak skillet. Add finely chopped shallots or onions, minced garlic and cook 1 minute. Pour in dry red wine and let it slowly reduce to almost nothing. Now add same amount of stock. Add tomato paste and reduce to slightly less than ¼ cup. Season and pour over steak or do as the French.

At the very end, take skillet and swirl in pat of butter, unnecessary but awfully good.

Au Poivre Vert

Sauté steak exactly as above. After removing steak, add   butter. When hot, deglaze with brandy and crème fraîche (see some unrelated ingredients) Bring to boil and return steaks to skillet to coat.

Beef Sauté a la Bourguignonne

½ lb. mushrooms
2 tbsp. butter
1 tbsp. oil
18 braised white onions
1 chunk bacon
1 clove mashed garlic
1 tsp. tomato paste
2 ½ lbs. cubed fillet of beef
1 ½ cups beef stock
¼ dried or ½ tsp fresh thyme
1 ½ cups dry white wine
1 tbsp. tomato paste
beurre mané (1 tbsp. each butter and flour)

Begin by sautéing sliced mushrooms and setting aside. Blanch onions by dropping in boiling water for 1 minute, Remove, run under cold water and slip off skins. Sauté in usual mixture of hot butter and oil for 10 minutes. Blanch bacon in boiling water for 5 minutes. Rinse, drain, pat dry and dice.

Pat meat dry and sauté briefly in the hot butter and oil for 2 or 3 minutes per side, in 1 layer or in batches. Remove and sauté bacon. Set aside and pour off fat. Dice.

In meat skillet, place the stock, wine, tomato paste and thyme. Boil down by half. Off heat, whisk in beurre manié (wich see) to thicken lightly. Back on burner, simmer 1 minute, stirring. Add sautéed mushrooms, bacon, and braised onions and simmer for 2 minutes. Correct seasonings and pour over meat.

Beef Stews and Daubes

Dress up a plain beef stew with wine and special seasonings, call it a daube or ragout, if you wish, and you have a dish for an informal dinner party. If you are a devoté of the current country cooking trend, you might serve it with a tossed salad and a loaf of crusty bread. If you are going away with such simplicity, make sure your ingredients are the best and cooked to perfection. The two cuts I like best for stewing come from the rump or the chuck pot roast. Allow ½ lb. per person. An inferior cut is liable to become stringy, while too good a cut will disintegrate in the long, slow cooking. The wine you use in the stew does not have to be expensive, but it should be a wine that you are willing to drink. I rely on the California mountain red and whites. Whether you marinate or not, brown or not brown the meat, thicken or not thicken, cook in 1 piece or cut it up. Use a red or a white wine. However the basics are the same -to simmer the meat in an aromatic mixture of wine, seasonings and vegetables.

1 tsp. salt
2 cloves mashed garlic
¼ cup olive oil
2 cups of dry wine
2 cups each onions and carrots
1 herb bouquet (a few parsley stems, fresh or dried)
6 peppercorns and an herb bouquet

My butcher has meat so tender that it would be a waste of time to marinate it. Should you wish to do so, start the day before? Mix salt, mashed garlic, cup olive oil, 2 cups if a dry wine, onions and carrots, herb bouquet with a few parsley stems, fresh or dried and peppercorns. Tie various herbs in a square of cheesecloth with string for easy removal. Marinate in covered dish (ceramic or glass) overnight in refrigerator. If recipe calls for browning, be sure to dry meat after removing from marinade. Of course this will serve as the braising or stewing liquid. A stew can be made a day ahead and refrigerated. Not only does the flavor improve but fat removal is easier

Beef Stew -Peggy's Boeuf à la Bourguigonne

This recipe differs from others in that the wine is not added in the beginning.

6 strips bacon
3 cloves mashed garlic
3 lbs. cubed rump or chuck
1 tsp. salt
½ tsp. pepper
1 large carrot, sliced
herb bouquet (see above)
1 large onion, chopped
½ cup dry red wine
2 tbsp. flour
1 cup sliced mushrooms
1 ¼ cups beef stock
1 small braised white onions
1 tbsp. tomato paste

Begin by sautéing mushrooms in butter (see). Braise onions (see). Brown bacon. Remove, pouring out most of fat. Brown meat well on all sides, Remove. Lightly sauté onions and carrots. Return meat to skillet. Season with the salt and pepper; sprinkle over the flour. Return bacon to skillet plus stock, herb bouquet and tomato paste. Bring to boil, turn down to the merest simmer, covered. After cooking for an hour, add wine to almost cover meat. Total cooking time will be 2 ½ or 3 hours or until meat is fork tender.

When done, put roast on platter to rest 15 minutes or so before carving. Heat up onions and mushrooms in the liquid. Pour over roast. If amount of liquid is excessive, boil it down to a cup or more

Daube à la Provencale

No two men can agree on what constitutes a daube any more than two Spaniards can agree on paella. The point on which they can agree is that a piece of meat is slowly simmered in wine and stock, surrounded by flavoring vegetables.

4 lbs. rump roast of beef, larded by your butcher
6 mashed garlic cloves
1 handful fresh herbs or tsp dried
½ qt. of beef stock
2 heaping tbsp. flour
1 large onion, chopped

3 or 4 cups dry red wine
2 cups tomatoes, peeled
3 tbsp. brandy

Spread half vegetables and herbs on bottom of casserole. Season and flour roast and place on top of vegetables. Top with rest of vegetables. Add garlic and wine almost to cover. Cover casserole tightly and cook at 250 degrees for 4 hours.

After 3 hours have elapsed, mash 3 anchovy fillets, 3 tsp. vinegar, 3 tsp. drained capers. Beat in 3 tbsp. of oil from anchovy can and beat into casserole liquid with fork. When done, transfer meat to warm platter. If casserole liquid is excessive, boil down to 1 cup.

Chili

2   lbs. chuck hamburger
2 cups water
3 tsp. chili powder
1 tbsp. oil
15   oz. can tomato or 1 ¾ cups concentrated tomato
1/8   tsp. red pepper flakes
2 tsp. oregano

Sauté meat only until it loses its pink. Add water and simmer for 1 ½ hours. Add rest of ingredients and cook another 45.

Veal

Unless you have access to the ethnic markets of a city, the desirable, pale pink, almost white veal is not always easy to find. The best comes from a very young, milk-fed calf. European calves are milk-fed while ours are generally grass fed, producing reddish, tougher meat.

Except for the following sautés, veal is better braised rather than roasted, because it is lean meat.

While you can roast a leg, it requires constant basting.

Veal Escalopes

Call it a scallop, escalope, scaloppini or even schnitzel; it is still a small, boneless medallion of veal, generally cut from the leg. Depending on appetites, allow two per serving. These escalope recipes are designed for the tender, pale pink variety. Although expensive, you are paying for exactly what you get; there are no bones and no waste.

The recipes that follow are so basic that they make excellent examples of the sauté.

Escalopes must be patted thoroughly dry, the fat very hot and the skillet uncrowded. Use oil alone or a mixture of butter and oil in the proportion of two butter to one oil, just enough to film bottom of skillet by 1/8 inch.

½ pound veal escalopes, 1/8 –inch thick, fat removed

2 tbsp. butter

1 tbsp. olive oil
1 cup all-purpose flour for dredging
salt and pepper to taste
juice of half a lemon

Pat dry escalopes thoroughly. Lay escalopes between two sheets of wax paper and press down (gently) with rolling pin until thin and of uniform thickness. Dry dust with flour seasoned with salt and pepper (at the last minute). If using oil alone, heat skillet until a light haze forms over the pan; if using a mixture of butter and oil or butter alone, place scallops in skillet at the very moment the butter stops sizzling. Turn escalopes to coat, lowering heat so that they do not burn. Lightly brown both sides. Remove to warm serving platter.

The Italians have as many ways of finishing escalopes as they have of preparing chicken breasts. Here are some options:

After removing browned escalopes, wipe out pan, removing any burned grease. Add lemon juice, a pat of butter and a little finely chopped parsley. Take pan off heat, swirl pan around and pour over escalopes.

To make a deglazing sauce, wipe pan clean and melt pat of fresh butter. Add one tablespoon of finely chopped green onions and cook for one minute. Deglaze skillet with ¼ cup each stock and a dry white wine. Boil down by half and pour over the escalopes.

Lamb

Lamb is a staple in many countries but apparently not in this one. On several occasions, guests have told me that they tasted lamb for the first time at my house. Lamb used to be a seasonal animal, and you knew exactly what you were getting. Born in late winter, there was the expensive baby lamb followed by spring lamb, available until October.

Legs could weigh from 4 ½ to 7 lbs., the flesh pink, the fat a pearly white. Then came the heavier winter lamb or yearling with legs weighing up to nine pounds. After a year, lamb became mutton, a rarity in this country. Today, not only has the lamb-breeding season been extended, but marketing methods have also changed. The heavier winter lamb, which can weigh up to nine pounds, now dominates the market. The approximate age can be determined by the weight of the whole leg.

A butcher can confuse the issue by halving the leg. If so, you have a choice between the shank and the butt end. The shank is meatier, easier to carve and more expensive. As some lamb is now shipped frozen to the market, then defrosted and sold as fresh, check this out at your market if you plan to refreeze.

Unlike beef, lamb is slaughtered at such an early age that tough muscle fibers have not had time to develop. For this reason, much of it can be roasted or broiled. The leg is probably the most popular cut. It can be roasted and, if boned, flattened out (butterflied) and broiled in no time at all. Even the tougher, cheaper cuts, such as the shoulder, can be deboned, rolled and roasted, but better yet, save it for stews.

Lamb yields some elegant and very expensive cuts, among them the saddle and the rack. Cut from the rib section, the rack serves three at the most and is often the most expensive entree on a restaurant menu. Two racks tied together make a crown roast fit for the finest dinner party. You will not find these cuts at your local supermarket, nor will you find the top-grade prime, but there is nothing wrong with the second-grade choice generally carried by supermarkets.

Leg of Lamb

Allow ½ lb. per person. Ask your butcher to remove tail and hipbone for easier carving. Cut off most of the fat. Some will remove the parchment-like covering known as the fell, and others leave it on the theory that it holds the roast in place. Boiling potatoes cooked in roasting pan along with the roast are delicious. Allow one or more small boiling potatoes per person. Do not peel.

12 small unpeeled boiling potatoes cut in half, if large
¼ tsp. each salt and pepper
4 ½ lb. leg of lamb
2 slivered garlic cloves
1 tbsp. olive oil
1 cup all-purpose flour for sprinkling
1 tbsp. sherry vinegar
1 tsp. lemon juice
1 tsp. thyme or basil (optional)

Place potatoes in a saucepan and cover with water; bring to the boil, reduce heat, cover and simmer for 10 minutes. Drain in colander and run under cold water to facilitate peeling. Pat potatoes dry with paper towels. Place around roast when it goes in oven and turn occasionally during roasting to ensure that they brown. If not brown enough, brown briefly in pan fat before making the gravy.

Preheat oven to 350 degrees. Remove roast from refrigerator some 30 minutes before cooking and place in shallow roasting pan, on rack, fat side up. Season leg of lamb with salt and pepper and, with a sharp knife, make six or seven half-inch slits in the surface. Insert small garlic slivers in each slit. If desired, rub surface with cold bacon grease or oil, sprinkle lightly with flour and pour over a little vinegar, an old- fashioned Southern way (Mediterranean cuisine recommends dousing roast with lemon juice and covering it with chopped thyme or basil.) Place pan in middle level of preheated oven. Roast 15 to 20 minutes per pound, or until meat thermometer reads 135 degrees. Remove roast to warmed serving platter, cover loosely with foil and allow to rest for 20 minutes before carving. The temperature will continue to climb five or ten degrees during this period. Prepare gravy. Serves 4 to 5.

Once again, an instant-read meat thermometer is indispensable. Insert in thickest part of roast; leave for 15 seconds or until needle stops moving, roast, 140 degrees for medium rare and 150 degrees for medium. In accordance with FDA's directives and avoiding eating rare meat, roast lamb for 15 to 20 minutes per pound, when meat thermometer reads 135 degrees, remove roast to warmed serving platter, cover loosely with foil, and allow it to rest for 20 minutes before carving. The temperature will continue to climb five or ten degrees during this period.

Make gravy in roasting pan. Spoon   off all but 2 tbsp. of fat leaving all brown bits in bottom of pan undisturbed. Turn up heat under burner. When pan is good and hot, throw in heaping tablespoon of flour. Turn down heat to low and stir into the hot fat to brown. Two important points are that the pan must be hot and the flour browned before adding a liquid. Add ¼ cup dry red or white wine. Let this bubble a minute or so and pour in 1 cup of beef, chicken stock or even water, if you must. Stir well for a few minutes, adding more liquid if necessary to get a proper consistency. Season to taste. If gravy is properly made, straining will not be necessary

Lamb Chops with Dijon Sauce

A lamb stew can be made exactly as this recipe, substituting two pounds of cubed stewing lamb for the chops.

2   cloves mashed garlic
1   tsp. anchovy paste
2   tbsp. chopped rosemary
4 loin lamb chops, each 1-inch thick (4 ounces)
1 tbsp. unsalted butter
2 ¼ tbsp. chopped shallots
1 clove garlic
½ cup dry red or white wine
½ cup beef or chicken stock
1 tsp. Dijon mustard

In a mortar, make a thick, paste-like mixture of garlic, anchovy paste and rosemary. Warm cast iron skillet without fat. When very hot, place seasoned lamb chops in pan reduce heat and sear chops about three minutes per side. Season again and remove cooked chops to warmed platter.

Prepare a pan sauce by adding butter to skillet. When moderately hot, add shallots and garlic. Cook for one minute. Raise heat; add wine and stock. Scrape and stir pan bottom. Reduce liquid to ½ cup. Incorporate Dijon mustard until smooth. Pour over chops. Serves 2.

Braised Shoulder Lamb Chops

Lamb chops lend themselves to a presentation, that is, they can be arranged on a serving platter, surrounded by neat, attractive alternate piles of cooked vegetables, such as new potatoes browned in unsalted butter, green beans or perhaps lightly sautéed cherry tomatoes. Veal or pork chops can be substituted for the lamb.

4 shoulder lamb chops
all-purpose flour for dredging
2 tbsp. olive oil
1 chopped celery rib
1 small chopped yellow onion
1 tbsp. finely chopped garlic
½ cup dry red wine
½ cup stock, chicken or beef
½ tbsp. Worcestershire sauce
½ tsp. tomato paste
1 finely chopped rosemary or thyme
salt and pepper to taste
1 tbsp. chopped parsley

Pat chops dry with paper towels and dredge lightly in seasoned flour, shaking off excess. In a Dutch oven, heat one tablespoon of oil. Brown chops on both sides. Remove and reserve. If fat has burned, wipe out pan and add second tablespoon of oil. Reduce heat, add and soften celery and onions for about 10 minutes; add garlic and cook for one minute. Add wine, reducing it to a tablespoon. Add stock. Season to taste with salt and pepper. Add Worcestershire, tomato paste and sprig of rosemary or thyme. Add chops. Bring to boil, immediately reducing heat to simmer. Cook covered for 45 minutes.

Again remove chops, skim off any fat and then boil until thickened. Remove rosemary or thyme and sprinkle with parsley. Taste for additional seasonings and serve.

Curried Lamb Stew

This personal favorite, derived from all the Indian curries that I have encountered throughout the years, is, in spite the long list of ingredients, as follows:

3 lbs. of cubed lamb shoulder
2 tbsp. unsalted butter
1 tbsp. oil
3 small sliced yellow onions or 2 sliced leeks
3 celery ribs
1 tbsp. flour
1 clove of mashed garlic
¼ grated fresh ginger
1 tbsp. all-purpose flour
2 tbsp. mild curry powder
1 tsp. turmeric
big pinch cinnamon
1 tsp. Dijon mustard
salt and pepper to taste
4 chopped dates
1 tbsp. minced crystallized ginger
2 tsp. lime juice
4 tbsp. mango chutney
1 ½ cups beef or chicken stock
1 bouquet garni (6 parsley stems, 1 bay leaf, and 2 fresh sprigs of rosemary)
1 tbsp. all-purpose flour
½ cup light cream
2 tbsp. sherry wine vinegar

Preheat oven to 400 degrees. Cut lamb into cubes; heat oil and pat meat dry. Working in batches, sauté over moderately high heat until lamb is slightly brown. Do not crowd skillet. Remove lamb and set aside.

Reduce heat to very low; soften onion or leeks and rib of celery, about 10 minutes. Add clove of garlic and fresh ginger. Cook for one minute. Meanwhile mix together tablespoon each of flour, curry powder, cinnamon, mustard, salt and pepper. Stir in well and add dates, and crystallized ginger, limejuice, mango chutney, beef stock and bouquet garni. Bring to the simmer. Place in oven and cook, covered, for 1 ½ hours. Taste for seasonings and add remaining flour dissolved flour in light cream. Do not let it boil. Once sauce is thickened, remove bouquet garni. (Can be frozen at this point.)

Could add, if you wish, cubed honeydew and simmer 5 min. more. Skim and correct seasonings.

Optional: add toasted coconut flakes. Serve over rice to which you have added grated orange peel.

Lamb Chops

I prefer the loin chop, cut 1-inch thick, to the smaller rib chop. You can cook them as is or you can marinate. I like to paint chops with a thick mixture of finely chopped garlic, anchovy paste and chopped rosemary. Or you might marinate several hours at room temperature in

1/3 cup minced onions
¼ cup each minced basil and honey
3 tbsp. oil
1 tbsp. each soy sauce and minced garlic

In any event, to cook, place iron skillet over high heat, without fat. When good and hot, throw in chops, immediately turning down heat. A 1 inch thick chop will take 3 minutes per side. To make a sauce, remove cooked chops to warm serving platter.

Add:

2 tbsp. butter
1 tbsp. finely chopped shallots
1 tsp. finely chopped garlic
¼ cup red wine
¼ cup beef or chicken stock
2 tbsp. Dijon mustard

Heat butter in pan. When hot, add shallots and garlic. Cook 1 minute. Raise heat and add red wine. Scrap pan, add beef or chicken stock. Reduce to ½ cup and add mustard. Pour over chops. Alternate piles of vegetables around chops, such as new potatoes browned in butter, green beans, lightly sautéed cherry tomatoes.

Lamb Curry

3 lbs. cubed stewing lamb
3 tbsp. butter
4 celery ribs
4 sliced leek or onion
1 tbsp. flour
1 tsp. curry powder
2 tsp. currant jelly
¼ tsp. cinnamon
salt, pepper to taste
1 tbsp. candied ginger, minced
2 tbsp. currant jelly
2 tsp. lime juice
1 smashed garlic clove
¼ cup raisins
½ cup beef stock
½ cup milk
5 cups cubed honeydew melon
¼ cup light cream

Sauté lamb in the butter just until it loses its pink. Remove and soften celery and leeks in the fat. Mix flour, curry, cinnamon, salt and pepper. Put in skillet and stir 1 minute over moderate heat. Add minced ginger, current jelly, lime juice, garlic, raisins, stock and milk. Return meat to skillet and bring to boil. Cover, turn down heat and simmer for an hour. Can be frozen at this point. Could add, if you wish cubed honeydew and simmer 5 min. more. Skim and correct seasonings. Add mixture of tbsp. flour and ¼ cup light cream. Let thicken. Can add toasted coconut flakes.

Lamb Stew Romagnolis

1 minced garlic clove
1 sprig rosemary, chopped
1/8 cup oil
2 lbs. cubed stewing lamb
½ cup flour
1 cup canned, Italian plum tomatoes
1 tsp. tomato paste

Start by sautéing minced garlic clove and chopped sprig rosemary briefly in cup oil. Now add stewing lamb which has been flowered by shaking with cup flour in paper bag. Brown well, season and add cup dry red or white wine. When it evaporates, add cup canned, Italian plum tomatoes plus tomato paste. Bring to boil and simmer for an hour

Lamb Stew and Mushrooms in a Velouté

2 lbs. stewing lamb
4 cups stock
2 garlic cloves, mashed, peeled
1 tbsp. small mushrooms
2 tbsp. herbs
2 tbsp. parsley
1 tbsp. butter
1 ¾ cups flour

Cover stewing lamb, -just cover, with any kind of stock. Add garlic cloves. Half cover pot with lid and simmer ½ hour. Add small mushrooms, herbs, parsley. Season to taste and simmer another ½ hour. Drain through colander, reserving. Make velouté, starting with roux of butter and tbsp. flour plus 1 ¾ cups.

Abbacchio alla Cacciatora

2 peeled garlic cloves
2 tbsp. olive oil
1 ½ lb. cubed flavored lamb
1 sprig rosemary
½ cup dry white wine
½ cup peeled, Italian plum tomatoes
1 tsp. tomato puree

Sauté peeled garlic cloves in a little olive oil. When they start to turn golden, remove and add cubed flavored lamb, a small bit of rosemary. Brown thoroughly. Season and add cup dry white wine. Let it evaporate and then add cup peeled, Italian plum tomatoes and tsp tomato puree which has been diluted in a small amount of water, the previously, sautéed garlic. Bring back to boil, turn down to the simmer and cook uncovered, for about 1 hour.

Lamb and Beans

1 lb. of beans
3 lbs. leg of lamb
2 sliced onions

¼ cup butter
1 clove garlic, mashed
1 tbsp. each dried rosemary and thyme
2 tsp. salt
1/8 tsp. pepper
2 cans Italian plum tomatoes, drained

Begin by soaking of beans overnight or the quick soak, covering them in 6 cups of water. Bring to boil and do so for 2 minutes. Take off heat, cover and let stand 1 hour. Drain and reserve liquid. Add enough water to this to make 2 qts. Bring this to boil, cover and simmer for 1 hour or until just tender, but not mushy. Drain.

Sauté sliced onions in butter. As they soften, add mashed garlic. Put this plus beans, dried rosemary and thyme, salt, pepper, Italian plum tomatoes, drained, in shallow roaster and top with dried-off lamb and sprinkle with extra rosemary. Cook at 325 degrees for about 3 hours (medium rare).

Lamb Stew - Simca

4 lbs. cut up lamb
1 head of garlic
1 bouquet garni
¼ sliced mushrooms
3 tbsp. butter
3 ½ cups stock.
3 tbsp. flour
2 cups stock

½ cup vinegar

Make a stock of the lamb bones. Use this just to cover cut up lamb. Add head of garlic and bouquet garni. After cooking for 30 minutes, add sliced mushrooms. Season and cook another half hour.

Strain, discarding bouquet garni and garlic. Keep meat warm while making roux. Wipe out skillet. Add butter, and stock. You might try flour, same butter and stock. Try adding vinegar.

Ham

A leg of fresh pork becomes ham after it has been cured in brine or dry-cured in salt. It can then be smoked (usually, but not always), followed by aging. On the other hand, a leg of fresh pork that has not been cured is confusingly known as fresh ham. This term applies only to the leg. There are many varieties of salt-cured ham, such as Bayonne ham, the Westphalian ham from Germany, Parma ham, or prosciutto, from Italy or the delicious hams from acorn-fed mountain pigs, known as Serrano ham from Spain. These dry-cured hams are usually eaten with no further cooking. The wonderful American Smithfield ham is salted and smoked.

In Virginia, when choosing a ham, you have several options. At the top of the list is the country ham. It has been smoked and aged for one year. Troublesome and expensive, yes, but if you are a ham fancier, they have no equal. Mostly salt-cured, they are sometimes smoked. A country ham is salty and strongly flavored. They can be ordered through mail-order houses and are often available in fancy butcher shops. Make sure that you have a container large enough for the required soaking and simmering, such as an old-fashioned ham boiler, plus the necessary mouths to feed. The flavor is so rich and overwhelming that in the South, where fine hams abound, they are not generally served as the entrée but as an accompaniment, such as chicken at one end of the table, ham, sliced paper-thin, at the other.

What you will probably find in your supermarket are canned hams, or the completely (or sometimes partially) pre-cooked. Any meat tastes better if the bone is left in. Read the label. If there is any question about cooking or reheating times, consult the butcher. While convenient (except for deep cuts sustained when opening cans) canned hams vary in quality, some flavorful, some not. Precooked hams make up 90 percent of the market. They come in a wide variety of cuts.

There are whole bone-in hams, which can range from 8 to 20 lbs., and whole, boned hams, weighing from 8 to 12 pounds. Either can be cut in half by your butcher, giving you a choice of the butt or shank end. The butt end is meatier. There is also the smaller picnic shoulder, with more flavor, more fat, and costs about one third less per pound.

Avoid those labeled "water added".

Precooked Ham

These hams have been heated to an internal temperature of 138 degrees, high enough to kill any threat of trichinosis parasite, so you might infer that no further cooking is necessary. Such is not the case. Long, slow cooking is needed not only to heat them through, but also to bring out the flavor and enable you to glaze.

Reheating instructions generally come on the wrapper. Do not preheat the oven. Turn thermostat to 325 degrees. A whole ham, bone-in, weighing from 10 to   14 lb. will take from three or four hours to reheat; halved, from two to a little more than three hours. Once again, an instant-read meat thermometer is a must. In each case, the ham is ready when the thermometer reads 140 degrees.

Before   reheating, cut off rind and most of the fat, leaving only a thin layer. Score fat in a diamond pattern and insert a whole clove in each square. Let the ham rest for 1 ½ hours before placing in an oven-proof plastic bag so that it can come to room temperature. Place ham in bag in a shallow baking pan on lowest oven rack, scored side up. Turn oven thermostat to low, 225 degrees. When the instant thermometer reads 130 degrees, the ham can be glazed, roughly 45 minutes before ham is ready to serve. At that point, remove ham from oven, turning thermostat up to 400 degrees. Coat ham   with an appropriate   glaze (see below). Return ham to oven for some 45 more minutes, or until the proper temperature of 140 degrees is reached for a ham labeled "fully cooked" and the glaze is set. Other non pre-cooked hams must be cooked to an internal temperature of 160 degrees. After removing ham from oven, over loosely with foil and let rest for 20 minutes before carving. A 14 lb. ham serves 24 generously.

Simple Glazes

Heat up a jar of apricot preserves and push it through a strainer. Brush over ham surface.

Cover ham with brown sugar and press breadcrumbs over the sugar.

1 cup of brown sugar
2 tsp. allspice
2 tsp. dry ground mustard

1 tsp. black pepper
½ cup breadcrumbs
¼ cup bourbon or sherry

For a large ham, you might mix brown sugar, allspice, dry ground mustard and black pepper. Remove as much fat as you can from pan drippings and mix with the above to form a thick paste. After coating ham, rub in breadcrumbs. Baste with bourbon or sherry.

Remaining Ham Slices

You might call this a version of the Southern redeye gravy, which calls for strong black coffee instead of water.

½ cup warm water
½ cup of dry sherry or Madeira
½ cup light cream

Cut off fat, reserving just enough fat to grease a skillet. Cook over moderate heat, five minutes per side. Remove to a serving platter. Pour out the fat; add warm water to the skillet, reduce slightly. Pour over ham. If you have a disregard for calories, add dry sherry or Madeira to skillet and reduce it to a few tablespoons. Add light cream and allow to   thicken slightly.

Ham lends itself beautifully to leftovers. The Spanish add small pieces to flavor all sorts of dishes from soups to sauces to bean dishes, and both mashed and scalloped potatoes.

Jambalaya à la Creme

1 shallot, minced
1 tbsp. butter
½ lb. cooked ham, sliced
½ cup white wine
3 tbsp. Madeira or dry sherry
1 tbsp. brandy
4 tsp. tomato paste
1 cup heavy cream

Cook shallots in the butter for about 2 minutes. Add ham, white wine and bring to simmer. Let reduce by half which should take roughly 5 minutes. Remove ham and add the Madeira or sherry, the brandy and cook 2 minutes more. Whisk in tomato paste. Add cream and cook until slightly thickened. Season and return ham to pan. Heat through for a minute or so before serving.

Ham Leftover Dishes

2/3 cup bread crumbs
1 cup cooked ham
¼ cup hot milk
½ cup mayonnaise
2 grated carrots
½ tsp. each salt pepper
1 small grated onion
2 or more beaten eggs for topping
Mix in layers in oven casserole and bake at 350 degrees for 45 minutes.

Ham and Lima Bean Stew

2 cups soaked lima beans or Great Northern beans
6 cups water
1 ham bone or 12 oz. smoked ham
3 medium carrots
¼ tsp. dried thyme
1 bay leaf
2 medium onions
 2 medium celery ribs
1 14-oz. can whole tomatoes
12 oz. cubed cooked ham
¼ tsp. each of salt and pepper
8 oz. chopped spinach

Rinse and pick over beans (Great Northern could be substituted.) Add 6 cups water, bring to boil and let boil exactly 1 minute. Take off heat. Cover and let sit for 1 hour. (You could soak overnight, covered with water. The next morning, drain, add 6 cups of water, seasonings and continue with recipe.) Add remaining water to beans, ham bone, thyme and bay. Simmer uncovered for 45 minutes or until beans are just about tender. Remove ham bone. Add sliced onions, carrots, celery and tomatoes. Simmer partially covered for 1 minute. Add chopped ham, salt and pepper and simmer uncovered for 15 minutes. Add chopped spinach and cook for 5 more minutes. If you elect to use canned limas or cannellini beans, cook ham bone in the water for 30 minutes before adding canned beans.

Sliced Precooked Ham

Cut off fat and render or melt enough to keep ham from sticking. Sauté slice over moderately high heat for about 5 minutes per side for slice. In the country, they might do it like this; remove heated-through ham slice, pour off any fat and add either cup cold water or cup coffee.

Pork

All parts of the pig are edible, from snout to hoof, but the most desirable cut is the loin that runs from shoulder to rump. Roasts from this section are marked center cut (considered the best and the most expensive), boneless top loin, loin blade, and loin sirloin. If your roast has not been boned, ask your butcher to loosen the chine bone (backbone) to facilitate the carving. A three lb. boneless roast will serve four (½ pound per person); while a bone-in roast will serve perhaps three.

The USDA recommends that you cook pork to a temperature of 160 degrees, taking into consideration that all parts of the meat should reach this temperature. Even so, some years back, many either refused to serve pork or cooked it to a dried-out 185 degrees. Longer cooking is recommended not only to err on the side of safety, but also to develop flavor. The instant thermometer should read an internal temperature of 160 for a medium done roast or 170 degrees for a well done roast. Check temperature several times during the cooking. Insert the thermometer in the thickest part of the roast; do not touch the bone. Once it is done, cover it loosely with foil. Allow to rest for 20 minutes before carving (the internal temperature may rise as much as 10 degrees).

Bland pork always benefits from a dry marinade:

1 5 lb. pork roast

2 slivered garlic cloves
1 tsp. coarse salt
1 tsp. freshly ground black pepper
½ tsp. crumbled rosemary
1/8 tsp. ground allspice

Make four or five small slits in the roast, inserting garlic slivers. Rub the surface with a mixture of coarse salt, pepper, thyme or rosemary, and allspice. Place in plastic bag and allow to marinate in refrigerator for at least two hours.

The braising times below are based on unchilled meat; remove meat from refrigerator an hour before roasting. Do not remove from its plastic bag until ready to roast.

Before browning, scrape off marinade, and pat dry with paper towels

Oven Braised Pork

Preheat oven to 350 degrees. The moisturizing, tenderizing effects of braising are preferable to that of open pan roasting. The meat is first browned on top of the stove, and then braised in the oven in a covered casserole. It can be served alone or accompanied by sauerkraut.

3 lb. boneless pork loin
3 slivered garlic cloves
2 tbsp. olive oil
1 carrot, scraped, coarsely chopped
1 chopped celery rib
1 chopped medium yellow onion
2 tbsp. unsalted butter
1 bouquet garni
2 ¼ tbsp. unsalted butter

Allow roast to come to room temperature for an hour. Insert garlic into slits cut into surface of pork loin and marinate as above. Heat oil in a skillet over moderately high heat and brown roast well on all sides. Reduce heat to prevent burning (should it do so, pour oil off and replace with the butter). Remove roast and set aside. Add carrot, celery and onion to skillet. Lower heat and cook slowly, covered, for 10 minutes, or until softened. Add garlic and two minutes later take off heat. Place contents into a baking casserole; press herb bouquet down into vegetables. Cover with roast (if you have already marinated the loin, further marinating will not be necessary). Cover and bring to the simmer on stovetop, then place the covered casserole in lower third of the preheated oven.

Allow 35 minutes per pound for a boneless three to eight-pound roast, 30 for a bone-in (it is difficult to give exact times as they can vary with the type of the roast). Check roast with an instant thermometer after an hour or so into the cooking. A medium-done roast will be ready when temperature reaches 150 degrees. Place on serving platter, cover loosely with sheet of foil and temperature will rise to 160 degrees in 15 minutes or so. For a well-done roast, remove from oven at 160 degrees. Let the temperature rise to 170 degrees. Remove herb bouquet and make pan sauce: scrape roaster and pour contents into bowl. To facilitate fat removal, pour juices in a deglazing pitcher (or cup, if you must) and place in freezer for 10 minutes. Remove fat and pour juices back into casserole. Process reserved vegetables through food mill and add to juices. Boil down to a cup or so, adjust seasoning and serve in gravy boat.

Sauerkraut

Sauerkraut requires long, slow cooking to make it palatable, a total of 3 ½ hours. First braised on top of the stove, it is then cooked with the roast for the required cooking time, 1½ hours. The sauerkraut in a two- pound plastic bag is preferable to canned sauerkraut. You will need only one pound for a three pound roast. Freeze the balance.

Package directions will probably tell you not to drain or rinse sauerkraut, but if you do not rinse it under cold running water, the sauerkraut may be excessively salty. Taste, and if still too salty, cover with cold water and soak for an hour or so, changing water twice. Drain. Proceed with recipe.

1 small   slice salt pork
2 tbsp. olive oil
1 small chopped yellow onion
1 small chopped carrot
1 lb. packaged sauerkraut
1 cup dry white wine
1 3-lb. pork roast
2 cups chicken stock

1 cup dry white wine

Spice mixture of ½ tsp. each of allspice, cumin, ground cloves, 6 peppercorns, 6 juniper berries, all tied in a 100- percent cotton cheesecloth bag.

Cut rind from salt pork. Blanch in boiling water for five minutes. Rinse, drain, pat dry and cube. To keep salt pork from sticking, add a little oil to skillet and sauté cubes over moderate heat until they start to brown. Reduce heat and add carrot and onion, cooking slowly until they soften. Add sauerkraut, enough stock to cover by half, spices and the wine. Sauerkraut should now be almost covered. Bring to a boil, cover, reduce heat to low and simmer for two hours.

After pork roast has been browned and placed in baking casserole, surround it with sauerkraut, cover and braise. When done, remove to warm platter; allow to rest before carving. Drain sauerkraut and place around roast. Degrease pan juices. Reduce to concentrate flavor and pour over roast.

Roman Pork Stew

This one dish peasant dish has found its way into good cuisine.

¼ lb. salt pork
¼ tsp. each salt and pepper
5 sliced medium yellow onions
3 qts. beef broth, or stock
½ cup freshly grated parmesan cheese
½ pint half-and-half (half milk and half cream)
½ cubed fillet of pork
12 cups cubed day old bread
2 tbsp. unsalted butter

1 sprig of rosemary

In a saucepan, gently sauté the diced, fresh salt pork. When lightly browned, remove and set aside. In the same saucepan, slightly soften onions in the pan. Add broth, season to taste, and gently simmer, covered for 30 minutes.

Grease a four to five quart ovenproof casserole. Layer 1/3 of the bread in the bottom, followed by 1/3 each of the following ingredients: cheese, cream, fresh pork squares, and salt pork. Repeat layers two more times. Bring the broth to boil and carefully pour over casserole contents. In a 400-degree oven, bake 15 to 20 minutes, or until cheese melts.

Pork Chops a l 'Orange

Pork goes well accompanied by fruit.

4 to 6 loin pork chops
salt and pepper to taste
3 tbsp. unsalted butter
all-purpose flour for dredging
2 small oranges, peeled and sliced into rounds
mint leaves
½ cup fresh orange juice

Preheat oven to 350 degrees. Dredge chops in the seasoned flour and brown; transfer to baking dish. Top each chop with orange slices and pour over the orange juice. Cover and bake in oven for one hour. Serve garnished with mint.

10

CHICKEN

Admonitions

While these precautions apply to all types of fowl, this chapter deals specifically with chicken and turkey. Poultry is almost as perishable as fish, particularly in hot weather. Summer spoilage is so prevalent that chicken should be bought on the day it is to be cooked, bringing it straight home from the store.

Salmonella outbreaks prove that the bacteria is alive and well in this country. A well-cooked chicken is not a problem. Bacteria are killed at the relatively low internal temperature of 140 degrees on an instant-read thermometer, with the proviso that all parts of the bird be uniformly heated. A chicken would, of course, be raw and inedible at this temperature and further cooking to 180 degrees is recommended (see roast chicken). Exercise caution when handling a raw chicken; the skin is susceptible to bacteria. Because this is not detected by the naked eye, treat all raw fowl with care.

The main precaution is to avoid spreading any possible bacteria around your kitchen, known as cross-contamination. Certain reasonably simple sanitary measures are recommended (short of surgical mask and gown), namely:

Refrigerate chicken in its store wrapper. Avoid placing it directly on a bare kitchen counter. Cover counter with newspaper and place on cutting board, laying out all needed utensils.

When ready to cook, unwrap the bird over the sink and rinse, giblets included. Pat dry with paper towels and place on the cutting board. If not planning to make giblet gravy, freeze them.

Proceed with seasoning, flouring, disjointing, etc. A baked or roasted chicken can go directly into the roasting pan. Avoid spreading around any bacteria by washing your hands before touching anything else. After preparing the birds, discard papers, wash equipment and of course, your hands.

Selecting a Chicken

Chickens are classified as fryers, broilers or roasters, supposedly based on age determined by weight, but the lines are not always clearly drawn. A chicken weighing from 1 ½ to 2 ½ is ideal for broiling, while a 2 ½ to 3 ½ pounder is right for frying and sautéing. They can also be roasted. Four to 6 lbs. is a roaster, which can also be braised or poached. The neutered capon runs 6 to 9 lbs. If you have a yearning for stewed chicken, there is always the old stewing hen, if you can find one.

These classifications may vary from market to market. What one calls a fryer, another might label a broiler; then there are the three-pounders, which markets label broiler/fryer, a misnomer because they are a little large for broiling. This category dominates today's market, and it is now not always easy to find a young chicken between the 1 ½ pound Rock Cornish game hen and the fryer.

Look for freshly killed, plump birds without bruises or skin blemishes. Select chicken by its weight with a specific cooking method in mind. If you plan to broil, look for a young chicken of two pounds or so, while a three- pounder is better for sautéing.

Chicken can be bought whole, split, quartered, cut or disjointed into eight pieces, namely, two drumsticks, two thighs, two wings and two breast halves. The breast halves can be cut in two crosswise, giving you 10 pieces. For a whole chicken, allow ½ pound per person, slightly less if disjointed.

Disjointing and Boning

The advantages of doing your own disjointing are that it is cheaper pound for pound, plus you have giblets, scraps and bones for stock. However, if you are adverse to any forms of butchering and if the above sanitary measures are troublesome, let your butcher do the work. If you do wish to try it, rather than following a murky diagram, buy a whole chicken and ask your butcher to let you watch him disjoint. No matter which method of preparation you decide upon, always rinse the bird under running water and pat dry.

Marinade

Marinating will add flavor to your chicken. Rub the skin with olive oil, freshly squeezed lemon juice, salt, pepper and spices such as cumin and allspice, to be scraped off before cooking, plus a little olive oil and freshly squeezed lemon juice. Marinate in a closed plastic bag for 30 to 40 minutes at room temperature.

How to Cut Up a Chicken

Chickens are generally cut-up or disjointed for frying or sautéing, split for broiling, left whole for roasting and braising. Of course they can be bought at the supermarket both whole and cut up. There are two advantages to cutting up your own. It is cheaper than having the butcher do it and you have skin, gristle and bones to freeze against future stock.

It is a simple procedure to cut up a chicken, but to avoid first hacking away, buy a whole chicken and ask your butcher to demonstrate cutting it up. We disjoint our chickens into 8 pieces, 2 wings, 2 drumsticks, 2 second joints, 2 breast halves. They will cut the breast in two horizontally so that you have a total of 12 pieces.

Begin by removing giblets, liver and hearts and freezing them. You are now going to separate the thighs or second joints from the body of the chicken. Lay chicken breast side up, neck toward you. Hold leg away from body. Cut through skin to locate ball and socket joint and cut through it, severing thigh from body. Locate joint between thigh and drumstick and cut through it, Do same with the wings, cutting away from body.

Turn bird over. With a sharp knife cut on each of backbone from neck to tail. Remove backbone and cut through breastbone, Separate breast from back, gristle and bones to freeze for the stock pot.

Roast Chicken

Remove chicken from refrigerator 15 minutes before cooking. Preheat oven to 400 degrees. If you have not marinated, rinse off and dry the chicken. Place directly in shallow roasting pan, breast side up.

3 ½ lbs. roasting chicken
¼ tsp. each salt and pepper
1/8 tsp. ground cumin
1 peeled garlic clove
1 sprig of fresh thyme or rosemary
2 cups mayonnaise

Clip off wing tips and remove any excess fat from cavity. If the bird has not been marinated, rub it inside and out with salt, pepper and a little cumin. Insert a cut clove of garlic and a sprig of thyme or rosemary in the cavity.

To preserve the bird's shape, tie the two ends of the drumsticks together with a 12 inch length of cotton string. Loop the end of the string around the tail and tie to the drumsticks, which will bring them down over cavity.

Slather breast and legs with mayonnaise. This not only takes care of basting, but keeps the breast from browning too soon or too much. If the breast browns too excessively, add more mayonnaise.

Place bird into lower third of preheated oven. Roast for roughly 20 minutes per pound. Insert instant meat thermometer in thickest part of the thigh. New directives call for a reading of 180 degrees. Since temperatures will continue to rise during the all-important 20-minute pre-carving rest, remove the bird from oven at a reading of 170 degrees. Place on a warm serving platter and cover loosely with a sheet of foil.

The thermometer can, of course, be left in chicken, a good way to avoid an overdone 190 degrees. If a thermometer is not available, the time-honored method of checking is to make small slit in thickest part of the thigh. If juices run clear with no traces of pink, the chicken is done.

Giblet Gravy

Start an hour prior to putting the chicken into oven. (As only gizzard and heart are used in this gravy, the liver can be frozen).

½ cup   all-purpose flour
3 tbsp. unsalted   butter
giblets from one chicken
3 cups beef or chicken stock, to cover
½ cup dry white wine
1 whole yellow onion, unpeeled and studded with 2 clove nails
1 peeled garlic clove
3 sprigs parsley stems
1 tbsp. beurre manié

Knead softened butter and flour together. It is added in little pieces, at the last minute. Serve sauce immediately. Rinse off giblets and heart and pat dry. Trim away any green from gizzard. Over high heat cover gizzard and heart with cold water or stock. Add a few tsp. of dry white wine and add an unpeeled, clove-studded onion (two clove nails) and parsley stems. Heat to boiling and then reduce to the simmer in a partially covered pan; simmer until giblets are fork-tender, about an hour. Monitor carefully and add boiling water as needed if the liquid boils away. Strain giblets, reserving liquid, and discard onion and parsley. Purée   giblets and heart in a food processor or a blender, and set aside. Once chicken is done, remove from roaster. Skim off as much fat as possible from pan juices, or pour into deglazing pitcher. Heat degreased roasting pan on stove stoop. Add purée and the reserved liquid bit by bit until customary gravy consistency is attained. (As the purée will thicken gravy, it should not be necessary to add flour.) Season   to taste.

Southern Smothered Chicken

There are as many recipes in the South for this popular down-home dish as there are for fried chicken. The gravy is what makes it; serve it with rice or mashed potatoes.

2 ½ to 3 lb. chicken
½ cup seasoned all-purpose flour (salt and pepper)
2 tbsp. unsalted butter
stock or water to cover
1 tbsp. all-purpose flour for slurry: optional

Preheat oven to 375 degrees. Rinse a 2 ½ to 3-lb. chicken and pat dry. Halve by laying breast side down on a cutting board with a sharp knife or poultry shears, slitting from neck to tail on either side of backbone, staying as close to it as possible. Free backbone and free for future stock. Turn bird over. Spread open and cut through breastbone on each side, separating the carcass.

Place seasoned flour and chicken halves in a paper bag and shake vigorously. When chicken is coated, remove from bag and place breast-side down in a medium sized baking pan, just large enough to hold chicken. Add enough cold water or stock to cover bottom of pan by one inch. Dot chicken well with butter.

Cook 45 minutes, turn chicken over to cook for another 30 minutes, or until tender. If water level drops appreciably, add a little boiling water to the pan, but do not overdo it, as this will become the gravy, which should not be on the watery side. If chicken has not browned properly, run it briefly under broiler. Remove bird to warm serving platter. If pan liquid is too thin, either reduce by boiling or thicken it the old fashioned way, by dissolving a heaping tablespoon of flour thoroughly in ¼ cup of cold water, known as slurry. Simmer pan juices; slowly add the flour/water mixture to pan juices, whisking well. Season to taste. (A beurre manié can also be used for this purpose, which is a mixture of half and half softened butter and flour.) Cooking time: 1 ½ hours.

Chicken Baked with Onions

There are similarities between our Southern country cooking and European country cooking. Smothered chicken is similar to this recipe. The techniques and cooking times are the same, although no water is added. You might say that this chicken is "smothered" in onions.

2 ½ lb. chicken
2 tbsp. softened, unsalted butter
½ cup seasoned all-purpose flour for dredging
1 ½ cups thinly sliced yellow onions
1 tbsp. olive oil
1 minced garlic clove
½ cup seasoned bread crumbs

Preheat oven to 375 degrees. Wash, dry and halve the chicken by laying breast side down on a cutting board and slitting from neck to tail on either side of the backbone with a sharp knife or poultry shears, staying as close to backbone as possible. Free backbone and freeze for future stock. Turn bird over, spread open and cut through the breastbone on each side, separating the carcass. Rub the skin well with softened butter and dredge lightly in seasoned flour. Lay bird, breast side down, in a shallow roaster and place in the oven. Bake for 45 minutes before turning and adding onions. Meanwhile, soften onions slowly in just enough oil to coat the bottom of the skillet, about 10 minutes. Add garlic; cook one minute more. Pour in the contents of the skillet, plus breadcrumbs. Spoon over pan drippings; continue to cook for an additional 30 minutes. Remove chicken and onions to warm platter. Skim off fat from roaster, or degrease with the aid of a deglazing pitcher. Add ½ cup of water or stock and bring to the simmer, scraping up all brown bits from bottom of pan with a rubber spatula. Reduce and season.

Sautéed Chicken

Once again, the definition which says it all is: brown small pieces of tender food, chicken in this instance, quickly in a small amount of very hot fat, cooking continued in covered pan until chicken is done, about 30 to 40 minutes. As chicken pieces should not be tough, sauté in batches, and, as white meat cooks more quickly than the dark, either remove them temporarily or pile on top of the dark meat.

1 2 ½ to 3-lb. chicken cut into 10 serving pieces
salt and pepper to taste
2 tbsp. unsalted butter
1 tbsp. olive oil

Sauce:

1 tbsp. unsalted butter
1 tbsp. finely minced shallots
½ cup dry white wine
½ cup chicken stock
1/8 tsp. lemon juice

Season. Heat butter and oil in heavy 10 inch skillet. When very hot, place chicken pieces, skin-side down, moderating heat so that the chicken browns, but does not burn. Brown for 2 to 3 min. per side. As chicken pieces should be separated from each other, sauté the chicken in batches. As white meat cooks more quickly than the dark, either remove them temporarily, or pile breast and wings on top of the dark meat. Add the wine and reduce until almost gone. Add the stock and simmer for a minute or two. Add lemon juice. Cover pan and cook at a mere sizzle for 10 minutes. Arrange all the pieces in one layer, turning once.

Chicken is done if juices run clear if bird is pricked by knife tip at the thigh. Remove pieces to a warm serving platter.

Oven "Fried" Chicken

This is a chicken dish placed into a very hot oven, a misnomer, for it is not really fried chicken.

1 stick melted butter
2 ½-3 lb. chicken pieces, disjointed
½ cup buttermilk
1 cup buttered breadcrumbs
1 cup seasoned all-purpose flour, seasoned with salt and pepper
1 tsp. baking powder
2 tbsp. sesame seeds
2 tbsp. pecans, chopped
1 egg (optional)
Cornmeal for dredging

Preheat oven to 425 degrees. Marinate disjointed chicken pieces in buttermilk. Place in plastic bag; refrigerate for several hours. Drain well on a rack. Coat chicken pieces in breadcrumbs mixed with pecans and sesame seeds, or, if desired, dip them first in seasoned flour and egg beaten with a teaspoon or so of cold water, then in cornmeal. They can be done in the cornmeal alone. Place coated pieces on a greased baking sheet for 35 minutes or until done, turning once during cooking.

Spanish Chicken Stew

2 tbsp. olive oil
6 chicken thighs
2 medium onions
¼ cup flour
2 medium peppers
½ tsp. paprika
½ tsp. salt
10 frozen artichoke hearts
1/8 tsp. cayenne
1-pound can tomatoes
2 sliced onions
3 garlic cloves
1 ½ chopped bell peppers
2 halved artichokes
1 tsp. chopped rosemary
1 cup chicken stock
1 cup frozen peas
salt and pepper to taste

Cut thighs in half, and in batches, dip in mixture of flour, paprika, salt, pepper, and cayenne.

Heat oil in skillet over moderately high heat. Brown chicken thighs in batches for about 8 minutes. Drain on paper towels.

Preheat oven to 350 degrees. Sauté onions for 3 min., add garlic and brown for minute or so, add chopped peppers, halved artichokes, rosemary, drained tomatoes, stock. Add chicken and heat through.

Place in oven and cook, covered for 30 minutes. Uncover and cook another 30. Stir in peas and cook another 15 min.

Arroz con Pollo (Chicken with Rice)

To my way of thinking, you have to be a Mexican to make a proper tortilla, a Southerner to make baking powder biscuits and Spanish to make paella. This is much easier to make than paella and the last minute baking ensures that the chicken will be done, which is not always the case if all the cooking is done on top of the stove.

1 3-lb chicken, cut into serving pieces
1 tsp. each salt and pepper
2 tbsp. olive oil
1 large green pepper, chopped
1 cup onion, minced
3 medium tomatoes, peeled, chopped
2 pimientos, chopped
2 garlic cloves, minced
4 tsp. paprika
1 tsp. saffron   threads
2 cups short-grain rice
1 cup dry white wine
3 cups of chicken stock, heated to the boil
1 cup minced parsley

Pat chicken dry and season with salt. Heat   oil in large skillet   over moderately high heat. Fat should be hot but not smoking. Add chicken pieces, turning heat down a bit. If skillet is not large enough to hold chicken pieces in one layer, do them in batches. Sauté on all sides until golden brown. This will take 15 minutes or so. Transfer chicken to plate. If fat is excessive, pour out all but a couple of tablespoons.

Turn heat to low and add green pepper and onion and cook, uncovered, until they soften. Now add tomatoes, pimientos, parsley and garlic and continue to cook for 5 more minutes.

Add paprika, saffron followed by the rice. Stir around

3 minutes. Add the wine, the heated broth, followed by the chicken. Season   to taste with salt and pepper. Cook for an additional 7 or 8 minutes, stirring now and then.

Transfer rice to 2-quart baking dish and top with chicken pieces. This goes, uncovered, into an oven preheated to 325 degrees. Bake 25 minutes or until the rice has absorbed the liquid. Sprinkle with parsley and serve.

Pollo al Ajillo (Chicken with Garlic)

1 3-lb. chicken, cut into small serving pieces
1 head of garlic, separated, peeled and minced in food processor
1 tbsp. oil
1 tsp. each salt and pepper
1 cup dry white wine
4 tbsp. olive oil
1 sprig parsley, minced for garnish

As in above recipe, heat up oil over moderately high heat. Add dried, seasoned chicken pieces and turn down heat a bit. Brown on all sides, which will take about 15 minutes. Remove chicken temporarily and add all but a tablespoon of the garlic. Regulate heat so that it does not brown. Season chicken and return to skillet. Add the white wine. Cover and cook for 15 minutes more. Add tbsp. reserved garlic and serve.

African Chicken

¾ cup salted peanuts
2 tbsp. oil
3 medium onions, chopped
3 medium carrots, diced
½ tsp. Tabasco
¼ tsp. nutmeg
1 cinnamon stick
2 tomatoes, diced
1 ¼ cups chicken broth
3 whole boned chicken breasts
2 tbsp. lime juice
1 tsp. lime zest
1 medium green pepper, chopped
2 tbsp. cornstarch

Process peanuts for 3 minutes. Add cornstarch and process 15 seconds. Reserve. Chop or process onions, carrots and tomatoes.

Heat   oil in skillet - medium high. Add cubed chicken breasts in batches and stir until lightly browned all over, 2 min. per batch. Remove with slotted spoon, reduce heat to medium. Add onions and lightly brown them. Add carrots and remaining ingredients. Bring to boil and cook slowly, covered, for 12 minutes, stirring now and then. Stir in chicken, peppers and cook, covered, until vegetables are tender, 8 to 10 min. Stir in peanut/cornstarch to thicken.

A Fried Chicken to Try

In soup kettle, bring 2 ½ inches of water to the boil. Put whole 2 ½ or 3-lb. chicken in kettle on rack. Cover and steam until bird is almost tender, 15 min. Cool and cut into 6 serving pieces.

Dip pieces in mixture of 1 beaten egg and 1 ½ cups buttermilk. Now dip in mixture of tsp. salt, ½ tsp. pepper and cup of flour, shaking off excess. Heat up vegetable oil over medium high heat to 365 degrees. Cook chicken pieces 7 minutes. Turn down heat and cook 7 min. on other side or until brown. Drain.

Child's Broiled

2 ½-lb. chicken, split or quartered.
3 tbsp. melted butter
1 tbsp. of oil
3 tbsp. melted butter
1 tsp. salt
3 tbsp. Dijon mustard
dash pepper
2 tbsp. finely minced shallots
herbs such as thyme and rosemary
2 cups fresh breadcrumbs

Dry and paint with mixture of   butter and   oil. Place skin side down in broiling pan, 6 inches from element. Broil 10 minutes per side, basting every 5 minutes. Salt lightly.

Mix Dijon mustard, pepper, herbs, and shallots. Into this, almost by drops, beat in half of basting fat and coat chicken. Roll chicken with breadcrumbs.

Again skin-side down, paint with basting fat and broil and put this time under moderately hot broiler. Brown 10 minutes. Turn and broil 10 minutes more or 40 minutes in all.

Poached Chicken

2 ½ to 3-lb. chicken
1 slice of lemon
6 cups water or chicken stock
small bunch parsley
3 tbsp. butter
2 tbsp. flour
1 ½ cups liquid
2 egg yolks
¼ heavy cream

Season chicken, insert slice of lemon in cavity. Bring water or preferably chicken stock to the boil. Add chicken, breast side down, small bunch parsley and immediately turn down to the merest simmer. Do not let it boil. Partially cover with lid and cook until chicken is tender. You can now serve chicken as such with sauce. You can turn it into chicken salad or a chicken pot pie.

To serve as such, remove chicken, cover and keep warm.

Degrease pot as well as you can. Make 1 ½ cups of béchamel or velouté (butter, flour, liquid) Beat egg yolks with fork and add heavy cream. Heat to the boil and boil 1 minute. Strain (sauce parisienne).

Jellied Chicken

3   chicken pieces
5 cups water
1 onion, sliced
2 celery ribs, sliced
1 carrot, sliced
1 onion, slivered
2 celery ribs with leaves, chopped
1 carrot, sliced
2 bay leaves

¼ tsp. each salt and pepper
2 envelopes gelatin
½ cup sour cream
½ cup mayonnaise
2 tsp. Worcestershire
3 tbsp. finely chopped parsley

Cover chicken pieces with water plus onion, celery rib with leaves, bay, salt and pepper. Simmer for 35 to 40 minutes. Strain cooking liquid and cut chicken into pieces and return to saucepan. Add gelatin (softened in water, dissolved over very low heat and set aside to cool).

In deep bowl, whisk sour cream and your own mayonnaise, Worcestershire and finely chopped parsley. Slowly incorporate this into stock, stirring until smooth. Set over bowl of ice water, stirring with metal spoon until it thickens enough to flow sluggishly. Stir in freshly grated carrot and chill 6 to 8 hours.

Turkish Chicken

12 boneless chicken thighs
2 tsp. cumin seeds, toasted in skillet 2 to 3 min. until fragrant
1 small onion, quartered
2 garlic cloves, peeled
1 cup yoghurt
1 ½ tsp. paprika
½ tsp. pepper
2 tbsp. melted butter
2 tbsp. lemon juice or 1 tbsp. Dijon mustard
½ cup dry white wine.

Process   cumin, onion, garlic, yoghurt, paprika, pepper, and lemon juice. Purée.

Rinse and dry 12 boneless chicken thighs. Marinate in above for 4 hour or overnight in refrigerator. Broil 7 minutes per side.

Pull second joint away from body of chicken. With sharp knife, cut a slit in skin to locate ball and socket joint and cut through it. Remove wings from body and the drumsticks from second joints in the same way.

Skin   side down, cut along backbone on both sides from neck to tail, removing backbone. Cut through breast bone, in two. Rub with melted butter and lemon juice or Dijon mustard in which case, let it sit for a few hours. Add ½ cup dry white wine. Start with dark meat, covered at 350 degrees for 20 minutes. Add white meat and cook 20 minutes more.

Oven Fried Chicken

2 beaten eggs
½ cup milk
2 tbsp. sesame seeds
2   pecans, chopped
2   tsp. salt
1 chicken, cut up
1 cup flour
1 tsp. baking powder
8 tbsp. melted butter

Mix eggs and milk well. Mix other ingredients except butter. Dip chicken in first mixture and then in flour. Place on baking dish and pour over butter. Skin side   down   for 30 minutes Turn and cook at 350 degrees until done.

Baked Chicken Breast

Could be marinated overnight in 1 tsp. each lemon and lime juice, half as much white wine, salt and pepper, crushed garlic, tarragon. Roll in hot butter. Cover supremes with buttered waxed paper. Bake 6 min. at 450 degrees or until tender, springy to the touch. Remove and make sauce.

Pour marinade, ½ cup stock into baking casserole. Boil down until syrupy and then strain in 1 cup heavy cream. Boil this down until cream thickens. Off heat, season with drops of lemon juice.

Chicken Breasts

Each whole breast has 2 halves or in culinary parlance, two supremes. You can cut the supremes yourself from a whole chicken or you can buy the supermarket packaged breasts unboned with the skin left on or boned and skinned.

I would suggest buying them unskinned as they are much moister. Before boning, put in freezer for half an hour. Starting at rib end, slide knife between rib cage and meat separating meat from bones.

4 skinned whole breasts
2 lemon rinds, minced
4 minced garlic cloves
1 tsp. salt
¼ cup olive oil
1 tbsp. oregano
¼ tsp. pepper
½ cup each ground
½ cup bread crumbs
4 cloves of peeled garlic
1 tbsp. melted butter over chicken.
1 cup dry white wine
1 tbsp. lemon juice

Marinate chicken breasts for 4 hours in minced rind of 2 lemons, garlic cloves, salt, olive oil, oregano, pepper. Put in shallow dish in ground and bread crumbs. Let stand 30 minutes.

Meanwhile blanch peeled garlic for 10 minutes in chicken stock. Remove and reduce stock by half. Pour garlic and melted butter over chicken. Bake loosely covered with foil for 15 min. at 375 degrees. Uncover and broil 3-inches from element for 3 minutes. Remove chicken, add dry white wine and boil down to ¼ cup. Season with drops of lemon juice.

À la Milanese

2 halved chicken breasts
2 tbsp. flour
1 beaten egg
2 tbsp. oil
2 tbsp. water
1 cup crumbs
¼ cup parmesan
4 tbsp. clarified butter

1 tbsp. minced parsley
1 tbsp. lemon juice

Dip 2 halved breasts in first flour, then in egg beaten with oil and 2 tbsp. water and finally in crumbs into which has been beaten. Let sit for half an hour. Sauté in clarified butter, about 3 min. one side, 2 on the other.

Make sauce by adding clarified butter and let it turn a light golden brown (mod, high heat for about 1 min). Off heat, season, add parsley and lemon juice.

Claiborne's Hash

2 cups cooked chicken
1 cup cream
1 tsp. salt
Roux:
1 ½ cups milk
2 ½ tbsp. butter
2 ½ tbsp. flour
3 egg yolks
¼ grated onion
2 tbsp. grated Swiss cheese

Simmer chicken in cream until cream is reduced by half. Make roux with milk, butter and the same amount of flour. Add half this sauce to the chicken. Season and add 1 yolk. Mix other 2 yolks with reserved half of the sauce (beat yolks lightly with a little of the hot sauce). Add rest of milk to this plus other ingredients plus remaining butter.

Moroccan Chicken or Chicken with Chick Peas

1 tsp. salt
1 inch fresh gingerroot, finely chopped
5 garlic cloves, chopped
1 tsp. pepper
1 tsp. turmeric
2 tbsp. butter
4 quartered chickens
½ cup sliced scallions

1 cinnamon stick
1/8 tsp. saffron
5 cups water
1 thinly sliced onion
1 cup chick peas, cooked
5 tbsp. butter
1/3 cup raisins
2 tbsp. parsley or fresh coriander

The night before, blend turmeric, salt, ginger, pepper,

garlic and rub into chicken. Chill, covered, overnight. Soak chick peas overnight in water to cover. Next day, drain, cover with cold water and simmer 1 hour. Skins will come to the top.

Chicken and marinade juices go in pan. Add salt, turmeric, butter, scallions, cinnamon and water. Bring to boil, reduce, cover and simmer an hour, turning now and then. Remove, keep warm. Add onion, cooked chick peas, raisins and cook until onions soften. Return and reheat chicken.

Time and Life Chicken with Sauce à la Provencale

3 chicken pieces
¾ cups dry white wine
1 chopped tomato, peeled, chopped
2 cloves minced garlic
1 bay leaf
¼ cup fresh herbs
1 tsp. anchovy paste
½ cup black olives

Sauté pieces from chicken, a matter of 10 minutes. Remove and cover bird loosely. Deglaze pan with dry white wine. Add chopped tomato, garlic, bay leaf, any fresh or dried herbs on hand, good squirt anchovy paste. Add black olives. Cover and cook slowly together for 5 min. Return chicken and cook slowly, covered, until done.

Chicken Lyonnaise
1 young split chicken

2 tsp. soft butter
3 cups onions
2 tbsp. butter
2 chopped garlic cloves
1 cup breadcrumbs

Season young, split chicken and rub with soft butter. Lay skin-side down in baking dish at 425 degrees for 20 minutes. Turn and cook another 15 minutes.

Meanwhile sauté onions in butter for 12 minutes or so. Add garlic and cook 2 minutes more. Pile onions on top of chicken which is skin side up. Top with breadcrumbs and moisten with accumulated fat. Back in oven for 25 minutes. Put chicken on serving platter.

Sauce for 6 Pot Pies

½ cup onions
6 tsp. butter
7 tsp. flour
3 cups chicken stock
1 tsp. salt
¼ tbsp. rosemary
¼ cup chopped pimientos
10 oz. package of drained peas.

Soften onions in butter. Make roux with flour, adding chicken stock, salt, rosemary, chopped pimientos and drained peas.

Breasts with Balsamic Vinegar

4 boneless chicken breasts
2 tbsp. flour
2 tbsp. olive oil
1 tbsp. butter
6 peeled garlic cloves
¾ lb. small mushrooms, rinsed, dried, sliced
¼ cup balsamic vinegar
¾ cup chicken broth
¼ tsp dried thyme

1 bay leaf

Dredge chicken in seasoned flour. Brown in oil heated over medium high heat - both sides. Add garlic and scatter over mushrooms.

Cook and shake for 3 minutes. Add vinegar, broth, thyme, bay leaf. Cover tightly and cook over medium heat for 10 min., turning pieces now and then. Remove chicken, uncover and cook for 7 minutes. Swirl in butter.

Creamed Chicken - Cook's

1 boneless chicken breast, cubed
salt and pepper to taste
3 tbsp. butter
¼ tsp. dried thyme
¾ cup mushrooms, sliced
2 minced shallots
½ cup dry white wine
¼ cup chicken broth
1 cup heavy cream

Brown chicken seasoned with salt, pepper, thyme in 2 tbsp. of the butter until pale golden - for 3 or 4 minutes. Remove and add mushrooms and cook for several more minutes. Remove and add extra tbsp. of butter and shallots. Add wine, stock and reduce, scraping pan, by half. Back to medium heat, add cream and reduce by 1/3   for 5 minutes. Put everything back and season.

Various Sautés

All chicken sautés begin in the following fashion: Disjoint 3 chicken pieces. Dry with paper towels. Over moderately high heat, heat up 2 tbsp. butter or margarine and 1 tbsp. oil. As the butter stops sizzling, drop in chicken pieces, skin side down. As pan should not be crowded, you may have to do this in batches. Brown 4 or 5 minutes on one side. Turn and brown on the other side.

In order not to overcook white meat - breast and wings, cover and keep warm. Return dark meat to skillet, cover and cook slowly for 10 minutes.

Return white meat to skillet and finish sauté in any one of the following ways:

1. Before returning white meat to skillet, remove dark meat. If fat has burned, replace with fresh butter. Sauté 3 tbsp. sliced mushrooms. Remove and sauté 2 tbsp. finely minced shallots for 2 minutes. Return all ingredients to skillet cover and cook slowly for 18 minutes. Again remove chicken and pour in ½ cup dry white wine. Reduce a bit and pour over chicken

2. As above. Remove chicken and sauté 2 tbsp. shallots for 2 minutes. Add 15 peeled garlic cloves which have been blanched in boiling water for 10 minutes. Add parsley, bay, 2 tsp. tomato paste, ¾ cup chicken broth. Cover and simmer for 30 minutes or until chicken is tender.

Turkey

Here are 4 admonitions: never stuff a turkey the night before. Make your stuffing, yes, but bring this to room temperature stuffing the next day. Do not cook turkey all night in a very low oven and last of all, do not let turkey sit around after dinner. Refrigerate it or throw it in the soup pot.

The following chart does not allow for stuffing. Add extra 30 minutes if you elect to stuff. Some will put their stuffing in a covered casserole, set it in a pan of hot water, and cook it along with the turkey. I find this way troublesome as you should lade in a little of the turkey juices now and then.

I make my stuffing the old-fashioned way, that is, with only butter, bread cubes, celery and onions. I would use the following proportions for an 18-lb. turkey.

2 cups finely chopped onion
2 cups finely chopped celery
¾ cup parsley
1/3 cup butter
8 cups dry bread cubes
½ tsp. salt
½ tsp. pepper
½ tsp. poultry seasoning
½ tsp. sage

½ cup water or chicken broth

Cook onion and celery in slowly butter until tender. Mix seasoning and sprinkle over bread cubes. Add water or broth if a moist dressing is desired. Stuff turkey and roast right away. Do not stuff it the night before.

11

VEGETABLES

Some familiar vegetables are omitted from the following recipes, which are generally simple, on the premise that if you are a beginner, you can proceed to more complicated preparations. Particularly in the case of greens, the flavor of the vegetable is allowed to predominate. In short, resist the temptation to drown fresh asparagus with hollandaise sauce.

Vegetables must be selected with care, only buy the firmest, freshest and crispest available. This will probably involve shopping at a vegetable market at a farmer's market. Except for tomatoes, onions and garlic, vegetables should be placed in the refrigerator vegetable drawer. Tomatoes do not necessarily have to be refrigerated, for they ripen with light. Once fully ripened, they should be refrigerated.

The current advisories on nutrition, vitamin content, the parental "eat-it-because-it-is-good-for-you" or the "no-dessert until-you-eat-your-spinach" approach makes it easy to forget what a properly blanched green vegetable, fresh to begin with, can add to a meal.

First of all, do not soak a green vegetable in water before cooking. Rinse under running water, looking for blemishes. Blanching not only involves dropping certain foods (such as tomatoes, garlic) briefly into boiling water to loosen their skins, but it is also a method of cooking green vegetables. In order to preserve the green color, they are dropped, a few at a time, into a large quantity of rapidly boiling, salted water, so that the boiling processes is diminished as little as possible. Calculate as much as four or five quarts per pound of vegetables, is used. The pan should be covered only long enough to bring water back to the boil, at which point remove the lid.

Blanch as briefly as possible, a few minutes, or until just tender. Larger vegetables should be checked for doneness with a fork. Taste smaller vegetables. Drain in colander, season and serve. The French regard vegetables so highly that if they are blanched and not to be served immediately, they will be drained and refreshed by running them under cold water to stop the cooking and set the color. When ready to serve, they will be seasoned, heated briefly in a little oil, and then sprinkled with lemon juice. Many recipes call for this method of refreshing, and pan reheating.

Broccoli and Brussels sprouts respond particularly well to this method. Blanching results in crisper vegetables than does steaming. Lately, however, there has been a new emphasis on roasting vegetables in the oven, rather than steaming or blanching them. Place root vegetables, such as, beets or potatoes in a saucepan, cover with cold water and bring to the boil. Cover the pan and simmer 20 minutes or so, until vegetables attain desired tenderness.

Asparagus

Wash each individual spear under running water. Remove tough part of stalk and peel with vegetable peeler. I find the stalks much easier to handle if cooked in a large pan of boiling water rather than large saucepan. Drop stalks into the skillet and start testing after 5 minutes. Drain and season as above.

Allow five or six large spears per person. While there is nothing like freshly picked asparagus, the expensive winter asparagus is surprisingly flavorful for a shipped-in vegetable.

To prepare, cut off the tough end portion of the stalks, and peel balance of stem with a swivel-blade vegetable peeler, a time-consuming but necessary process, except for baby or white asparagus. Wash each stalk individually under running water to remove grit. Some people will use a large saucepan to cook asparagus, tying them together in a small bundle with a piece of string. This can be avoided by dropping asparagus into a skillet full of boiling, salted water. Blanch as above, uncovered. Depending on size, start testing for doneness after five minutes; very large spears may take up to 10 minutes. Season, adding a small pat of unsalted softened butter, if you wish. To roast in an oven preheated to 400 degrees, place fairly thin asparagus in one layer in a small baking pan. Douse with a little olive oil and place pan in center of oven, which has been preheated to 400 degrees. After 10 minutes, turn the asparagus over and roast for another five. Again, the larger spears will take a good five minutes longer. Season, and if you desire, pour over a little melted butter.

Beans, Green Wax

One pound of green beans will serve three. Buy loose, rather than packaged beans. Cut off stems and cut diagonally into one-inch lengths. Blanch for two or three minutes. When just tender, drain, season with salt, pepper and a sprinkling of lemon juice.

In the South, beans would be put into a saucepan, covered with several slices of bacon. Add a cup and a half of water, Cover and simmer for 40 minutes. Despite the unusual length of the cooking time, Southern-style beans are very tasty.

Beets

Cut off stems an inch or so from the top of beets. If cut too close, beets will "bleed." Scrub with brush. Place beets in saucepan. Cover with cold water and bring to the boil. Cover pan, turn down heat to the simmer and cook until tender. Drain and when cool, slip off skins, running under cold water if necessary. I like them dressed with salt, pepper, a little lemon juice and a dab of softened butter, in other words, as simple as possible. You can reheat beets in this or you might reheat in the following sauce:

½ cup sour cream
1 tbsp. of vinegar
2 scallions, finely chopped
1 tsp. salt
¼ tsp. pepper

Blend ingredients and add to 4 cups cooked beets.

Purchase small to medium-sized beets (large ones tend to be old and tough). If at all possible, buy them with their leaves attached (if they are fresh and green in color, this is an indication of their age). Cut off the tops, leaving an inch or so attached to the beets, which will prevent them from bleeding; save them to sauté on another occasion. If not to your taste and you are a gardener, assuage your conscience by saving them for the compost pile.

Another recipe calls for dousing cooked beets in a little sour cream to which chopped shallots and a dash of wine vinegar have been added. However, this could be considered gilding the lily.

Scrub with brush under cold running water and place in saucepan. Cover with cold water. Bring to the boil, add salt, cover pan, turn down to the simmer and cook until fork-tender, between 30 to 60 minutes, depending on size and age.

Drain in colander. Allow to cool just enough to slip off skins. Blanching is easier than roasting for rendering outer skins. Chop. Reheat briefly in a little hot butter, season and sprinkle with lemon juice or a little vinegar. The flavor of the beets, usually intense, requires nothing more than the above seasonings.

Leftover beets, incidentally, are good in a tossed vegetable salad (Incidentally, lemon juice will remove beet stains from your hands).

Broccoli

Broccoli is one of the healthiest of vegetables. When used in soup, both stalk and are cooked together.

2 broccoli heads, trimmed, cut into 2-½ "by 2" pieces (florets & stalks)
1 tsp. lemon juice
¼ tsp. each salt and pepper
¼ tsp. grated nutmeg

Allow ½ lb. per serving. Heads should be compact and smooth, with dark green or purplish florets; there should be no trace of yellow.

Remove florets, leaving two inches or so of stem; shave stem slightly. Do not soak but rinse well under running water, keeping an eye out for possible crawlers.

In a 5-quart saucepan, bring water to boil.

Blanch florets and test for doneness after two minutes. (It may take three or four minutes.) They should be tender-crisp rather than soft. Drain, season and flavor with a few drops of lemon juice.

Broccoli stalks can be added to the florets, if desired. Peel them with a vegetable peeler, then thinly slice lengthwise or chop. Because they take a little longer to cook, drop them into the boiling water two minutes before adding the florets.

Another option is to blanch stems for one minute, then lightly sauté in olive oil or unsalted butter until tender, about a minute or so. Season with   salt, pepper and a dusting of nutmeg.

Brussels Sprouts

Brussels sprouts awake passions in people, those for and those against.

2 cups trimmed Brussels sprouts
few drops lemon juice
1   tbsp. olive oil, optional
1   tsp. unsalted butter: optional
1 clove peeled garlic: optional

Allow one pound for four servings. Pick out small, firm, green sprouts with no trace of yellowing. Cut off base and remove any discolored leaves. Cut a cross in the bottom of each sprout to ensure faster, uniform cooking, wash under running water and, as with the above broccoli, examine carefully for any possible insects. Depending on the size of the sprouts, blanch from 10 to 12 minutes, or until fork-tender. Drain, season and add a few drops of lemon juice.

If you wish to finish the cooking in sauté pan, blanch for only five minutes, drain and pat dry.   Heat   butter and oil in skillet. Sauté garlic until slightly golden and discard. Add sprouts and sauté slowly for five minutes, until tender and lightly browned.

Cabbage

You will find that cabbage goes further than any other vegetable, one pound serving three generous portions. Green, Napa and the Savoy cabbages are favorite choices. Choose firm, heavy heads with no wilted leaves. Unless cooking for a large number of people, the smaller the head the better. Of course, leftovers can always be made into coleslaw, vegetable soup or Irish colkennon for the next night. Cabbage tastes better when sliced, not chopped. The slicing disk of a food processor (not the shredder) is perfect for this chore, and it is a chore.

Braised Cabbage

1 lb. head of thinly sliced, cored, thinly sliced green cabbage, outer leaves removed

1   tbsp. olive oil
1   tbsp. unsalted butter
¼   tsp. ground cumin
¼   tsp. ground allspice
1 medium chopped yellow onion
1 clove garlic
1 tsp. each salt and pepper
1/8 tsp. paprika
Optional:
1 cup stock
1   tsp. caraway seeds, optional
2   white wine vinegar
2   tbsp. finely chopped parsley

Carefully rinse cabbage under cold running water. Melt butter and oil in a skillet. Add the following: cumin and allspice, onion and cook until softened. Add chopped garlic clove. Season with salt and pepper. Add drained cabbage strips, and stock just to cover. Add optional caraway seeds. Cook slowly, covered, for some 15 minutes or until tender. Sprinkle with paprika.

Variation: add cream instead of stock and cook as above. Caraway seeds that have been toasted by heating two to three minutes in a warm, dry skillet can be added to the cabbage slices. Stir in white wine vinegar to taste, and an equal amount of finely chopped parsley.

Coleslaw

Like potato salad, the success of coleslaw is dependent on the fact that the cabbage is sliced, not chopped or shredded. The slicing disk of a food processor is perfect for this job. Other than that, slice with a sharp knife as thinly as possible.

1 ½ pounds trimmed, quartered, cored, thinly sliced green cabbage
1 small sliced yellow onion
1 tsp. celery salt
1 tsp. celery seed
2 tsp. dried dill weed
2/3 cup of mayonnaise

First remove any wilted outer leaves, Rinse well under running water and pat dry, or use a salad spinner. Slice or process in the food processor with onion. Season to taste with both celery salt and celery seed. Add dried dill weed. Fold in 2/3 cup or more of mayonnaise. Cover and chill for an hour.

Carrots

Carrots with tops attached are always fresher than those in plastic bags with tops removed. Peel and cut into julienne which is more attractive than rounds. Add 5 or 6 tbsp. each of water and butter. Bring to boil. Cover, turn down heat and simmer until almost all of the liquid has evaporated and the carrots are tender. Season with salt, pepper, softened butter and chopped mint.

Allow 1 to 1 ½ carrots per serving. Buy them in a bunch, tops still attached, not in plastic bag. When ready to use, rinse, peel and pat dry. No matter how you serve them, carrots not only improve in appearance, but also in flavor when cut into neat, julienned strips.

Carrot Casserole

It is as easy as good.
2 cups peeled, rinsed and julienned carrots
1 tbsp. unsalted butter
1 or 2 parsnips, optional
½ tsp. salt

¼ tsp. ground cumin
1/8 tsp. grated ginger root
2 thinly sliced Bermuda onions
1 tbsp. fresh chopped thyme or ½ tsp dried thyme
1 tbsp. freshly chopped mint

Preheat oven to 350 degrees. Butter casserole heavily. Toss carrots with salt, cumin, and ginger root (a parsnip or two can also be julienned and added to this dish, if desired); alternately layer carrots with the onions. Dot each layer liberally with butter, salt and pepper to taste.

Add fresh or dried thyme or fresh mint.

Cover tightly and bake in oven at 375 degrees for one hour. Serves 3 or 4.

Carrots, Glazed

1 lb. peeled, rinsed, julienned carrots
1 tbsp. melted unsalted butter
juice of freshly squeezed lemon
4 tsp. light brown sugar

Place julienned carrots in saucepan with cold water to cover; bring to the boil, and simmer until tender, about 20 minutes. Drain. Meanwhile, in the same saucepan, mix butter, lemon juice and brown sugar.

Return carrots into pan toss and glaze until slightly caramelized; brown, about seven minutes.

Colcannon

1 lb. peeled and quartered boiling potatoes
2 peeled garlic cloves
1 lb. washed, cored and shredded green cabbage
4 sliced green onions
5 tbsp. unsalted butter
3 tbsp. chopped ham
½ cups scalded whole milk
3 tsp. parsley
salt and pepper to taste
½ cup grated gruyère cheese

Boil potatoes plus two cloves garlic until tender; drain. Meanwhile, prepare cabbage. Slice green onions in a food processor. Melt three tbsp. butter; add ham to onions and cabbage and sauté slowly, covered, until cabbage is soft, about 10 minutes. Run potatoes and garlic through potato ricer; add to them scalded milk, chopped parsley, cabbage mixture, the remaining two tbsp. soft butter and season to taste. Stir in cheese.

Corn

It is amazing how many corn products turn up in our diet: corn meal, corn syrup, cornstarch, and grits, to name but a few. It is a mystery to me why Europeans, ordinarily so appreciative of good food, turn up their noses at corn on the cob, relegating it to the livestock. They grow fodder corn, suitable for cows, etc.

Corn-on-the-cob is a distinctly American tradition. Zealots are so concerned with the freshness of their corn that if they grow it, they will not pick it until ready to cook, insisting that it be that day's harvest. Consequently, there is no excuse for buying the shipped winter ears; better the frozen kernels if hankering for corn. If you do buy fresh corn, refrigerate ears when you get them home; do not shuck them until ready to cook.

Everyone has his or her favorite method of cooking fresh corn. One of the best is also the simplest: cover corncobs with cold water and bring to a full rolling boil over high heat. Remove immediately, season with salt and pepper, and roll on a platter.

Corn Pudding

8 ears scraped corn
½ cup half-and-half (half milk and half cream)
2 tbsp. unsalted butter
salt and pepper to taste
a grating of onion
2 tbsp. chopped parsley

Allow two large ears per person. The nice thing about this old-fashioned dish, in addition to being the best corn dish around, is that it can be made with day-old corn. Scrape corn into top of double boiler. You can do this, if you must, with the back of a table knife. (Exercise caution when using the back of a knife, as is sometimes suggested as corn can end up on your face or even on the ceiling). The best tool for this is a so-called corn cutter, almost never to be found except in the back of a seed catalogue.

Bring water to the boil in bottom portion of a double boiler. Set top half over boiling water; add corn, cover, lower heat to the simmer, cook for three to four minutes. Add a little cream, a pat of butter, onion, parsley and cook two to three minutes more. Season with salt and pepper and serve. Frozen uncooked corn may be substituted if the kernels are first defrosted and then pulsed, no more than once or twice, in the food processor. One ear of scraped corn will yield a good half-cup of kernels.

Corn Oysters

1 cup scraped corn
1 tbsp. milk, if corn seems dry
2 tbsp. flour
1 tsp. each salt and pepper
1 tbsp. bacon grease for frying
1 tbsp. butter
1 egg yolk (reserve white)
Place corn in bowl. Add milk if corn seems dry, flour, salt, pepper to taste, bacon and butter, egg yolk. In another bowl, beat egg white just to stiff peaks and fold into first mixture.

Heat up the 2 shortenings until moderately hot but not smoking by any means. Drop in above mixture by heaping tbsp. in batches, 3 min. per side.

Corn Fritters

1 egg
2 tbsp. milk
¼ cup flour
¼ tsp. salt
2 cups oil
1 cup scraped corn

Mix egg, milk. Add flour, salt to taste, mixing with oil until blended. Add scraped corn and tbsp. milk. Should be the consistency of buttermilk.

Drop in fat and cook 4 or 5 minutes in all. Can be   kept warm in 200 degree oven.

Fried Corn

12 ears corn, scraped
6 tbsp. bacon grease
1 cup water
1 cup milk

Cook scraped corn 30 minutes in mixture of bacon grease and water, covered. Add cup of milk at end.

Eggplant

The optimum size is about 5-inches in diameter, a size which you will never find in your local supermarket. The skin should be firm, the vegetable, heavy. It will be bitter and watery unless blanched or salted. To salt, sprinkle well with salt and drain in colander for 30 minutes. Scrape off salt and proceed with recipe.

Eggplant Casserole

Eggplant should be used the day you buy it. It is no longer necessary to follow the old instructions that required salting the eggplant before cooking; new strains have been developed so that one no longer has to leach out the bitterness, which was the point of salting. This recipe is refreshing, as it is one of the few, which does not call for the addition of cheese. Its success depends solely on the addition of herbs. As a variation you may add a cup and a half of canned tomatoes with which you have mixed the vinegar and sugar.

1 medium eggplant, about two pounds, peeled, cut into 1-½ inch cakes
½ cup olive oil
1 ½ cups sliced Bermuda onion
2 chopped garlic cloves
¼ cup finely chopped, fresh herbs, parsley, basil and touch of rosemary
¼ cup vinegar
½ tsp. sugar
½ cup seasoned fresh breadcrumbs

2 tsp. butter

Optional:

1 ½ cups of canned tomatoes with which you have mixed the vinegar and sugar.

Preheat oven to 375 degrees. Place eggplant cubes in a saucepan and cover with water. Bring to a slow boil; better yet, blanch for five minutes. Drain. Meanwhile, in a 10-inch skillet, heat oil until hot. Add onions, reduce heat; add half the garlic and cook slowly for 8 or 10 minutes, or until softened. Do not brown.

Grease a small baking casserole. Place a layer of eggplant in bottom. Sprinkle with salt and pepper and a sprinkling of the herbs. Top with a layer of onion. Continue alternating layers and seasoning to fill casserole. Mix vinegar and sugar together and pour over top layer of eggplant. Top with breadcrumbs processed with the remaining garlic. Dot with butter and bake for 25 minutes.

Sally's Eggplant

4 tbsp. olive oil
6 oz. fresh Spanish cheese such as Manchego, mildly sharp
1 tsp. grated ginger
1/8 tsp. hot pepper (if desired)
1 ½ tsp. cumin seed
½ tsp. mustard seed
½ bay leaf
2 medium bell peppers, steamed, seeded and stripped lengthwise
1 tsp. garam masala
1 eggplant, cut into 1 inch cubes and steamed until tender
1 tsp. salt
3 medium tomatoes, chopped
4 tsp. coriander or basil
1 tsp. turmeric
few sprigs of coriander or basil for garnish

Heat up oil and when hot, not smoking, add cheese pieces and brown evenly. Remove and set aside. In same pan, add rest of oil, follow right away with ginger, chili pepper, cumin, bay leaf and mustard seeds. Let fry until mustard seeds pop and turn gray. Add bay and in a second, bell peppers. Sauté for 3 or 4 min. Stir in tomatoes, coriander, turmeric plus fresh herbs. Stir chopped herbs and eggplant.

Simmered Button Mushrooms

The common button mushroom is featured in these recipes. Like their exotic cousins, the common mushrooms should never be washed, as they will absorb the water. The advantage of this recipe is that there is no fat to be absorbed by the mushrooms; if you want to avoid excess sautéing fat, try serving simmered mushrooms.

With a damp cloth, wipe clean one pound of small mushroom caps. In a saucepan, place the mushrooms with just enough water to cover Add 2 tsp. of freshly squeezed lemon juice and ½ tsp. salt; pour over mushrooms. Simmer for five minutes, or until tender.

Mushroom Casserole

Baked vegetables are generally first braised or sautéed (broccoli, leeks and spinach come to mind), and sprinkled with cheese and breadcrumbs.

½ cup dry breadcrumbs
2 tbsp. unsalted butter
1 lb. button mushroom caps
3 tbsp. chopped parsley
¼ tsp. finely minced garlic
2 tbsp. freshly grated parmesan cheese
2 tsp. lemon juice

Preheat oven to 350 degrees. Lightly toast breadcrumbs in butter. Place mushroom caps in baking dish. Sprinkle with parsley, garlic, cheese, lemon juice and half the breadcrumbs, reserving balance for the topping. Season to taste. Mix well and sprinkle over the remaining crumbs. Cover and bake 20 minutes.

Okra

If you can find baby okra, not easy in the North, all you have to do in the way of preparation is to rinse them off and snip off their stems. If okra is large, cut off the ends and halve. Small pods are preferable, as the larger ones can be fibrous and tough. If necessary, frozen okra can be substituted in gumbos at the ratio of one box (10 ounces) per pound of fresh okra. But fresh is best for this dish, which is cooked briefly in the pan. The okra is then topped with a tomato sauce and cooked until tender.

2 lbs. fresh okra, rinsed and stemmed, or 2 (10) oz. packages
2 tbsp. olive oil
1 clove of minced garlic
1 small minced yellow onion
1 small minced, seeded, sliced green pepper
2 cups canned tomatoes

Soften garlic in the heated oil for a minute or so; add onion and green pepper and cook until softened. Add the okra and cook slowly over, stirring constantly for five minutes. Run tomatoes through a vegetable mill and cook slowly for 10 minutes or so until okra is tender, stirring occasionally

Cornmeal-dipped Okra Sautéed in Oil

Straight from the South, brought by the slaves from Africa.

2 tbsp. olive oil or mixture of oil and butter
1 lb. rinsed and stemmed okra
1 cup cornmeal for dredging

Rinse and drain okra; dredge in cornmeal seasoned with rosemary while the okra is still damp. Sauté until crisp for some 10 or 15 minutes or until done. Be careful not to burn the cornmeal.

Onions

Onions are a powerful tool in the hands of those who want to flavor soups, stews and sauces. There are many varieties: red, pearl, yellow globe, Spanish, Bermuda, shallots, scallions, chives, leeks and the seasonal Vidalia. Irrespective of chives, scallions and red onions, which all can be eaten raw, sauté the balance. Vidalias bake beautifully.

Baked Onions

You can use any type of onion, but the Vidalia, when available, is among the best.

4 jumbo Vidalia onions with the skins on
4 tbsp. melted unsalted butter
1 tsp. lemon juice
salt and pepper to taste
3 sprigs chopped parsley

Preheat oven to 450 degrees. Cut one-quarter inch from bottom of each onion. With apple corer, make cavity in top of each onion and place them on tinfoil. Pour the melted butter mixed with the lemon juice into the cavities. Season with   salt and pepper and sprinkle with parsley. Pull up the sides of the metal paper to cover and for roughly 1 hour. Test with fork. Serves 4.

Pearl Onions

Pearl onions are miniature onions. Cut cross in stem end of each of twelve pearl onions. Drop in boiling, salted water for two minutes; refresh under cold water and drain.

Dry with paper towels. Drop in skillet containing two or three tbsp. of hot olive oil. Dry with paper towels. Brown until tender, about 20 minutes.

Green Peas

One pound or about 1 cup of shelled peas serves two people. Tender, small peas are increasingly harder to find in my vegetable market, but if you are lucky enough to find tem, you are in for a real treat. The easiest way to cook fresh, shelled peas after shelling is to add to a fairly large saucepan of boiling salted water and cook until done for 5 to 10 minutes, depending on the size of peas.

Potatoes

Potatoes are divided roughly into starchy potatoes, boiling potatoes and all-purpose potatoes. Although it doesn't always hold true, baking potatoes, such as the Idaho, are generally used for baking and mashing while the boiling potatoes, such as the red skinned or yellow, can be used for casseroles and salads. Look for firm, smooth unbruised potatoes; remove any spots or sprouts. The sprouts are poisonous. New potatoes, so called because they have not been put in storage, are excellent for salads and boiling.

Oddly enough, potatoes are low in calories; it is what you add to them that increases the calories. Use the starchy potatoes, such as russet and Idaho for baking, mashing and fries.

Perfect Baked Potato

Preheat oven to 400 degrees.
4 (7-ounce) russet potatoes
1 chopped clove garlic
4 tbsp. olive oil
2 tbsp. chopped parsley
small pinch rosemary
2 tbsp. gruyere cheese

Scrub potatoes, slice across each potato, without slicing through; drench slices with garlic, oil, parsley, and chopped rosemary. Remove potatoes after 35 minutes. Fluff potato with a fork, sprinkle with grated gruyere and bake 10 minutes more.

Mashed Potatoes

A word of caution: never mash your potatoes in a food processor; it will wreck them.

4 large Idaho potatoes
salt   to taste
¼ cup sliced onions
4 cloves peeled garlic
½ cup whole milk
1 tbsp. soft unsalted butter

Place potatoes in saucepan with salt, sliced onions, peeled garlic and water to cover. Over high heat, bring water to a boil, reduce heat and simmer 15 minutes, or until tender.

Drain and process the potatoes, onions and garlic together in a food mill or with rice, adding butter, blending with a wooden spoon. Meanwhile, heat milk until hot.

Add milk gradually and season to taste. Spoon potatoes into ovenproof dish. Smooth top and run briefly under broiler.

Remaining Mashed Potatoes

Leftover mashed potatoes make wonderful potato patties. Form cooked mashed potatoes into small patties. Dredge in seasoned all-purpose flour, shaking off excess. In a skillet, melt one tbsp. unsalted butter. Brown patties on both sides.

Baked Potato Slices

Preheat oven to 425 degrees. Peel six medium baking potatoes. Cut into 1/8 inch slices (no thinner). Rinse under cold water until water runs clear. Dry with paper towels or spin in a salad spinner. Put slices in a bowl and toss with one tablespoon melted butter or olive oil. Arrange slices on a baking sheet so that they touch, but do not overlap. Bake for 20 to 25 minutes until brown and crisp. (If they do not brown properly, run under broiler).

Grated Potato Cakes

Use starchy potatoes such as Russets.

2 lbs. potatoes
2 egg yolks
2 tbsp. melted unsalted butter
1 tsp. salt and pepper
2 tbsp. chopped parsley
½ cup grated gruyere cheese
½ cup all-purpose flour

Grate potatoes and drain in colander. With your hands, squeeze out as much of their liquid as possible. Add egg yolks, melted butter, salt and pepper to taste, parsley, and enough all-purpose flour to make a firm dough, in roughly ¼ cup portions. Mix thoroughly with hands and shape into patties. Drizzle with melted butter and bake at 400 degrees for 15 to 20 minutes, or until brown.

Spinach

Spinach is washed thoroughly like lettuce, whether bagged or not. Fill a large bowl with cold water and add spinach. Shake back and forth in the bowl. Remove to colander, strip off stems and tear leaves into small pieces.

Rather than cooking in boiling water, transfer damp spinach to saucepan. Cover pan; increase heat to high and cook for three or four minutes, frequently shaking pan for three or four minutes. Spinach will be barely cooked. Return to colander, and press out as much remaining water as possible with back of wooden spoon. Season with salt and pepper. Return spinach to saucepan if reheating is needed. Add a small pat of unsalted butter just before serving.

Sautéed Spinach

This dish comes straight from Rome.

1 tbsp. unsalted butter
1 tbsp. olive oil
1 ½ lb. fresh baby spinach leaves or 2 10-ounces packages thawed frozen spinach
1 anchovy fillet or squirt anchovy paste
½ garlic clove

Heat butter and oil in skillet, preferably cast iron, over moderate heat. Add canned, well mashed anchovy fillet or a good squirt of the paste. Add garlic clove; discard garlic when it starts to brown. Add rinsed spinach, patted dry and sauté until tender, about three minutes. Serves 2.

Squash, Acorn

Preheat oven to 375 degrees. Halve squash lengthwise and scrape out the seeds.

In a small baking pan, put squash cut side down in a half-inch or so of water. Bake 45 minutes. Turn squash cut side up. Fill with applesauce seasoned with lemon peel and red wine. Bake 15 minutes more.

Tomatoes

There are not many tomato recipes in this book as there is little you can do to improve the original. The season is short, so enjoy while you can. In my part of the country, east Coast, it runs only from mid June through Mid September. From force of habit, I suppose, I continue to buy the expensive, winter, hothouse tomatoes which have so little flavor that they would be difficult to identify as tomatoes in a so-called blindfold test. You can substitute the canned Italian plum in winder soups and sauces.

Stuffed Tomatoes

Tomatoes have deteriorated, largely because new varieties are bred for shipping.

If you can grow your own, do so. If not, substitute imported, canned Italian plum tomatoes in soups and sauces.

6 small tomatoes
salt and pepper to taste
2 ½ cups dry breadcrumbs
3 tbsp. olive oil
3 tsp. chopped parsley
2 minced garlic cloves
3 mashed anchovy fillets

Preheat oven to 350 degrees. Cut tops off six small tomatoes; scoop out pulp, and set aside. Salt the inside of tomatoes and turn them upside down to drain. Sauté   breadcrumbs in olive oil until a rich brown. Add parsley, garlic cloves and (optional) anchovy fillets plus a teaspoon of their oil.   Simmer, stirring constantly.   Add pulp.   Cook five minutes. Stuff tomatoes and bake in muffin tins in a 425 degree oven for 10 minutes.

Winter Stewed Tomatoes

1 small onion, chopped
4 tbsp. butter
1 ½ cups dry bread cubes
½ cup light brown sugar
5 cups canned tomatoes
1 tsp. salt
½ tsp. pepper

Soften small chopped onion in butter. Add dry bread cubes and light brown sugar and cook 3 to 5 minutes. Add tomatoes, salt, pepper. Put in greased, shallow casserole and bake at 350 for 30 to 40 minutes.

Franey's Tomato and Zucchini Casserole

With a salad and good bread, this constitutes a pleasant dinner.

2 small zucchini
2 thinly sliced tomatoes
½ cup sliced yellow onions
1 small sliced green pepper

Optional: breadcrumbs and ½ cup parmesan with cheddar cheese for topping

Preheat broiler. In a greased casserole, layer the vegetables, seasoning each layer with salt and pepper; sprinkle each layer with chopped parsley and basil. Run under broiler for five minutes. Turn oven to 400 degrees and bake for 25 minutes.

Fried Green Tomatoes

A Southern standby. Dredge sliced green tomatoes in cornmeal seasoned with salt and pepper. Sauté until lightly browned in small amount of hot olive oil.

Turnips

An excellent way to cook turnips. (They must be small and young.)

2 lbs. small turnips

2 tbsp. unsalted butter
1 tsp. Dijon mustard
2 tbsp. maple syrup

Peel and slice turnips into ½ inch slices. Drop in boiling salted water and blanch for five minutes. Drain.

Melt butter with a little Dijon mustard in skillet. Add maple syrup.

Mix and add drained turnip slices, stirring. Cover skillet and cook over low heat for 30 minutes.

Yam Casserole

I specify yams rather than sweet potatoes, because they are much more flavorful. European cooks often write about American cooking and refer to the following yam casserole as a dessert. In the South, this dish is served with the entree, often part of a holiday meal. Yams and/or sweet potatoes tend to become watery when boiled, so it is preferable to bake them at 400 degrees for 40 to 60 minutes. They can be baked and the casserole mixed the day previous to serving and refrigerated overnight. If children are involved, top with marshmallows. My culinary reputation was damaged when caught by a so-called gourmet friend as I purchased marshmallows for this dish. Adults will not appreciate the marshmallows, but children love them. Canned pineapple bits make a very nice addition, as does any dried fruit.

8 medium yams
½ tsp. ground cinnamon
a good grating of nutmeg
½ cup unsalted butter
2 tbsp. dry sherry
3 tbsp. light cream
1/3 cup chopped pecans
¼ tsp. salt
optional: 10 marshmallows
can drained pineapple bits

Preheat a 350-degree oven. In an ovenproof casserole or baking pan, bake the yams in their skins until tender, about 45 to 60 minutes. Cool sufficiently to slip off skins.

Run through a vegetable mill and beat in the spices, melted butter, dry sherry, light cream, pecans and salt; mix well and turn into well-greased two quart-casserole.

Yam Pudding

4 cups raw yams
1 tsp. cinnamon
½ tsp. ginger
½ tsp. nutmeg
¼ tsp. ground cloves
1/3 cup honey
¾ cup chopped pecans
1 ½ cup milk
½ stick softened butter
3 eggs

Grate raw yams. Add cinnamon, ginger and nutmeg, ground cloves, honey, chopped pecans. Mix well. Add milk and softened butter. Heat this mixture through. Transfer to well- greased casserole. Beat eggs lightly. Slowly beat into casserole. Sprinkle with remainder of nuts and bake at 350 for about 1 hour, 15 min. or until puffy and firm.

Vegetable Ragout

This so-called stew is similar to ratatouille, but there is no sautéing involved. It consists of layers of eggplant, butternut squash, zucchini and mushrooms, each layer generously topped with onions, garlic and sliced tomatoes. These vegetables do not require precooking, but if you add leeks or fennel, 30 minutes of softening in butter is required.

1 medium unpeeled and thinly sliced eggplant
3 chopped yellow onions
3 finely minced garlic cloves
3 large peeled and seeded tomatoes
3 tbsp. chopped parsley
3 tbsp. chopped basil
4 small unpeeled zucchini, sliced
10 thinly sliced mushroom caps
1 thinly sliced medium butternut squash
2 tsp. unsalted butter

2 tsp. olive oil
3 finely minced garlic cloves
5 basil leaves, chopped
1 pat of softened unsalted butter or olive oil

If available, us a heavy, greased enamel-over-iron casserole that can go over direct heat and is nice enough to be brought to the table

Season all vegetables to taste. Start with layer of eggplant and cover with a thick layer of onions, a sprinkling of garlic, a slice or two of tomatoes and mushrooms. Continue with a layer of zucchini thickly covered with onions, some garlic, tomatoes and mushrooms. The third layer begins with the squash and continues in the above fashion. Sprinkle top with parsley and basil. Add soft butter or tablespoon good olive oil. (If desired, substitute enough chicken stock to keep vegetables from sticking, about ½ cup.) Bring casserole to the boil. Cover and immediately reduce heat the merest simmer and simmer slowly for 45 minutes.

Roasted Vegetables

Most vegetables can be roasted in a 500-degree oven, preferably in the winter to avoid excessive heat in the summer. On a lightly oiled sheet pan, place vegetables in a single layer, not touching. Asparagus can be lightly oiled and baked for 6 minutes, then turned and cooked for five more minutes. Beets should be cooked 30 to 40 minutes, depending on size. Carrot slices should cook for 15 minutes turned and cooked for 10 minutes more.

Rutabaga and Sweet Pepper Gratin

4 tbsp. softened butter
1 lb. rutabaga, quartered, peeled, ½ inch slices
2 medium onions, chopped
1 medium green pepper, cut into 2 inch rings
1 medium red pepper, cut into 2 inch rings
1 cup heavy cream
¼ tsp. each salt and pepper
1 tsp. grated nutmeg
¾ cup gruyere or Swiss cheese

Layer above in buttered casserole. Pour over cream, nutmeg. Top with cheese and bake at 350 for 50 minutes.

Scalloped Tomatoes

2 medium sized chopped onions
4 tbsp. butter
1 ½ cups dry bread cubes
½ cup white sugar
1 small tomato, chopped
5 cups canned, or if possible, tomatoes
½ tsp. salt
¼ tsp. pepper

Preheat oven to 350 degrees. Grease casserole. Sauté onions   in butter, lightly.   Add bread cubes and sugar and stir for several minutes. Add tomatoes, seasoning and cook until bubbly, 30 to 40 minutes.

Leeks
3 leeks, chopped
2 tbsp. olive oil
2 skinned, halved tomatoes
12 pitted olives
½ cup lemon juice
1 tbsp. grated rind of lemon

Cut off and discard green portion and root of 3 leeks. Slice from top to bottom and rinse thoroughly under running water. Cut into 3-inch lengths. Place in skillet which contains 2 tbsp. warm, not hot, olive oil. Cover and cook 10 minutes. Add tomatoes, olives, lemon juice, grated lemon rind. Cook slowly 10 minutes more.

Leeks with Cheese and Crumbs

3 leeks, sliced
1 garlic clove
¾ cup bread crumbs
1 cup gruyere

Cover sliced leeks with boiling water and cook at high heat for 8 minutes. Drain well and preheat oven to 425 degrees. Put leeks in buttered casserole well rubbed with garlic and spread with breadcrumbs. Add another layer of leeks plus rest of crumbs. Add cup gruyere. Bake 10 to 15 minutes.

Spinach

3 chopped onions
1 tsp. salt
1 stick butter
2 10 oz. package frozen spinach
2 hardboiled eggs, sliced

Soften onions and salt in butter. When soft, remove to bowl. Add another half tsp. salt, other half of butter and frozen spinach. Cover and cook over moderate heat, stirring now and then. Add onion to spinach. Off heat, add cup of room temperature sour cream. Garnish with sliced, hard boiled eggs.

Onions Confit

1 lb. onions, sliced
2 tbsp. of butter
1 tbsp. white vinegar
1 tbsp. sugar
1 tbsp. drained peppercorns

Soften 1 lb. thinly sliced onions in 2 tbsp. of butter, covered over moderate heat. Soft but not golden. Add tbsp. each white wine vinegar, sugar, drained green peppercorns. Continue to cook, stirring until slightly thickened, Season. Can be made ahead, chilled and micro waved.

Glazed Onion Confit

1 lb. small white onions
2 tbsp. butter
2 tsp. sugar

Drop onion in boiling water, take pan right off stove and allow to sit for 2 minutes, run under cold water and skin slips off. Put in pan with butter, sugar. Season. Cover with cold water. Cook over mod. high heat until liquid is reduced to ¼ cup and onions are tender. Shake pan. Onions should be golden and a light glaze is formed.

Montaguesque

¼ cup oil
3 tbsp. sugar
3 lbs. onions, 1 inch in diameter, blanched and peeled
½ cup white wine vinegar
4 tomatoes, diced, peeled
½ clove garlic
1 tsp. coriander
1 tsp. pepper corns
2 bay leaves
1 cup dry vermouth

Heat up oil. Sprinkle with sugar. Add onions. Cook until they start to color. Add white wine vinegar. Increase heat and cook until liquid is syrupy -about 3 minutes. Now add diced, peeled tomatoes, halved garlic, coriander and peppercorns, 2 bay leaves, dry vermouth, Cook until onions are tender, 30 minutes.

Another

30 small onions, blanched and peeled
½ cup dry white wine
3 tsp. oil
2 tbsp. wine vinegar
½ tsp. thyme
½ crumbled bay leaf
1 large garlic clove
½ tsp. salt
1 ½ tsp. tomato paste
pinch saffron
¼ cup raisins

Put all of this in pan, just covering with water. Cover and cook slowly for 20 minutes.

Perrier's Gratin Savoyard

1 clove garlic
1 tbsp. butter
6 large potatoes, peeled and sliced
¼ cup gruyere
3 strips bacon, sautéed
4 cups chicken stock

Rub 1 ½ qt. dish with garlic and butter. Wash potatoes, dry and layer in dish. Season layer and add a sprinkling of gruyere and julienned sautéed bacon, 3 layers in all, no bacon on top. Enough chicken stock to almost cover.

Bake at 450 degrees for 40 minutes.

Baked Potatoes

The 2 simplest ways of doing potatoes are often improperly done. To bake a potato, preheat oven to 425 degrees. Wash potatoes and rub lightly with oil. A potato of medium size should take roughly 55 minutes. Check by pricking with fork. When soft, cut cross in top and push up to expel steam.

Here is another way. Make several slits in red boiling potatoes but do not go all the way through. Spread out potato and pour over a little olive oil, a little chopped garlic and parsley. Bake at 450 degrees for 40 minutes.   -

Mashed Potatoes

3 lbs. potatoes
1 ½ cups milk or cream
1 cup minced scallion or onions
½ to 1 stick butter

Mashed potatoes are the other culprit. Start by covering boiling potatoes, unpeeled, with cold water and cook until fork tender. Remove and drain potatoes.

Put in saucepan and dry out, covered, shaking pan. Skin and mash with wooden spoon. Meanwhile, you should have been heating up milk or cream with minced scallions or onions.

With wooden spoon, beat in softened butter, cut into pieces. Beat in enough of the hot milk to make fluffy mixture. Season.

Soufflé Potatoes

8 eggs
1 qt. half and half
¼ tsp. each salt and pepper
¼ tsp. nutmeg
¼ cup grated Swiss cheese
10 potatoes

Make custard. Slice peeled potatoes 1/16 of an inch. Lay half in baking pan. Sprinkle over half the cheese. Lay rest of potatoes. Pour over custard and rest of cheese. Place in double boiler or bain marie for 45 minutes or in the oven, 350 degrees for 40 minutes.

Gourmet's Potatoes

1 lb. potatoes, peeled and grated
2/3 cup milk
2/3 cup heavy cream
1 small onion, minced
1 clove garlic, large, minced
½ cup Swiss cheese, grated

Mix potatoes with milk and heavy cream, onion, large garlic, both minced. Bring to boil, stirring. Put in greased 1 ½ qt. casserole. Add and sprinkle over grated Swiss. 25 minutes at 400 degrees. Let stand 10 minutes.

Roesti

2 ½ lbs. boiling potatoes
3 tbsp. butter
2 tbsp. oil

Cover potatoes with water and simmer 10 minutes. Drain, cool, chill for 2 hours. Heat up butter and oil in 7-inch skillet. When moderately hot, add warmed up seasoned potatoes. Spread evenly and tamp down. Cook uncovered for 8 minutes or until bottom is brown. Invert in another skillet containing butter and oil. Cook 8 minutes more. Try cooking in hot grease at 400 degrees for 30 to 45 minutes.

Vegetable Stew

1 medium eggplant
4 small zucchini, both unpeeled and thinly sliced
3 chopped onions
1 medium butternut squash, peeled and sliced
3 tomatoes, skinned and sliced
3 chopped garlic cloves
3 cups small mushrooms, stems removed
diced parsley

A vegetable stew consists of layers of various vegetables, each covered with chopped onions, chopped garlic and sliced tomatoes. Any vegetable is acceptable. I like to use eggplant, zucchini, butternut squash, mushrooms and the above onions, garlic and tomatoes.

I use a heavy enamel-over-iron casserole which can be used over direct heat and is nice enough to be brought to the table.

Cuisinart Scalloped Potatoes

3 medium potatoes (6 oz. each), thinly sliced
2 cups skimmed milk
½ tsp. salt
½ tsp. pepper
¼ cup parsley
4 oz. Swiss cheese or parmesan
½ medium red onion, chopped
2 tsp. cornstarch

Preheat oven to 400 degrees. Pour milk over mixture of salt, pepper and cornstarch. Mix well. Put this mixture over medium heat and stirring constantly, let this thicken - about 5 minutes- Add cheese. Overlap potatoes in 3-qt. baking dish. Bake until brown and bubbly -about 20 minutes.

Potatoes Sliced and Roasted

4 medium potatoes
1 tbsp. salt
3 tbsp. melted butter
2 or 3 fresh herbs or 2 to 3 tsp. dried
4 tbsp. grated cheddar cheese

If skin on 4 medium is tough, peel, otherwise don't peel and slice thinly but not all the way through. Put in baking dish and fan. Sprinkle with tsp. salt, and melted butter. Sprinkle over fresh herbs or dried.

Bake at 425 for 50 minutes. Take out of oven and sprinkle with grated cheddar. Put back for another 10 or 15 minutes or until cheese is melted and potatoes are soft.

Ratatouille

1 unpeeled eggplant, small
3 tbsp. oil
1 zucchini, cut into rounds
2 onions, sliced in rings
2 tomatoes, large

Slice eggplant and salt (see eggplant). Sauté lightly in a small amount of oil. Set aside. Sauté salted zucchini and set aside. Sauté 2 ringed onions until softened. Top with tomatoes, skinned and sliced. Cover with lid, take off heat and allow to sit for 15 minutes.

Layer these sautéed vegetables in heavy casserole, scattering each layer with salt, pepper and chopped fresh herbs. Cover pan and cook slowly for 30 minutes.

Butternut Squash

2 ½ lbs. butternut squash
½ cup packed brown sugar
1 stick butter
4 Granny Smith apples
½ cup plus 1 tbsp. sugar

2 cups rinsed, picked-over cranberries
½ tsp. cinnamon.

Bake at 450 degrees for 45 to 50   or until tender. Cool for 15 minutes. Halve, discarding seeds. Put flesh in food processor with half of the brown sugar and butter, processing briefly until smooth. Put peeled, cored apples, cut into eighths, ¼ cup of remaining sugar in heavy saucepan and cook until apples are tender, 10 minutes. or so.

In another saucepan, cook berries over mod. heat with ¼ cup of the sugar, stirring until they pop. Put berries, apples and squash mixture in bowl and mix gently. Fill squash cases with this and sprinkle with mixture of rest of sugar and cinnamon and bake at 350 degrees for 15 or 20 minutes.

(Why not just cook apples, add cooked squash and fill cases?)

Moroccan Vegetable Casserole

½ lb. white mushrooms, steamed 5 minutes.
1 ½ cups cooked garbanzos
1 cup pitted black olives
¼ cup chopped green onions
2 cups chopped red peppers
12 cherry tomatoes
1 cup yoghurt
½ cup mayo
2 smashed garlic cloves
2 tbsp. oil
1 tsp. lemon juice
1 tsp. cumin
¼ tsp. turmeric

Mix mushrooms, beans, olives, green onions, red peppers and the tomatoes. Chill for 2 hours. Also chill dressing ingredients. Coat mushroom mixture lightly with dressing and toss rest. Serve on lettuce leaves.

Mushrooms

If trying to avoid excessive fat, cook your mushrooms in boiling water instead of butter. Cut off stems and drop caps into boiling water to just cover to which has been added 1 tsp. salt, 2 tsp. lemon juice. Boil for about 5 min or until tender.

Sweet and Sour Red Cabbage

2 to 2 red cabbage finely shredded after discarding outer leaves
2 tbsp. butter
1 medium onion, chopped
¾ cup good red wine vinegar -secret of the dish
6 cloves
4 tsp. brown sugar
1 bay leaf
6 juniper berries
1 tsp. salt
½ tsp. pepper
2 cups water
½ medium lemon

Heat butter and sauté onions until soft, about 3 minutes. Add vinegar, cloves, sugar, bay, juniper berries, salt, pepper 2 cups water. Bring top boil. Add cabbage, return to boil, and simmer covered about 45 minutes until cabbage is tender. Off heat, stir in flour, 1 tbsp. at a time until thick. Cover and keep cabbage warm.

Cook's Savoy with Caraway

1 small onion, sliced
1 head Savoy cabbage or other cabbage, derribed, and shed into small thin strips
1 tbsp. caraway toasted over low heat, stirring until fragrance is released.
4 tbsp.butter
¼ cup white wine vinegar
¼ tsp. each salt and pepper

Melt butter and cook cabbage over low heat until tender, -about 12 minutes. This much can be done ahead. Reheat if made ahead, stirring in seeds and vinegar.

Sautéed Savoy Cabbage with Apples

1 medium tart apple, cored, sliced
1 small onion, sliced
1 head Savoy cabbage, coarsely chopped (1 ½- lbs)
2 tbsp. oil
½ tsp. salt
¼. tsp. pepper
¼ cup dry white wine

Sauté onion and oil in skillet until softened, 4minutes, and add caraway and cabbage, stirring constantly until it wilts, about 2 minutes. Add wine and seasonings, Simmer, stirring now and then until cabbage is tender, 6 to 8 minutes

Braised Savoy

1 medium head, quartered and cored
2 tbsp. oil
¼ lb. tart apples, peeled, cored, diced
Large pinch grated nutmeg
15 juniper berries
1 cup dry white wine

Add cabbage to large pan, salted boiling water and cool 5 minutes. Drain and shred. Put cabbage in heated oil in oven- proof casserole. Add apples. Bring to boil on top of stove, Add seasonings, junipers, wine. Cover and braise 35 to 45 minutes. Check to make that liquid does not boil away. If so, add boiling water. If too watery, boil down.

If cabbage were initially shredded initially, it would probably save cooking time. I would think that juniper berries and caraway seeds could be interchangeable.

Creamed Cabbage Hazleton

1 medium cabbage, or 2 lbs., shredded
2 tbsp. butter
1 cup of half and half
salt and pepper to taste
nutmeg to taste

Plunge into large kettle boiling water (cabbage that is). Boil, uncovered for 5 minutes. Drain and try to squeeze dry.

Add to heater butter and after mixing well, add seasonings, half and half. Simmer covered over low heat for about 5 minutes.

Stirring often. Should still be crisp.

Gratin Savoyard

Rub garlic over dish. Slice potatoes thinly, wash, dry. Put a layer of potatoes in dish. Season. Sprinkle on layer of grated, layer of julienned bacon (sauté ½ lb.). You will have 3 layers of potatoes in all, potatoes on top, no bacon on top layer. Pour over just enough chicken stock to almost cover. Bake at 450 degrees for 40 minutes.

12

LEGUMES

The dried seeds of peas, beans and lentils are legumes, that is, they belong to the plant family leguminosae. To name only a few of the many, there are the white beans, which include pea and the great northern, kidney, red, black turtle, chickpeas (also known as ceci and garbanzos), flageolets, lentils, limas, black-eyed and split peas. Not interesting in themselves, the long, slow cooking allows your seasonings to permeate them and the lowly bean is turned into something special.

With the exception of lentil, black-eyed and split pea, all dried legumes must be soaked in order to re-hydrate them. There are two soaking methods. Whichever you use, always begin by rinsing beans under running water and picking them over. This is to ensure that no possible pebbles have crept in during the harvest. The older method, which I am more comfortable with, consists of covering beans with cold water and letting them stand for ten hours or overnight. So many beans are used in Spain that the presoaked can be bought in their markets.

The quick-soak method calls for placing rinsed beans in saucepan, covering with cold water and bringing them to the boil. Let them boil hard, uncovered, for exactly two minutes. Take pan off heat, cover and let stand for two hours. In both instances, rinse beans under running water, discarding soaking water. They are both then ready for cooking.

Cooking times vary with the type, age and size of the bean. The larger great northern and chick pea should be tender within 1-½ to 2 hours although some recipes call for longer cooking of 3 to 4 hours. The smaller peas and lentils should take roughly 45 minutes. As to the age of the bean, you, of course, have no way of telling how long they have been on the grocery shelf but do not let them gather dust on yours.

While the following recipes call for two different types of beans and each dish has its own distinctive flavor, the procedures are similar, the purpose of which is to get as much flavor as possible into the beans. It is a flexible process. The soaked beans can be simmered in water or in a mixture of water and dry white wine or stock. Aromatic vegetables are added, sometimes sautéed, sometimes not. Cooking can take place on top of the stove or in the oven. Remember not to salt until just about when beans are done as it will toughen them beyond repair. Watch your temperatures. If the liquid boils, the beans toughen but if they fall below the simmer, it is almost impossible to soften them.

One pound of dried beans, 2 or 2-½ cups will expand to yield six or more servings.

Spanish Bean Casserole, known as Fabada

This is a specialty of northern Spain and there are many ways of doing it.

1 lb. soaked white beans
6 parsley stems
sprig rosemary tied, chopped, fresh
2 cups canned, peeled tomatoes
1 head garlic, whole, unseparated
2 tbsp. tomato paste
1 ½ lbs. chorizo, a garlic, paprika sausage, or andouille sausage
1 unpeeled onion, studded with 2 cloves nails
¼ tsp. each salt and pepper
1 bay leaf
½ cup fresh herbs

Place soaked, rinsed, drained beans in casserole or saucepan. Add all ingredients except sausage, salt, pepper and fresh herbs. Add water just to cover. Cover with lid and bring just to simmer on top of the stove. Continue to cook for an additional 2 or 3 hours, until tender, stirring now and then - always with wooden spoon. Check water level and add a little boiling water if it has dropped below that of the beans. Add salt and pepper to taste. During the last half hour, add sliced sausage to beans and cook the 30 minutes. Remove parsley, onion, garlic cloves and bay. Sprinkle with fresh herbs and serve.

Black Beans and Rice

¼ cup olive oil
2 green peppers
2 medium onions
1 lb. black turtle beans
1 cup dry white wine
3 cloves garlic, peeled
small ham hock
1 herb bouquet (2 bay leaves, sprig, rosemary and 6 parsley stems)
¼ tsp. each salt and pepper

Heat up oil in skillet and soften onions and green peppers. Add garlic. Meanwhile, place beans in stovetop casserole and add cup of wine and enough water to cover. Add the contents of the skillet plus bouquet garni and ham hock and bring just to a slow simmer. This may require the use of a flame tamer. Continue to simmer for some 3 hours. Make sure the water does not fall below the level of the beans; if so, add boiling water. Season with salt and pepper during the last hour. When ready to serve, remove bouquet garni and ham hock, scraping off any meat clinging to bones back into casserole. Cook one cup raw rice; pour contents of casserole over and serve as an entrée in soup bowls.

Great Northern Beans as a Vegetable

1 lb. any white beans
4 garlic cloves, unpeeled
5 or 6 parsley stems, tied
1 onion, unpeeled studded with 2 cloves
2 bay leaves
2 tbsp. salt
½ cup olive oil
2 medium onions, chopped

3 peeled tomatoes, or 3 cups canned tomatoes, peeled, seeded and chopped
2 tbsp. tomato paste

Soak lb. of Great Northern or any white bean as above. Drain and place beans in saucepan. Add garlic cloves, parsley stems, unpeeled onion studded with cloves and bay leaves. Add cold water to cover beans by 1 inch. Bring to simmer, cover and simmer gently for 2 hours

Do not let the bean water get above the boil or you will toughen the beans. Add salt and continue to simmer for another half hour. Check water level now and then. If it has fallen below the bean level, add boiling water.

Meanwhile, heat up cup olive oil and add medium onions, chopped. When soft, add tomatoes which have been peeled, seeded and chopped plus 2 tbsp. tomato paste. Simmer for 15 minutes or so. Add to beans and simmer uncovered for 20 minutes more. Remove clove-studded onion and serve.

These beans are delicious partially cooked, finished in the oven around a leg of lamb or cooked with stewing lamb. (See lamb.)

Baked Beans

1 ½ cups Great Northern Beans, soaked, drained   salt
6   oz. salt pork, rind removed
1 tbsp. Worcestershire sauce
4 cups cold water
4 pepper grinds
½   cup chopped onions
1 bay leaf
2 mashed garlic cloves
1 tsp curry powder or grated
3 tsp. catsup   ginger
3 tsp. unsulphured molasses
6 oz. salt pork, rind removed
2 tbsp. Dijon mustard
salt and pepper to taste

Preheat oven to 250 degrees. Place all of the above in baking dish or casserole, topping with diced salt pork. Cover and bake at 250 degrees for a good 6 hours, 9 if possible. Stir now and then. If water level has dropped below that of beans, add a little boiling water.

Black Eyed Peas with Onion

2 medium tomatoes, peeled, seeded, chopped or 15 oz. can of whole
1 cup rinsed black-eyed peas
1 medium onion, chopped
1 garlic clove, minced
1 tsp. salt
½ tsp. pepper
2 tbsp. parsley, minced

Bring beans and 4 cups of water to the simmer and cook until tender -about 30 min. Meanwhile, heat up oil and soften onions. At last minute, add garlic and then tomatoes and stew until soft about 10 minutes. Season and add to beans. Cook about 5 min. Add parsley.

Cajun Red Beans and Rice

½ lb. pinto beans
1 tsp. salt plus pepper to taste
1 qt. water
¼ lb. salt pork or bacon
1 cup chopped green pepper
1 cup chopped onion
¼ tsp. cayenne
¼ tsp. dried oregano and thyme
1 cup canned tomato sauce
½ link crumbled fresh bulk pork sausage
½ cup chopped scallions, green included
3 cups Cajun rice

Mix beans, salt, qt. water and bring to boil for 2 min. Set aside, covered, off heat for an hour. Now bring this back to the boil, covered and cook, stirring now and then for some 45 min. Now add herbs, peppers, onions, cayenne, and tomato sauce. Again simmer covered for 45 minutes, adding more boiling water if necessary. Add sausage and scallion and simmer 15 minutes more. Serve with rice.

Black-Eyed Peas Vinaigrette

1 lb. black-eyed peas
1 clove-studded onion
1 bay leaf
1 garlic clove
¼ tsp. each salt and pepper
½ cup chopped onions
2 tbsp. minced shallots
1 clove garlic, peeled
2 sprigs parsley
3 tbsp. vinegar
2/3 cup oil

Cook peas 90 minutes with clove-studded onion, bay, garlic, salt and pepper. When down, put in bowl and give them a 15 minute rest, drained of curse. Add chopped onions, minced shallots, garlic, parsley, vinegar, oil.

Black Turtle Beans

2 lbs. black turtle beans
½ cup cider or wine
water to cover
8 chunked onions
2 green peppers, sliced
1   tbsp. each salt and bacon
2 cups of hot, not smoking, oil
4 bay leaves
2 tbsp. vinegar
6 sliced garlic cloves
1 tsp. salt

Soak, drain and rinse beans. Put in bowl, cover with cider or wine, add water to cover and place in 300 degree oven while you do the following: sauté onions and green peppers, salt and bacon until lightly browned in 2 cups of hot -not smoking- oil. Take pan out of oven and add contents of sauté pan to it. Stir in -with wooden spoon- bays, vinegar, garlic, salt, a few pepper grinds. Cover pan and put back in oven, adjusting oven temperature so that is simmers gently. Add hot water if necessary, it is edible in 2 hours but better in 5 or 6 hours. As these beans are much better if allowed to cool and then reheat.

13

MISCELLANEOUS SIDE DISHES

Boiled Rice

The thousands of varieties of rice can be neatly divided into two categories: long grain and short grain. You will occasionally come across a medium grain that can be relegated to the short grain. Basically the short grain, preferably the Italian Arborio and the Spanish Valencia, are used for national dishes such as the Italian risotto and the Spanish paella. In both cases a creamy texture is desired. In other instances where a fluffy consistency is desired, such as in boiling and steaming and the pilaf, our long grain Carolina rice is called for.

When boiled or steamed, 1 cup of raw rice will expand to 3 cups of cooked but when sautéed such as in risotto or a pilaf, the yield drops. In this instance, 1 cup of raw rice will yield 3 servings. I go by the Chinese saying, allowing ½ cup of cooked rice per male, ¼ cup per female.

When a recipe calls for a fairly small amount of rice, say 1 cup or less, I use the following method: place 1 cup of long grain rice in small saucepan. Add 1 to 1- ½ cups of cold, salted water.

Steamed Rice

Turn up the heat and just as it nears the boil (do not let it come to a full boil), immediately turn heat to lowest possible setting, cover tightly and cook for exactly 18 minutes.

For larger amounts of rice, I find the old fashioned rice steamer indispensable and also foolproof. I use the type that resembles a double boiler but with slots in the sides of the inset. Begin by bringing a large saucepan of salted water to the boil. The suggested proportion of rice to water is 2 qts. of water to 1 cup of rice. Dribble in rice and when water comes back to the boil, turn down heat a bit but let it continue to boil at a good clip, uncovered, for 10 minutes. An added teaspoon of oil will keep it from boiling over.

Place rice in colander and cool down by running cold water over it. Drain and place in inset. Season with salt, pepper and dot with butter if you wish. Bring water to the boil in bottom of steamer, turn down heat and insert top portion. Cover and steam for 12 minutes at which point, rice will be done.

The nice thing about this method is that if you are having a party and want to get as much cooking as possible out of the way, rice can be boiled and rinsed off in the morning and then steamed when ready to use. I might add that electric steamers are available.

Rice Pilaf

For this method which is essentially sautéing followed by simmering in a liquid, I use the more absorbent Italian or Spanish short-grain rice. As opposed to boiling, do not forget that your yield will drop to 3 servings per cup of raw rice.

Heat up 2 tbsp. butter or oil over moderate heat. If you wish you can soften a few chopped scallions in the oil, add your rice, cook, stirring until translucent. Add two cups of stock per cup of rice cover and cook slowly for about 18 minutes, unlike risotto stirring only once or twice.

Isolina's Risotto

This recipe comes straight from Milan. It is a great party or company dish, but I say do not serve it unless you have a guest who does not mind being stationed at the stove, stirring for some 20 minutes.

2 tbsp. butter
1 small onion, thinly sliced
½ cup dry red or white wine
3 ¼ cups boiling chicken stock
½ tsp. saffron
¾ cup grated cheese
1 ½ cups Arborio, Italian short-grain rice
¼ to ½ cup heavy cream or light cream

Melt butter and soften the onions in it. Add wine and reduce to a few tablespoons. Add rice and continue to cook until rice turns translucent but do not let it brown.

Red Beans and Rice

1 ½ lbs. red kidney beans
1 ham hock
1 large ham bone
½ lb. coarsely chopped salt pork
2 tbsp. olive oil
3 or 4 large chopped green onions
2 celery ribs
3 minced garlic cloves
1 tsp. fresh or dried thyme
1 tsp. oregano
1 bay leaf 2 tbsp. chopped parsley
½ tsp. ground black pepper
½ tsp. chopped basil
1 tsp. Tabasco sauce
½ lb. chorizo or andouille sausage
salt to taste
2 cups Carolina rice, cooked separately
1 cup orange juice
sprinkling grated lemon rind

Soak dried kidney beans; sauté green onions, celery ribs in oil and butter until tender. Add garlic and the beans.

Then add pepper, andouille sausage, stock, if available, or water. Add garlic and the beans. Bring to boil; simmer, partially covered for three hours. At the end of cooking, mash some of the beans against pot with a wooden spoon. Serve over boiled rice (see rice), adding, if desired, a few drops of hot pepper sauce.

Rice

Add the stock at half-cup increments after each half cup has been absorbed, stirring constantly. Continue to add stock by half cupfuls, always stirring constantly and only adding more when previous half cup has been absorbed, but rice has not become dry. When rice is almost done, dissolve saffron threads in a little of the hot stock and the other half of the butter and the cheese. Take pan off heat and let it settle for a moment or so, stirring it in gently but thoroughly. Now stir in the ¼ to ½ cup of cream. Bring back to the boil and you will have a creamy mixture.

An interesting way to cook rice, particularly if you are going to serve it with a curried dish, is to substitute orange juice for half the water. Sprinkle with grated rind.

Spoon Bread (Batter Bread)

There are two versions of this dish, one, a soufflé-type in which beaten egg whites are folded into the mixture and this is the other version.

Rub 1-½ quart baking dish well with butter. Scald two cups milk until bubbling, stirring constantly with wooden spoon, slowly add cup stone-ground cornmeal. Cool a bit. Off heat, beat in 2 tbsp. butter by bits, salt, and baking powder. When butter is absorbed, beat in 3 beaten eggs. Bake at 375 degrees on middle level of oven for 40 minutes.

Grits

Grits and polenta have their similarities. This Southern specialty begins by bringing 4 cups of salted water to the boil and adding 1 cup of non-instant grits very slowly, stirring constantly until a smooth consistency has been obtained. Turn heat to low and cook, stirring now and then for some 20 minutes. Remove from heat and add 2 tbsp. butter, a grated garlic clove and 1 cup grated sharp Cheddar cheese. It can be served as such or it can be turned into the following soufflé. Cool a bit and then add two beaten eggs, salt and pepper to taste and ¼ cup milk. Put into greased 1-½ quart casserole. Bake 40-60 minutes in 300 degree oven.

Hopefully you will have enough left over for breakfast, as to my way of thinking there is no better breakfast dish than fried grits (actually sautéed) and applesauce. We will assume that it has been chilled overnight.

Fried Grits

Heat up a tablespoon or so of butter in a heavy skillet. When sizzling hot, break off biscuit-size squares of grits and drop into the fat, turning down heat. When brown on one side, flip and brown on the other.

Applesauce

3 lbs. red Delicious apples, sliced, uncored, unpeeled
3 tbsp. red wine
1 tbsp. unsalted butter
1 handful fresh cranberries
sugar and ground cinnamon to taste

My only cooking discovery was in finding out that applesauce cooked in a little red wine turns the apples into an attractive pink. I was once accused of serving canned applesauce.

My feeling is that using red unskinned apples, such as Red Delicious will also enhance the color, as does the wine.

I recently learned that a handful of cranberries added to the applesauce will have the same effect. Applesauce will require more apples than you would think to give you a substantial amount. For four or five servings, put apples in heavy saucepan and add 2 or 3 tbsp. of red wine.

Cover and cook slowly until the apples are tender, possibly 10 or 15 minutes. Stir in butter. Run through vegetable mill. You may now, if you wish, add sugar and cinnamon to taste. I do not.

Fried Apples

As in the above grits, frying actually means sautéing. Peel, core and chop apples. Drop into skillet with small amount of moderately hot butter. Sprinkle over a teaspoon or so of sugar and allow to brown, stirring. When apples are brown, cover pan, turn down heat and cook until tender, a matter of 5 or 10 minutes.

Serve with above grits as breakfast dish.

Pancakes

1 cup all-purpose flour
1 tsp. double-acting baking powder
1/8 tsp. salt
3 tsp. unsalted melted butter
1 egg, separated
1 cup milk

Measure flour by scooping into cup with spoon, level off excess and sift with baking powder and salt. In separate bowl beat egg yolk with fork and stir in milk and melted butter. Stir gently into dry mixture. Beat egg white until stiff and fold into mixture. Heat well greased griddle until very hot and ladle batter into four inch pancakes, turning when bottoms are brown. It is often said that the first batch should be discarded and subsequent batches served. Pancakes with the above fried apples and bacon or sausage served with pure Vermont maple syrup make a wonderful breakfast.

14

EGG DISHES

These are completely unrelated dishes, the soufflé, baked eggs and cheese, and Spanish tortilla.

The Soufflé

To oversimplify, define a soufflé as a thick, flavored béchamel or white sauce into which beaten egg whites are folded.   As it bakes, the air trapped in the beaten whites expands and causes the soufflé to rise and puff. In some circles, the soufflé is considered synonymous with trouble, an undeserved reputation unless egg whites are not both beaten and folded in properly.

There is also trouble if you cannot get people to the table right away.   Five minutes out of the oven and it will sink.

Egg Whites

There is no better spot to discuss egg whites. First of all, refrigerated eggs are easier to separate than the room temperature but room- temperature whites mount more readily. To this end, remove eggs from refrigerator, separate and allow to come to room temperature for some 20 minutes before beating.

Secondly, if there is any dampness or grease on beater or bowl or if even a trace of yolk gets into the whites, they will refuse to mount. It is not always easy to fish out these bits of yolk (with piece of eggshell) from a large bowl of whites.

To avoid trouble, I will break each egg separately into cup and then add each individually to beating bowl. You can beat whites with whisk, rotary beater or hand-held electric beater, my preference. Start beating at low speed. You will note that whites become frothy and foamy. This is a good time to stop and add a ¼ tsp. of salt and ¼ tsp. cream of tarter, which is said to stabilize the whites. Increase speed a bit and continue to beat, circulating beater around bowl. Hold up beater. When the whites that cling to it stand up in vertical peaks, they have been beaten sufficiently. They should be stiff but not dry, that is they should not lose their wet, glossy look. In other words, do not over-beat or they cannot be folded in properly.

Folding

To fold connotes incorporating a delicate substance such as beaten egg whites into a thicker sauce or perhaps whipped cream into a dessert. A folding motion is actually used. Before the beaten whites can be -folded into the soufflé base, you must first lighten base by stirring in big spoonful of the beaten whites. You can now fold in balance. Turn the bowl of whites onto top of sauce. Center rubber spatula on the surface and cut right down to bottom of bowl. Come back up against sides, flipping contents of spatula onto surface. Continue this motion, rotating bowl with one hand, "folding" with the other until whites have been just about incorporated. Do not be too thorough about this. There should be flecks of white on the surface. Do this delicately and quickly. It should not take more than a minute or so. Again restraint is the key word. Mixture is now   ready   to be turned into mold and baked.

Cheese Soufflé

If you have experienced tasteless cheese soufflés it is possibly because supermarket cheese was used. Even though their may be marked "made in Switzerland", it has nothing in common with the aged and this of course applies to as well. They make excellent brunch or supper dishes. You are better off with a deep, 6-cup, straight-sided, porcelain, so-called charlotte mold, available in all kitchen stores, believe in giving yourself every advantage.

In addition to cheese, there are all manner of soufflés, among them, oyster, garlic, lobster and crabmeat. Master the ever-popular cheese and try them all. While seasonings will differ and the solid ingredient is perhaps handled differently procedures and proportions of ingredients to the other are the same for the 6-cup mold. They are:

3 tbsp. soft butter
1 cup scalded milk
1 cup shredded Swiss cheese
3 tbsp. flour
½ tsp. salt
3 tbsp. butter
pinch red pepper or Tabasco sauce
4 egg yolks
4 egg whites
grating of nutmeg

Preheat oven to 400 degrees. Prepare mold by buttering sides and bottom and sprinkle with tablespoon of the cheese. Reserve 3 more tbsp. for sprinkling on top before it goes in oven.

Roux or Sauce Base

(See sauces.) Heat butter over moderate heat. Add flour and stir well with wooden spoon for 2 or 3 minutes. Take pan off heat; allow to cool for a moment. Now pour in half of the milk, which has been heated to the scald. Stir in remaining milk.

Back over moderately high heat, stir constantly for 5 minutes. Stir in seasonings and cheese. Set aside to cool a bit while you beat whites. After 5 minutes or so, beat in yolks followed by folding in whites. Spoon mixture into prepared mold, sprinkle with cheese and place in middle level of preheated oven. Turn oven down to 375 degrees and do not open oven door for some 20 minutes.

It should rise and puff in 25 or 30 minutes. Arrange for guests to take; allow cooling for a moment their places at the table. Give it 5 more minutes to firm up and serve immediately.

Omelet Savoyard

5 or 6 slices of bacon
2 medium potatoes, peeled, sliced
2 sliced leeks
8 eggs
6 tbsp. butter
1 tbsp. each salt and pepper
½ cup finely diced chopped herbs
3 parsley sprigs

Blanch bacon, drain, dry, sauté, set aside. Sauté potatoes in hot fat 4 or 5 minutes. Lower heat, add leeks and cook 2 minutes more.

Beat eggs with salt and pepper to taste with chopped herbs and add skillet contents. Melt butter in 12- inch skillet or 2 skillets. When butter stops sizzling, add egg mixture to skillet, stirring as it cooks. Do not overcook. Eggs should not be overcooked. Run under broiler for a moment or so.

Tortilla Espanola (Spanish Omelet)

In this salmonella-conscious age, you might say that this replaces the 2 minute omelet. It is long cooking and can be tested with internal meat thermometer. It should reach 150 degrees. This dish is quite common in Southern Spain where it is served as a light meal or as an appetizer.

4 tbsp. olive oil
2 small onions, chopped
1 peeled garlic clove
1 medium potato, peeled, diced
4 whole eggs
1 medium potato, peeled and diced
¼ tsp. each, salt and pepper
chopped parsley

Heat up 2 ¼ of the oil over moderate heat, preferably in heavy iron skillet. Add onions and garlic. Soften onions. When garlic clove starts to brown, remove and discard. Add diced potato and cook until tender. Watch heat. You do not want them to brown.

With slotted spoon, remove onions and potatoes to bowl. Pour out oil in skillet and replace with remaining 2 tbsp. While this heats up -moderate heat - beat eggs until frothy and pour into bowl containing potatoes and onions. Season to taste.

Pour this into hot skillet and cook until underside is set and brown. Place plate over skillet and invert, turning tortilla onto plate. Slide back into skillet and cook until second side is cooked.

This has great similarities with the Italian frittata in which the potatoes are omitted, tomatoes, onions and green peppers substituted. This is added to the egg mixture exactly as above. Instead of flipping the egg mixture over, as in the tortilla, the skillet is placed in the oven under the broiler until the top browns; it is then turned into the serving plate.

Favorite Cheese Dish

Neither a fondue nor a soufflé; makes an excellent luncheon or dinner dish.

6 slices bread, buttered, decrusted
5 whole eggs
2 ½ cups milk
½ cup gruyere cheese
1 tsp. dried mustard

Layer bread   in greased baking dish, sprinkling with cheese.   Rest of ingredients beaten and poured over bread and cheese. Let stand for 2 hours or overnight in refrigerator. Put casserole in baking pan half filled with hot water and bake it at 350 degrees for an hour.

15

GUMBO

In Louisiana, almost every recipe begin with a combination of onions, celery and peppers, which is known as the "holy trinity."

Does this mean that the onions, celery and carrots known as mirepoix should be known as their "holy trinity"?

Serve it over rice as an entrée. If no fish stock is available, make your own by shelling the shrimp, browning them briefly in butter and adding 1½ qts. of water. Simmer for 20 minutes; then strain and set aside.They might contain rabbit, chicken, shrimp oysters, crabmeat, either alone or all together. The name comes from the African word for that vegetable. It either contains okra or file powder, a thickener, is made from dried sassafras leaves.

Roux for Gumbo

½ cup olive oil
½ cup all-purpose flour

Before making your roux, assemble and prepare the gumbo base listed below. In a large heavy skillet or stockpot, heat oil. Add flour, a little at a time, stirring constantly. Reduce heat to medium; keep stirring until roux turns a golden brown, some 20 minutes, taking care that it does not burn.

Gumbo Base

2 medium chopped tomatoes, or 1 ½ cups of canned Italian plum tomatoes
3 Louisiana andouille sausage or kielbasa
1 tbsp. minced garlic
2 qts. shrimp stock
2 lbs. whole fresh, deveined shrimp
1 ½ cups chopped yellow onion
½ cup chopped green onions including tops
½ cup chopped green pepper
2 sliced okra, tips removed
2 tbsp. minced parsley
1 can crabmeat, picked over for any bits of shell (about 2 ½ cups (or 2 6 ½ oz.) cans crabmeat
salt to taste
1/8 tsp. cayenne
3 tsp. lemon juice
2 crushed bay leaves
5 allspice berries
1 ½ tsp. dried thyme or 3 sprigs fresh parsley
1/8 tsp. nutmeg
To the hot roux, add yellow onions, green onion tops,
  peppers, okra and parsley.

In Louisiana a combination of onions, celery and peppers, with which just about every recipe begins, is known as the holy trinity. Does this mean that the onions, celery and carrots known as mire poix should be known as their holy trinity?

This is not a true Cajun gumbo, but more of a New Orleans type.

To the hot roux add onions, scallion tops, peppers, okra and parsley. Cook, stirring, for about ten minutes. Add tomatoes, sausages and garlic; mix thoroughly. Add roughly 2 quarts of your shrimp stock, half the shrimp, crabmeat and the seasonings. Cover and simmer very gently for an hour. At the end of the hour, add 2 cups of water and let stand for 30 minutes. At the end of this time, bring back to the boil, add remaining shrimp and cook until they turn pink, roughly 5 minutes. Serve over boiled rice. This will serve approximately 8 people. You will need 2 cups of raw rice (see rice).

This is a great party dish. It can be made well ahead as it freezes beautifully. A good time to freeze is after it has cooked for the first hour. When read to use, defrost and cook remaining shrimp.

Some consider this a soup. I serve it over rice as an entrée and really feel that it deserves its own chapter. If you do not have fish stock on hand, you can make your own by shelling the shrimp before beginning the recipe, browning them briefly in butter and adding 1-½ quarts of water and simmer for 20 minutes; then strain and set aside.

Shrimp

Boiling Shrimp in White Wine

Serve over rice with or without the liquid. Cover unpeeled shrimp with cold water   to which has been added salt, pepper, Worcestershire, juice of half a lemon, a   smashed garlic clove, ½ cup dry white   wine and a good ¼ tsp. of crab boil, if   available. When water starts to boil, remove from heat and let shrimp cool in cooking liquid.

16

PASTA

Italians are critical of our use of sauce; they use just enough sauce to coat the pasta. In this brief chapter dried pasta is served as the main course, and not the first course, as the Italians do.

Also, the Italian way to cook pasta is until al dente or firm to the bite. Having invited Italian friends for dinner, I asked my daughter, who had lived in Italy for some years, to help prepare an Italian dinner. Her answer was, "I wouldn't dare".

Calculate four quarts of water per pound of dried pasta. For a pound of pasta, bring four quarts of water to a boil. Add pasta: add 2 tsp. of salt. Cover pot until water returns to a rapid boil. One pound of pasta will serve three if you serve nothing else, and six if it is a side dish. Stir up occasionally.

Cook according to package directions. Drain pasta in a colander and reheat briefly in the sauce.

Sauces

Tomato Sauce

Imported canned Italian plum tomatoes make an excellent sauce. If you can find good fresh tomatoes, by all means use them. Try this quick version of the old-fashioned simmered sauce of yore.

3 tbsp. olive oil
4 cloves minced garlic
2 cups canned tomatoes, drained, or 2 cups fresh, peeled and seeded tomatoes, coarsely chopped
¼ tsp. each salt and pepper
4 tbsp. chopped parsley
5 basil leaves
2 anchovy fillets or a squirt of anchovy paste
½ cup of sliced black olives
1 tbsp. capers

In a large saucepan, heat olive oil over moderate heat. Add garlic. After a minute or so, add canned tomatoes, drained and coarsely chopped. Increase heat to medium high. Add salt and several grindings of pepper. After a minute or two, turn heat down to the merest simmer and continue to cook for 10 minutes, stirring often. Run through food mill, sprinkle with chopped parsley and serve. In the summer, fresh, chopped basil leaves are a welcome addition. Liven it up a bit by increasing oil to four tbsp; add two rinsed-off anchovy fillets or a squirt of anchovy paste to the oil. Add capers and ripe olives. The yield is small, about two cups, enough for one pound of pasta.

Bolognese Sauce

This sauce is of northern Italian origin and contains far less meat than cooks generally put into it.

2 finely chopped medium yellow onions
2 tbsp. unsalted butter
3 tbsp. olive oil
3 tbsp. chopped celery
3 tbsp. chopped carrots
½ lb. ground lean beef, preferably chuck or the meat from the neck
salt to taste
¼ teaspoon pepper to taste
1 cup dry white wine

½ cup whole milk
2 cups canned Italian tomatoes

In large skillet, soften onions in oil and butter. Add celery and carrots and wilt for two minutes. Crumble in beef and add one-tablespoon salt and the pepper. Stir, cooking only until it has lost its raw color. Add wine. Increase heat to high and cook until liquid has almost evaporated, stirring occasionally. Reduce heat down to medium, add milk and let it evaporate. Add tomatoes and continue to stir. When the tomatoes have started to bubble, turn down heat to low. Add salt to taste. Cover and simmer for a minimum of two hours. Serves 6. Makes   2 to 2 ½ cups sauce, enough for 1   lb. of pasta.

Pesto

This green sauce can be bought in stores but is a thousand times better when home-made

2 cups loosely packed basil leaves
½ cup olive oil
1/3 cup pine nuts
2 to 3 cloves garlic
1   tsp. salt
1/3 cup Pecorino cheese

Place the basil leaves, olive oil, pine nuts, and cloves of garlic, salt and cheeses in the blender. Blend at medium speed for several minutes until mixture is puréed. If pesto is too dry, add a little more oil. Heat but do not boil.   Enough for 1 ½ lbs. pasta, preferably over linguine, flat spaghetti.

Creamy Fish Sauce

Make this sauce with either smoked salmon or canned tuna fish.

1 6 ½ or 7-ounce can tuna fish or 1 cup finely diced smoked salmon
1 cup light cream

Drain the tuna or smoked salmon. Put it in a blender with the lemon juice and cream, blending with a fork until it is the consistency of mayonnaise. Heat gently in a small saucepan and serve over   1 lb. of pasta.

Tomato Sauce with Tapenade Paste

In the summertime, make this sauce with fresh, rather than canned tomatoes if you can. It takes more time to peel them, but they have more flavor.

2 tbsp. olive oil
2 cloves chopped garlic
2 cups chopped, peeled, fresh tomatoes
2 tsp. tapenade paste (see below)

In a medium-sized skillet, heat olive oil and garlic. Sauté until golden, monitoring closely that the garlic does not burn. Add tomatoes and simmer 10 minutes. Remove from heat and add tapenade paste, stirring with a fork to incorporate it into the tomato sauce.

Enough for one pound cooked pasta.

Tapenade

Buy this black olive paste in gourmet specialty shops. Use it in chicken and rabbit dishes or over focaccia bread. But you can easily make your own.

1 cup canned black olives, pitted and drained
1 tsp. drained, rinsed capers
4 canned anchovy fillets, rinsed and drained or 4 anchovy paste
2 tbsp. lemon juice
1 tsp. Dijon mustard
freshly ground black pepper to taste
½ cup virgin olive oil

Blend olives, capers, anchovy fillets, lemon juice, mustard and pepper in a food processor or blender until paste-like. Continue blending, adding a stream of olive oil until you obtain a thick paste.

17

DESSERTS

Fruit Desserts and Sauces

There is nothing prettier than a bowl of fresh fruit, arranged with an eye for color. If you feel that further adornment is needed, try one of the following simple sauces, also suitable for ice cream.

Strawberry or Raspberry Sauce

6 oz. frozen berries
½ tbsp. cornstarch
¼ cup water
¼ cup sugar
¼ cup apricot jam
1 tsp. buttermilk
¼ cup chopped walnuts or pecans
1 tsp. buttermilk
1 cup heavy cream

Frozen berries make it easier. Defrost package and drain thoroughly or use a pint of fresh berries. Purge by running through tomato/vegetable mill which of course both purges and strains, and put in saucepan, reserving a small amount of the purge to blend with cornstarch. Return cornstarch mixture to saucepan, cook over medium heat for a few minutes or until cornstarch taste is lost and sauce thickens. Or, you might make an apricot glaze: combine water, sugar and apricot jam in saucepan, stirring constantly over medium heat until boils and glaze thickens. Crème fraîche (Also see custard sauces below)

Cream is allowed to mature differently than ours and this is one of several approximations: add buttermilk to 1 cup heavy cream. Sweeten to taste with confectioners' sugar and let sit overnight at room temperature. It will thicken. Add a few chopped walnuts or pecans and spoon over fresh fruit.

Peaches and Vanilla Ice Cream

This dessert consists of scoops of vanilla ice cream surrounded by poached, puréed peaches. I would suggest avoiding the tasteless, shipped in winter peaches in favor of the locally grown.

It is not necessary to make a true sugar syrup f or fruit poaching. Simply add sugar to water in the proper proportions (¾ cup sugar to 4 cups water) and simmer to dissolve the sugar. Add teaspoon of vanilla or a piece of lemon rind. Drop whole, unpeeled peaches into the simmering liquid. As fruit should be covered by ½-inch of the liquid, you may have to increase these proportions.

Continue to simmer for about 8 minutes or until soft enough for a thin skewer to be inserted in them. Take pan off heat and let fruit cool in the liquid for 20 minutes. Remove, drain, peel and chill. Reserve a little of the poaching liquid for the puree which can be done in food processor or vegetable mill.

You can now place puree around scoop of ice cream, perhaps adding one of the above fruit sauces. Another alternative is to poach in red wine rather than in the above poaching liquid, very good when halved, cored and skinned pears are used. When done, let cool in pan of liquid. Spread each pear with Mascarpone cheese. Reduce wine to a syrup and pour over peaches before serving.

Baked Bananas

3 firm, ripe bananas
½ cup honey
2 tbsp. lemon juice
¼ cup chopped pecans
¼ cup of heavy cream

Preheat oven to 400 degrees. Peel bananas and lay in shallow baking dish. Pour over a mixture of honey and lemon juice and place in preheated oven. Baste frequently. You can sprinkle with chopped pecans and serve or, for a more festive occasion, top with heavy cream into which pecans have been folded. Bananas will be tender and puffy in roughly 30 minutes.

A la Minute

1 lb. fruit
3 tbs. orange liqueur
3 tbsp. brown sugar

This is a simple dessert but a good company dessert. Place fresh fruit such as strawberries, raspberries, and blackberries in individual serving cups. Just before serving, pour over a mere sprinkling of an orange liqueur such as Grand Marnier, a tbsp. or so of brown sugar, and run under broiler for a minute or so.

Sherry Gelatin

This is an excellent party dessert as it can be done ahead. Your special equipment will only include small dessert cups. Can be halved or doubled.

2 envelopes gelatin
2 tbsp. brandy
¼ cup sugar
2 cups sherry
1 cup orange juice
lemon juice to taste
dabs of whipped cream

Sprinkle gelatin over 1/3 cup of cold water. Stir to dissolve. Add ½ cup of boiling water. Dissolve and let cool to room temperature. Add sugar, sherry, orange juice, and brandy and lemon juice to taste. Pour into cups and chill for 3 or 4 hours. You can top with whipped cream.

Chocolate

The 3 types of chocolate I keep on my shelf are the sweet, the semi-sweet and bitter. For one reason or another, I do not use white chocolate. In each case, I make a point of buying a so-called name brand, avoiding the generally inferior supermarket label. The foreign brands are exceptional but very expensive. Begin by breaking up chocolate into small pieces. If melted at too high a temperature, chocolate can "seize" or harden. Any moisture in melting pan or stirring spoon will have the same effect.

To melt, fill bottom portion of double boiler with water, insert empty top and bring water to the boil. Be sure bottom of insert does not touch water in bottom pan. When the boil is reached, drop in chocolate, take off heat, and let top stand in bottom portion for some 5 minutes, stirring several times. If not properly melted, set bottom of double boiler briefly back over heat. Hot cream can be added to make a chocolate icing or butter to make a sauce to be poured over ice cream. An excellent chocolate sauce which will harden when poured over ice cream can be made by melting a pound of semi-sweet chocolate bits and a stick of softened butter in top of double boiler as above. An excellent chocolate icing (ganache) can be made by heating a cup of half- &-half or heavy cream with a stick of softened butter. Proportions for cake: you will of course have to increase these proportions for a large cake.

Charo's Flan

My Spanish friend Charo tells me that this is the way they do it in Seville. This is easier than our way which consists of baking custards in individual cups in pan of hot water (known as a bain marie). (This recipe calls for lining top of double boiler, a requisite). Custard will then be made in caramelized top. You will need:

Caramel

1 ¼ cup sugar

½ cup water

Place both water and sugar in top of double boiler and set top portion over direct, moderate heat. Cover pan and swirl until sugar melts, some 2 or 3 minutes. I would now suggest oven mitts as spattering sugar can cause a painful burn. Uncover pan and continue to swirl pan until sugar begins to caramelize, turning a golden brown. Now tilt pan so that caramel adheres to sides of pan. Set aside for caramel to harden.

Custard

5 whole eggs
¾ cup sugar or to taste plus 1/8 cup sugar
1 tbsp. water
2 cups half-and-half or if you wish, milk
1 tbsp. grating of nutmeg
1 tsp. vanilla extract
½ tsp. lemon rind
2 tbsp. sherry
¼ tbs. salt

In bowl, beat eggs and dry ingredients until eggs deepen in color and thicken. Stir in vanilla, sherry, tasting for possible addition of sherry and/or sugar. Pour this into caramelized double boiler top. Water is now placed in bottom of double boiler and brought to the boil. Set caramelized pan in top of double boiler and turn heat down to low. Fill with flan mixture. Cover pan and continue to cook some 35 to 40 minutes, stirring only for the first five minutes, until custard is firm, not shaky, particularly in the middle. Remove top portion, uncover pan and refrigerate until cold, several hours or possibly overnight. When ready to serve, run sharp knife gently around inside of pan. Place serving plate on top of pan and invert pan. If custard does not release, wrap pan in hot towel.

Trifle

This is one of several oddly named English desserts, such as slump, grunt and fool. It is a great party dessert even though it cannot be assembled until the last minute, which only takes a minute or so. It consists of slathers of sponge cake covered with raspberry jam and topped with crème anglaise and raspberries.

4 slices sponge cake
½ cup raspberry jam
1 cup crème anglaise
2 tbsp. sweet sherry wine
1 cup fresh raspberries

I like to serve this in individual dessert cups. Put circle of sponge cake in bottom of each cup and sprinkle lightly with sherry. The cake can be yours or from a bakery. Spread raspberry jam lavishly over cakes. Pour over ¼ cup or so of chilled crème anglaise. Above recipe should take care of 4 cups. Top with a few raspberries and serve.

Pie Pastry

Easy as pie. How could the above expression have originated when so many aspiring cooks are terrified of pie pastry? Does pie pastry belong in a beginner's cookbook? I would say yes; it will give you a feeling of accomplishment. Take heart; pie making is as easy as pie if you follow the rules.

First of all, you must get the feel of the dough as amounts of added liquid can vary with the humidity and that might take you a crust or two to achieve.

You must chill both liquid and shortening, work fast and never over-mix dough.

In warm weather, it is not a bad idea to chill both flour and mixing bowl. You will need a Pyrex pie plate or one of a dark metal, in this instance, 9 inches in diameter. You will of course need a rolling pin and, hopefully, a marble pastry slab, the advantage of which is that it can be chilled.

Flaky Pie Crust

They call this pâte brisé or savory piecrust as opposed to the pâte sucré, or sweet pie. The addition of sugar to the pâte brisée will turn it into a pate sucré. For starters, these proportions are for a 9 inch pie plate. For a two-crust pie, the proportion can be doubled with perhaps less water added.

1 ¼ cups all-purpose unbleached flour
2 tbsp. chilled vegetable shortening

¼ tsp. salt
3 tbsp. ice water
4 tbsp. chilled butter

Measure flour by gently spooning it into the appropriate size measuring cups, in this case, 1 ¼ cups. Do not shake cups nor tamp down flour. Scrape off excess with back of knife. Flour and salt are placed in mixing bowl and stirred together.

Cut butter into small bits and add both butter and shortening to bowl. With tips of fingers, (never hot palms), rapidly work shortening in flour. Do this until shortening has been reduced to the size of large peas. Now is the time to add the ice water. This is where getting the feel of the dough comes in. As water measurements can differ according to humidity and the condition of the flour, the optimum is that just enough water is added so that the dough can be formed into a ball. You do not want a soft, mushy dough. Begin by adding one tablespoon of water, again working it in with your fingertips. Add the additional water in drib-drabs until dough has reached proper stage. Do this quickly. Put dough on lightly floured board, hopefully a chilled marble slab. You are now about to perform what they call a fraisage or rubbing together of flour and shortening. Break off a piece of dough, roughly two tablespoons. Flatten dough by firmly pressing away from you with the heel of your hand. Break off another piece of dough and repeat this procedure, piling it on top of the first piece. Do the same with the entire ball of dough. When this is done form dough into a ball, wrap in plastic and store in refrigerator for an hour or so.

When ready to roll out, again place dough on lightly floured board. If at some point the dough gets too warm, it can go back into the refrigerator; if too cold when taken out of he refrigerator, it can sit to warm up a bit. On lightly floured board press dough into a circle. You will want to roll it out into a circle roughly 1/8 inch thick and 11 inches in diameter for a 9-inch piecrust. The crust can be cut out with a ravioli wheel. To this end, place rolling pin on center of circle and roll to the far side, trying not to roll over edge. Give dough a slight turn and repeat the same procedure, rolling from the center to the end and turning dough slightly after each rolling out. For the novice, the dough can be rolled between two lightly floured sheets of heavy plastic, even though I have heard it described by cookbook writers as a useless crutch. When this process is completed, fold one half of dough over the other and gently place in pie tin.

Unroll dough and gently press down into the sides of the pan, being careful never to stretch dough. You want an overhang on side of pie plate of roughly one inch. I will use shears to cut of f the excess. Turn this one-inch overhang under itself around the plate. You can decorate with tines of fork or flute it with thumb and forefinger as follows: hold rim of crust on far side of pie between thumb and forefinger; press in with forefinger and out with thumb; repeat this process, moving around pie crust until it has been fluted. Prick bottom with tines of fork. Pastry should probably be re-chilled at this point.

When your filling has been cooked or partially cooked, recipes will often call for baking "blind". This means that pie shell is first baked or partially baked before filling is added. This is usually done as follows: line pie shell with piece of aluminum foil. Spread with several handfuls of dried beans or rice, which you keep for this purpose, to keep crust from rising and place in bottom level of oven which has been preheated to 400 degrees. Cook for fifteen minutes at 400, remove foil and beans and cook for another five minutes at 375 degrees.

Apple Pie

Crumb topping :

6 tbsp. butter
1/3 cup brown sugar
all-purpose flour

Pie:

2 ½ lbs. Cortland, Northern Spy or Granny Smith apples or 7 medium
1 tbsp. lemon juice
1 tsp. grated lemon peel
1/3 cup sugar
1 tbsp. ground cinnamon
1 tbsp. all-purpose flour

Take pie shell out of the oven; as it cools make the following crumb topping: melt 4 tbsp. butter and pour into one third cup brown sugar and one cup all-purpose flour. Then, using fingers mix well and break into crumbs. Set aside while you assemble the apples.

You will need two and a half lbs. of Cortland, Northern Spy or Granny Smith apples, or a mixture of them. Peel, core, slice and cut rings in half. Mix lemon juice and of lemon zest, sugar, a good sprinkling of cinnamon and flour and toss with apples.

Sprinkle roughly a quarter of the crumb topping over the bottom of the cooled pie shell. Mound the apples on top of this and sprinkle with the balance of the crumb mixture.

Bake in preheated 450-degree oven for twenty minutes on the bottom rack of oven; lower temperature to 350 degrees and bake twenty to thirty minutes longer. Crust will be a golden brown. Let cool a bit before serving.

Fruit Desserts

There is nothing prettier than a bowl of fresh fruit, arranged with an eye for color. I do not think it needs further adornment but here are a few simple sauces also suitable for ice cream.

Strawberry Sauce

Use frozen berries. Defrost and drain thoroughly. Puree and push through strainer. Flavor with lemon juice or Kirsch.

Lemon Sauce

Mix 1 cup pineapple juice, 2 tbsp. honey, tsp. each grated lemon and orange rind. Add confectioner's sugar to taste and chill.

Crème Fraiche

2 tbsp. heavy cream
1 cup sour cream
 confectioner's sugar to taste
¼ cup chopped walnuts or pecans.

Add heavy cream to sour cream. Sweeten with confectioner's sugar and let sit overnight at room temperature. Add a few chopped walnuts or pecans.

Baked Peaches

3 ripe peaches (1 lb.)

1/3 cup brown sugar
1 egg lightly beaten with fork
1 cup heavy cream
¼ cup   sliced almonds
1 tbsp. powdered sugar

Slice peaches and arrange in circular pattern in bottom of shallow baking dish. Sprinkle with the brown sugar. Mix beaten eggs and cream and pour over peaches. Sprinkle with almonds. Bake at 375 degrees for 35 to 40 minutes or until peaches are lightly browned and slightly caramelized. Serve lukewarm.

Indian Pudding (serves 8)

2 cups milk
1 cup cornmeal
1 tsp. salt
1 tsp. cinnamon
¼ tsp. ginger
Powdered cloves and nutmeg to taste
2 tbsp. softened butter
¾ cup light, unsulphered molasses
1 beaten egg
2 more cups milk.

Scald milk. Gradually stir cup cornmeal. In the double boiler, cook stirring for about 15 min. or until it thickens.

Add salt and cinnamon, ginger, powdered cloves and nutmeg, softened butter, unsulphered molasses, beaten egg, and milk.

Put in greased 2 qt. casserole and bake at 250 for 5 hours. Let cool for 30 minutes and serve lukewarm

Another recipe says that after adding egg, pour in the 2 cups milk, cold, and don't stir. This one calls for 3 hours at 300 degrees. You can make what they call cream curls by scraping teaspoon against vanilla ice cream.

Cuisinart Tangerine Sherbet

Start early in day.

4 tangerines
2 lemons
1 cup sugar
1 cup of water

Process zests tangerines and lemons with ¼ of the sugar, for about 30 seconds. Rinse out work bowl with of the tangerine juice and the lemon juice and transfer to another bowl. In small sauce pan, over moderate high heat, bring cup of water and remaining sugar to the boil, let boil for a minute or so until liquid is clear. Add this plus remaining juice to above bowl, stirring mix. Strain through fine sieve and chill until cold.

Freeze in ice cream freezer or pour into shallow pan and freeze until firm, at least 4 to 5 hours. Cut into 1-inch pieces and process in batches until smooth, 15 seconds per batch, scraping down sides as necessary. Pour back in pan and freeze until firm and enough to scoop out, about 30 minutes.

Apple Guide

Best kept in cool, moist spot. Small quantities can be stored in refrigerator -away from freezer- in plastic bag with holes punched in it. Suit the cooking method to the apple variety.

Red delicious and Gravenstein are good for eating and in salads, (they do not discolor in a salad). Golden Delicious are an all around apple, good for anything as are the Jonathons, the McIntosh, Cortland, Winesap, Northern Spy and Staymans. Rome Beauty is good for baking as is the Newton Pippin.

Frozen Ring Mold (serves 8)

1 cup heavy cream
16 oz. pack of frozen strawberries, thawed
2 tsp. brandy
½ cup of sugar
1/3 cup lemon juice

Beat 1 cup of heavy cream in chilled bowl to Chantilly stage. Fold into processed berries. Put in oiled 3 cup mold, loosely covered and put in freezer for at least 4 hours or overnight. Before using, put in refrigerator for 30 minutes.

Sauce: Process raspberries (also not in syrup) with rest of sugar, lemon juice and brandy. Strain and pour unmolded strawberries.

Cold Lemon Soufflé (serves 8)

4 eggs, separated
1/8 tsp. salt
¾ cups sugar
1 cup heated lemon juice, slightly warmed
3 tsp. lemon zest
1 tbs. orange zest
2 egg whites
1 envelope gelatin (soaked in cup cold water)
5 cups heavy cream and an additional dollop
Make ½ inch wide wax paper strip for 6-cup mold. Set in

2-quart bowl   containing yolks, sugar,   lemon juice and zests over hot water. Beat until egg mixture ribbons. Take off heat and let it come to room temperature. Heat gelatin and its water very slightly and stir into yolk mixture. Chill until cool but not cold.

Beat cream to soft peaks and fold into yolk/gelatin mixture. Beat egg whites to soft peaks with the salt. Also fold in. Put in oiled 6-cup mold. Affix collar. Chill several hours. Remove collar and top with additional cream, whipped. Beat cream to soft peaks and fold in. Beat 6 egg whites and salt to soft peaks and fold in same mixture (yolk/gelatin). Pour into oiled 6 cup mold.

Pastry Crust (makes 6 4-Inch Tarts)

½ tsp. salt
½ cup sugar
1 cup flour
8 tbsp. butter
2 egg yolks
2 or 3 tbsp. water

Chill pastry. Bake at 375 for 7 minutes, 350 degrees for about 13 min., or until set and slightly brown. Set aside.

Pastry Cream

1/8 cup flour
3 egg yolks
½ cups sugar
1 tsp. salt
2 tsp. butter
1 tsp. vanilla
1 tbsp. of fruit liqueur

Mix flour, sugar, salt. Beat in egg yolks. Gradually beat in milk over low heat and cook until it bubbles and thickens -about 3 minutes. Let it boil for 1 minute, stirring constantly. Off heat, add butter, vanilla, and fruit liqueur. Cool, cover and chill.

Strawberries

1 tbsp. chocolate bits
1 tbsp. butter
1 pint berries

Mix and melt ingredients in double boiler. Paint top side of tart with this. Hull and halve berries. Dip halfway into chocolate mix. Spoon pastry cream into pastry shells and arrange berries on top, tops up.

Glazed Apples

4 apples, cored, peeled and cut into 1/2-inch rings
¼ cup butter
1 cup white wine or apple juice
1 tbsp. lemon juice
½ cup sugar

Melt butter over low heat. Sauté apple rings, several at a time, until golden. Return all to skillet. Pour rest of ingredients except sugar over apples. Now sprinkle over sugar, cover and continue until apples are tender

Glazed Oranges

6 orange navel oranges
5 cups water
1 tbsp. orange liqueur
1 cup sugar
1 cup water

Cut 6 navel orange skins into julienne. Drop into boiling water and simmer for 10 minutes. Drain and rinse. Halve and reform oranges. Make syrup of and water. Boil to 244 degrees. Surround oranges with julienned peel. Add orange liqueur. Spoon syrup over oranges and peel; chill.

Baked Bananas

4 peeled bananas
4 tbsp. lemon juice
4 tbsp. honey
1 cup whipped cream

Sprinkle bananas halved lengthwise with lemon juice and arrange layer in shallow baking dish. Thin out honey with a little water and pour over bananas. Bake at 450 degrees for 30 minutes, basting now and then. Should be tender and a bit puffed. Add whipped cream.

Another way would be to baste with mixture of orange juice and an orange liqueur. Dot with butter and cook 10 minutes, basting now and then. Sprinkle over brown sugar and broken walnut, baking until sugar melts and nuts are glazed.

Pecan Pie

1 9-inch unbaked pie shell
3 eggs
¾ cup sugar
8 tsp. butter
1 cup dark pecans, coarsely chopped

Use unbaked pie shell. Stir eggs lightly. Gradually add ¾ cups sugar plus melted butter, Karo corn syrup. Line shell with pecans. Pour over mixture. 50 minutes at 350 degrees.

Basic Pumpkin Pie

1 9-inch unbaked pie shell
4 tbsp. melted butter
1 ¾ cups canned pumpkin (much easier than using fresh)
1 ¾ cups milk
3 eggs
1 cup dark brown sugar
1 ¼ tsp. cinnamon
1 tsp. nutmeg
1 tsp. ginger
1 tsp. allspice
1 tsp. salt
¼ tsp. cloves

Mix and put in blind shell.

Use 9-inch pie shell baked "blind", that is 450 degrees for 10 min., 375 degrees for 30 minutes.

Key Lime Pie

1 9 or 10-inch unbaked pie shell
½ cup strained key lime juice
1 tbsp. grated rind (from 6 limes)
14 oz. can condensed milk
3 eggs, separated
¼ tsp. cream of tartar
4 tbsp. sugar
1 cup heavy cream, flavored with vanilla

Put lime juice in large bowl. Add grated rind and gradually, condensed milk. Add unbeaten eggs (except for reserved white) stirring each one in thoroughly. Beat white until stiff and fold in to above. Pour into cooled shell. Bake at 325 degrees for 15 min. Cool, chill and freeze.

Take pie out of freezer and make topping, as follows: Beat remaining egg whites with cream of tartar until stiff. Gradually add sugar and beat. In large bowl, beat vanilla flavored cream until stiff. Fold beaten whites into this.

Pile on top of frozen pie and let pie thaw. Refrigerate this.

My Mother's Cherry Pudding

2 tbsp. gelatin
small bottle Maraschino cherries, (reserve juice)
4 beaten yolks
1 cup powdered sugar
1 cup chopped nuts
12 crushed macaroons
4 beaten egg whites

Soak gelatin in the Maraschino juice. Heat slightly to dissolve.

Carefully heat yolk and sugar mixture, always under boiling point or eggs will curdle. To be perfectly safe, do this in double boiler. Cool mixture. Add rest of the ingredients and fold in beaten whites.

Watermelon Granite

1/3 cup sugar
3 cups watermelon, seeded, chopped
1 tbsp. lemon juice

Mix sugar and ¾ cups water in small pan. Bring to boil, stirring. When sugar is dissolved, take off fire and let cool. Purée melon and combine with above syrup plus the lemon juice. Chill 1 to 2 hours, covered. You can go this far a day ahead if you wish. Proceed by stirring and then put in metal ice cube tray (without dividers) or in shallow metal bowl. Freeze. Stir with fork every 20 to 30 min. for 3 or 4 hours, crushing large frozen lumps. Scrape to lighten texture and serve on chilled plates.

Upside-Down Apple Cake

10 tbsp. soft butter

1 large apple, peeled, cored, sliced
1 cup plus 3 tbsp. sugar
1 cup chopped pecans (4 oz.)
1 tsp. cinnamon
2 cups flour
1 tsp. baking powder
1 tsp. baking soda
1 tsp. salt
2 eggs
1 cup sour cream
¼ tsp. vanilla

Melt 2 tbsp. butter (this comes out of the above 10 tbsp.) in 9-inch skillet over medium heat. Add apple slices and sauté for about 2 minutes or until wilted. Transfer apples. Raise heat a bit and add ½ cup of the sugar, stirring until it turns golden. Off heat, arrange apple slices in skillet in a circular pattern. Set aside.

Toss pecans with 3 tbsp. of the sugar and the cinnamon. Set this aside.

Sift flour with baking powder, baking soda and salt. Beat remaining butter until soft. Gradually beat in 1 cup of sugar and the eggs, one at a time, sour cream and vanilla. Fold in dry ingredients.

Sprinkle half the pecans over apple slices in skillet. Carefully spread half the batter over apples. Sprinkle the remaining pecans over this and top with remaining batter.

Bake in middle level of 350 degree oven for about 45 mm. or until golden or inserted toothpick comes out clean. Cool on rack, still in pan, before inverting it. Let it cool to room temperature.

Craig Claibourne's Danish Loaf Cake

2 tbsp. butter for greasing loaf pans
2/3 cup chopped (don't use ground) almonds
2 cups heavy cream
3 cups flour
2 tsp. vanilla extract
2 cups sugar
½ cup butter
1 tsp. almond extract
4 eggs

¾ cups flour
4 tsp. baking powder
1 tsp. salt   cream, 2 tsp
½ cup pine nuts, coarsely chopped
¼ cup Kirsch
1 cup sugar

Butter 2 9 by 5-inch loaf pans heavily. Coat them with the almonds.

Beat cream to Chantilly stage. Add vanilla, sugar, butter and almond extract. Beat in eggs one at a time. Stir in dry ingredients (flour, baking powder, salt, sifted together). Beat at lowest mixer speed.

Pour half of the batter in each of the 2 loaf pans. Sprinkle each with 2 tbsp. of the pine nuts. Again add of the batter to each loaf pan. Smooth out and add the rest of the pine nuts.

Bake 1 hour at 350 degrees,   middle level of oven. It should take an hour. Test with toothpick. Glaze cake with above glaze and let cool in pan, on rack.

Angel Food Cake

1 ¼ cups cake flour
1 ¾ cups egg whites (12 large)
1 ¼ cups sugar
1 ½ tsps. cream of tartar
½ tsp. salt
1 ½ tsp. vanilla extract
½ tsp. almond extract
¾   tsp. lemon juice
1 cup each heavy cream and berries

Put whites in bowl and sift over cream of tartar. Add salt and beat to soft peaks, that is to say whites will flow, not run when bowl is tilted. Sprinkle over 2 tbsp. sugar and gently fold in. Continue until all of sugar is used. It is very important to use a light hand, the secret of this cake. Now do the same thing with the flour, 2 tbsp. at a time. Do same with vanilla, almond extract and lemon juice.

Batter goes in un-greased, 10-inch tube pan with removable bottom. Smooth top. 300 degrees for 70 minutes or until pale brown and springy.

Take out of oven and turn upside down for an hour before gently removing.

If cake pan has no feet (clips on side to hold it up when inverted), improvise by inverting pan over neck of a bottle. A tubular pan can be improvised by inserting wide mouthed bottle in pan to replace tube.

Serve with whipped cream and berries.

Bonnie Straus Tarte aux Cerises or Linzertorte

Pastry:

1 ½ cups of sifted flour
2/3 cup sugar
¼ cup ground, blanched almonds
½ cup butter
1 hard boiled egg yolk, mashed
1 raw egg
1 tsp. grated lemon rind
powdered sugar for dusting

Filling"

¾ cup cherry preserves
3 tbsp. Kirsch

To make crust, mix flour, sugar, nuts. Cut in butter and work in eggs. Add rind. Form into ball. Chill. Roll out 2/3 of the dough to fit 8-inch spring form pan removable bottom. Roll out ½ inch thick or so my directions read. I question this. The other 1/3 of the dough is to be rolled out for lattices, reserving enough to make a strip to be put around the rim. Lattices can be pressed into this rim to hold strips.

Cover bottom of crust with the jam and put on lattice strips. Bake at 400 degrees for 45 min. Dust with powdered sugar and serve with crème fraîche.

Crème Fraîche

2 ways: Put tsp. buttermilk in cup of heavy cream. Let sit overnight at room temperature, or thin out sour cream with a little heavy cream and add sugar to taste.

Various Ways to do Apple Pies, Single Crust

1. Slice peeled apples into rings and lay in circular pattern on crust. Sprinkle with a little lemon juice, zest and scatter on mixture of 2 tbsp. flour and cup of sugar. Dot with butter.

2. Or you might brush on 1 cup apricot preserves which have been brought to the boil and strained.

Mrs. Flagler's Chocolate Bread

1 cup milk
2 squares bitter chocolate
1 beaten yolk
1 heaping tbsp. butter
1 cup sugar
1 ½ cups cake flour
1 tsp. baking soda
1 cup hot water
½ tsp. vanilla

Scald cup of the milk, take off heat, drop in chocolate and let it melt. Let it cool a bit and add beaten egg.

Cream butter and sugar. To this add alternately the flour and remaining ½ cup milk. Dissolve baking soda in cup hot water and add all of this to chocolate mixture

Bake in bread pan at 350 degrees for 45 min. or until glazed.

Joan Purcell's Brownies

2 sticks butter
4 squares chocolate
2 tsp. tapioca
dash salt
2 cups sugar
4 eggs

2 cups flour

Melt butter and chocolate. Add tapioca, salt, sugar and eggs. Beat. Add flour. Bake in buttered, floured pan. 350 degrees for 25 minutes.

Gourmet Brownies

6 oz. unsweetened chocolate
½ cup butter, melted
3 large eggs
1 ¼ cup sugar
1 cup flour, sifted with ½ tsp. salt
2 tsp. vanilla
¼ cup chopped walnuts

Melt butter and chocolate and let it cool completely.

Beat eggs in mixer. Gradually add sugar and at high speed beat 7 or 8 minutes or until mixture is very thick and pale. Blend in everything but walnuts. Add them last. Bake at 375 degrees for 45 minutes.

Apricot Fool

1 cup water
4 oz. dried apricots
2 tsp. each sugar and a liqueur
1 cup chilled heavy cream

Add 1 cup of water to apricots. Simmer, covered, for 15 to 20 minutes, or until apricots are soft. Add sugar and cook 3 to 5 minutes more. Transfer to bowl and mash with spoon. Chill covered for an hour or two. Whip cream and fold in. Divide into cups.

Strawberry Fool

1 cup berries
3 tbsp. sugar
2 tbsp. water
¾ cup heavy cream, whipped, chilled

Cook the berries plus the sugar and water slowly for 5 minutes, stirring. Chill covered as above and then purée. Fold in whipped cream.

Banana Fool

2 to 3 bananas or 1 cup mashed
2 tbsp. plus 1 cup packed brown sugar
2 tbsp. lemon juice
¾ cup heavy cream
Mix. Chill covered as above and fold in cream.
Bon Appétit Hazelnut Torte (serves 8 to 10)
1 ½ cup hazelnuts, (measured before grinding
1 ½ cups flour
½ tsp. cream of tartar
¼ tsp. salt
1 cup plus 3 tbsp. sugar
6 tbsp. butter, melted and cooled
3 large eggs, separated
1 cup whipped heavy cream for topping

To toast hazelnuts, put them in baking pan-single layer-in 350 degree oven. Cook 8 or 10 minutes or until skins begin to split. Wrap in tea towel and leave them for minute or so. Then, still in towel, rub nuts together until skins slip off. Cool completely before proceeding to next step-grinding. When using food processor, be careful not to overdo it or the nuts will form a paste. Do them briefly in small batches, pulsing briefly. In this case, grind nuts with some of the sugar.

Transfer nuts and the sugar in which they were ground into small bowl. Thoroughly blend in flour.

Beat yolks with cup of the ½ cup of the sugar in large bowl until they ribbon. Beat whites with cream of tartar in another large bowl to soft peak stage. Beat in remaining 3 tbsp. sugar, one at a time and continue beating until whites are stiff but nit dry. Set aside for a moment.

Fold 1/3 of the nuts into yolks. Gently fold in 1/3 of the beaten whites. Do this in 2 more batches and just before the last whites are folded in, drizzle in melted butter.

Spread batter in prepared cans -2 9 X 1-inch round cake pans, bottom lined with buttered and then floured wax paper. Preheated oven of 350 degrees, center rack for about 17 minutes or until inserted toothpick comes out clean. Run knife around edge, turn out onto racks and cool.

Cajun Bread Pudding

1 loaf of day- old bread, cubed, crusts removed - 12 cups in all.
3 large eggs
2 cups milk
2/3 cup sugar
1/3 cup butter, softened
1 tsp. vanilla extract
½ tsp. cinnamon
2 ¼ tsp. nutmeg
¼ cup raisins
2 large ripe bananas, mashed (2 cups)

Let bread soften for 5 min. in 4 cups water. Press through colander and arrange in bottom of buttered 13 X 9 X 2 inches, with the butter. Sprinkle with remaining spices, sugar. Bake at 325 degrees, middle level, 1 hour and 15 min. Serve warm.

Gourmet's Plum Cake

1 stick of butter, softened
1 cup sugar
1 tsp. vanilla
2 eggs, room temperature.
1 cup flour
1 tsp. baking powder
1 tsp. cinnamon
5 plums, pitted and cut into eights

Cream butter   and half the sugar in mixer. Beat in vanilla and eggs, one at a time, beating well after each addition.

Sift flour and baking powder. Stir this into butter mixture. Mix well. Turn into buttered 9-inch spring form pan. Arrange plums skin side down. Mix remaining sugar and cinnamon and sprinkle over. Bake at 350 degrees for 45 min.

Swiss Florentines (yields 25 cookies)

1 cup sliced almonds
1 ½ cup sugar
½ cup honey
1 ½ cup cream
1 1/3 cup flour
1 cup candied orange peel
2 cups dark chocolate, melted

Cut up candied peel and almonds and mix the two and set aside. In heavy pan, put the sugar, honey and cream. Cook 35 minutes, mixing with wooden spoon. Cook to soft ball stage. Add and mix fruit and flour. Mound on oiled cookie sheet or sheets lined with baking paper. Bake at 350 degrees for 7 or 8 minutes, removing with spatula. For glaze, grate chocolate and melt in double boiler Spread on cooled cookies with a brush or knife.

Claiborne's' Florentines (34 cookies)

½ cup sugar
½ cup heavy cream
3 tbsp. butter
1/8 tsp. salt
2 cups flour
¾ cups candied orange peel
1¼ cups smashed almonds

Heat first 4 ingredients to the boil. Take off heat and add flour, nuts and candied peel. Spoon on to buttered sheet and bake at 350 degrees for 10 to 15 min. Watch.

Candied Peel:

Julienne peel of 4 large oranges (1 cup), 2 cups sugar plus additional handful to mix with cooked peel, 1 cup water. Bring water and sugar to the boil. When it reaches soft boil (238 degrees), add orange peel and turn down heat. Cook 10 minutes. Drain on wax paper and sprinkle over the additional sugar. For chocolate icing, melt 8 oz. semi-sweet chocolate, 2 tbsp. butter and dash of Grand Marnier. Dip cookies.

Cuisinart Meringue Tart Shell

5 egg whites at room temperature
¼ tsp. salt
1 cup sugar
4 tsp. cornstarch
1 tbsp. vanilla
1 tbsp. white vinegar
½ cup light cream
6 oz. frozen raspberries, thawed
2 cups assorted fresh fruit

Position oven rack in lower third of oven and preheat to 350 degrees.

Beat egg white until foamy. Add salt and beat to stiff peaks. Keep on beating while adding sugar, a little at a time. Then beat in cornstarch, vanilla and vinegar.

Draw a 10-inch circle in middle of parchment or waxed paper by tracing around bottom of 10-inch pan with pen. Spoon about half of the meringue mixture into middle of circle. Spread to flatten and make base. With large spoon, drop spoonfuls of meringue around circumference of circle.

Bake in a very slow oven for 1 hour 15 min., or until shell is firm. It should not color. Take out of oven and let it cool

Just before serving, force raspberries through a fine sieve. Put strained juice into another bowl.

Beat cream to soft peaks. Fold this into the berry sauce. Spread over bottom of nest and add the cut fruit.

Italian Meringue

This is made by adding hot sugar-syrup to beaten egg whites. No baking is required. It is used as a frosting, as a sherbet, and as a topping for tarts.

1 cup sugar
½ cup cold water
¼ tsp. cream of tartar
3 egg whites

267

¼ tsp. salt
1 tsp. vanilla extract

Stir water, sugar and cream of tartar together until sugar has dissolved. I assume this means that is heated. Stop stirring and cook over moderate heat for about 10 min. or until syrup spins a thread, 242 degrees.

Beat egg whites with salt to soft peaks. Add boiling syrup slowly in thin stream, adding about 3 tbsp of the syrup at a time, returning saucepan to heat for 30 sec. after each addition. Keep on doing this, beating constantly.

Add vanilla. The mixture will become firm and shiny and the whites will stand in soft peaks.

Parfait

To make a parfait, add cup whipped cream and pour into parfait glasses. For a sherbet, add cup of pureed fruit and freeze, butter cream, and fold in softened butter plus vanilla. Chill.

Meringue Kisses

4 egg whites
 pinch salt
1 ¼ cup of sugar
 pinch cream of tartar
1 tsp. cinnamon
1 tsp. ground cloves   -
1 tsp. allspice
2 cups grated almonds or pecans
1 tbsp. lemon juice
2 tsp. cornstarch for dusting cookie sheet   -

Beat whites until foamy. Gradually add salt and cream of tartar. Mix 1 cup of the sugar with the ground spices. Add to whites 1 tbsp. at a time, beating until stiff. Add additional cup of sugar and fold in nuts and lemon juice. Line cook sheet with aluminum foil, shiny side down. Trace 3-inch circle with glass. How many? Mound circles with meringue, Make hole in each with finger for any later filling. Bake at 225 degrees for an hour. Turn off oven and leaving door ajar; let them stay in oven for another hour.

Divinity Fudge

3 cups of extra fine granulated sugar
½ cup white Karo corn syrup
¾ cup water
¼ tsp. salt
½ tsp. cream of tartar
6 egg whites
2 cups chopped pecans
½ tbsp. vanilla

Cook sugar, Karo and water over low heat to soft ball stage. Cook at 250 degrees.

Beat egg whites, salt and cream of tartar until stiff. Quickly pour in the hot syrup, beating constantly at high speed. Fold in vanilla and nuts. Pour on marble slab. When cool, cut. Chill for at least 12 hours, wrapped in wax paper.

Inquirer's Coffee Gelatin Dish

1 envelope unflavored gelatin
½ cup cold water
½ cup sugar
¼ tsp. salt
1 cup of hot coffee
1 tbsp. lemon juice
½ pint heavy cream
2 to 4 additional tbsp. sugar

Sprinkle gelatin over cold water to soften. Add sugar, salt, hot coffee and stir to dissolve. Add lemon juice and pour into 4 small serving bowls. Chill until set. Serve with whipped cream to which the extra sugar has been added.

Espresso White Chocolate Dessert

This is a troublesome mixture of cream white chocolate and milk, thickened with cornstarch. Then you make an almost identical batch but this time with dark chocolate and coffee. One batch is placed on top of the other which gives a layered effect.

10 oz. white chocolate
1 ¼ cup heavy cream
¼ cup cornstarch
¾ cup skim milk
10 oz. dark semi-sweet chocolate
4 tbsp. freeze-dried espresso coffee
2 ½ cups heavy cream
3 tbs. cornstarch
5 oz. skim milk
3 oz. white chocolate

First break up the first 10 oz of the white chocolate into 1 inch pieces. Pulse, chop 30 sec. To further break up and run machine 30 sec. more. Heat the first 10 oz. heavy cream to the boil (medium high heat) and with processor running, pour in feed tube and process 15 seconds.

Mix cornstarch and skim milk. Add to work bowl and process 5 seconds. Put contents of bowl into small saucepan and cook over low heat until it thickens –about 6 min. Pour into serving dish and freeze. Wash out work bowl and blade and add semi-sweet chocolate and espresso. Again pulse-chop to break up chocolate and then process 30 seconds. Heat second batch of heavy cream to chocolate Espresso mixture and process 15 seconds. Now mix second batch of skim milk and cornstarch, as above, and add to mixture in work bowls, processing 5 seconds. Put work bowl contents in saucepan and again heat until it thickens – 6 min. or so.

Spread this on top of frozen white chocolate mixture and freeze for 3 hours.

Defrost in refrigerator an hour before serving. Invert on serving plate and shave over the rest of the white chocolate.

Cream Cheese Pastry

One of these is hard to handle but I don't remember which.

1 8-oz. pack of cream cheese, softened
2 sticks butter softened

2 ½ cups flour
1 tsp. salt

Beat cheese and butter in mixer at medium speed until smooth. Switch to low speed and slowly add flour and salt. Knead lightly only to mix. Wrap and chill for at least 3 hours. Makes enough for 2 8-inch shells.

Other Cream Cheese pastry proportions: 1 cup softened butter, 3-oz. package of cream cheese, softened, 1 cup flour, 1/3 tsp. salt.

Phyllo or Strudel Dough

These doughs are very difficult to work with as they dry out like lightening. If frozen, defrost completely before using. Before starting, have the filling ready as you have to work fast. Never let a sheet sit on counter without covering with wax paper top by a damp tea towel. The best directions I have seen are: unroll dough and take out what you need, placing it on waxed paper over damp towel. Immediately put what you are not going to use back in refrigerator, wrapped in closed plastic bag.

Another way of handling Phyllo or Strudel:

8 to 10 sheets per pastry
5 oz. skim milk,
10 oz. semi-sweet chocolate
4 tbsp. freeze-dried espresso coffee
10 oz. heavy cream
3 tsp. cornstarch
5 oz. skim milk
3 oz. white chocolate

Cover a damp towel with waxed paper. Put unfolded, unrolled package of phyllo on top. With the aid of towel and waxed paper, flip it over in half as though closing a book. Open book to first page which is the first phyllo leaf. Brush with melted butter ad sprinkle with bread crumbs or nuts. Do next page and continue till you reach the center of book. Now close the book and reverse the procedure. Spread filling on lower third. A whole package of phyllo will take ½ lb. of butter. Heat cream to the boil (medium-high heat) and with processor running, pour in feed tube and process 15 sec.

Cuisinart Lemon Berry Mousse

1 tbsp. gelatin
1 cup cold water
2 strips lemon zest
2 ½ cups sugar
2 eggs, separated
4 tbsp. lemon juice
1 cup heavy 1 non-fat dry milk
1 cup berries

Sprinkle gelatin in the cold water in small cup. Let soften for 2 or 3 minutes. Put this in shallow pan of simmering water and leave for several minutes until gel. Dissolve.

Meanwhile, in a food processor, process lemon zest and half the sugar for about 60 sec. Add egg yolks and process until lightly thickened, maybe 3 minutes. Scrape down work bowl. Add gelatin and lemon juice and process 30 seconds. Refrigerate work bowl and its contents.

In another bowl, beat egg whites to soft peaks. Slowly add remaining sugar and beat to stiff peaks.

In still another bowl, beat cream and dry milk (I think I might omit the dry milk) until stiff.

Now process the chilled lemon mixture for 10 seconds. Fold in half of this into egg whites. When combined, add or rather fold in the rest. Fold in whipped cream and berries. Spoon into individual cups or soufflé dishes. Chill at least 4 hours. Garnish with mint leaves.

Fried Milk, known as Leche Frita

This is basically crème patissière, chilled, cut into small squares and sautéed.

1 cinnamon stick
3 cups milk or preferably half-and-half
½ cup sugar

3 tbsp. butter
½ cup cornstarch
2 eggs, lightly beaten
1 cup fresh bread crumbs
1 tbsp. oil
1 egg for coating cubes
1 tsp. vanilla

Heat up cinnamon stick and milk. Bring to a boil and simmer 10 minutes. Beat eggs with whisk until light. Beat in sugar and then the cornstarch. Pour in a little of the hot milk, then gradually beat in the rest. Over moderate heat, stirring constantly, heat mixture just to the boil. Don't let it boil. Take off heat and remove cinnamon stick. Pour into greased 8 or 9 inch baking dish. Cool and refrigerate for at least 4 hours. Cut into 1 inch slices with knife dipped into hot water. Dip squares   first into the beaten egg and then in the crumbs. Put on waxed paper while you heat up the oil and butter moderately. When butter foam subsidizes, add squares and sauté for 2 min. per side. Remove, drain and sprinkle with cinnamon and powdered sugar.

Gourmet's Caramel Custard

2/3 cup of sugar
½ cup cream
1 ½ cups milk
2 eggs

Cook 1/3 cup of the sugar in heavy pan until it turns a deep gold. Carefully add cream and cook over mod, heat until caramel dissolves. Cool slightly. Bring milk to the boil. Take off heat. Put eggs in bowl and beat, adding remaining sugar. Mix well. Slowly add scalded milk. Cook to 175 degrees. Strain and chill.

Cook's Butter Cream

1 cup milk
1 tsp. vanilla extract
2 tbsp. maple syrup
1 egg
1 egg white
1/3 cup sugar

1 tsp. salt
1 tbsp. each flour and cornstarch
1/8   tsp. maple extract
6   oz. softened butter

In saucepan, heat milk, extract and syrup just to simmer.

Set aside, process egg, egg white, sugar, salt, flour, cornstarch just long enough to mix, 30 seconds. With motor running, slowly pour in hot milk. Return to saucepan and over medium heat, whisk constantly until mixture thickens, about 4 min. Boil. Transfer mixture to large bowl, cover with plastic and chill 1 hour. With hand mixer, beat butter into above, tbsp at a time.

Crème Anglaise (Soft Custard)

In my childhood, this was known as boiled custard, a misnomer if ever there was one, as if it comes anywhere near the boil, you will have a curdled mess on your hands.

It can be eaten as such (hopefully by me) poured over fruit but generally used as the basis for many desserts. Freeze it with cream and flavorings and you have ice cream. Add flour and you have pastry cream or crème patissière, gelatin and you have Bavarian cream, not to mention flan.

The proportions are as follows: For a thin custard which can be used as a dessert sauce, use:

2 egg yolks
¼ tsp. salt
¼ cup sugar
1 cup milk or half and half.

For thicker custard, such as for cream, increase egg yolks to 3. It can be made in a double boiler or on top of the stove. The double boiler method is time consuming but foolproof while the top-of-the-method is fast, simple but tricky.

 To   make in double boiler, heat water in the bottom to the boil. In   the top portion, mix egg yolks, sugar, salt and milk. Beat with fork only long enough to break up yolks. Place over the boiling water, turn down heat and stir constantly until custard coats the back of a metal spoon which may take 10 or 15 minutes. Transfer to bowl and beat with fork or spoon until cool.

If on top of the stove, scald milk. Add sugar and salt. Gradually pour hot milk over slightly beaten yolks, stirring all the while. Pour into heavy-bottomed saucepan and set over moderately high heat. Stir constantly and keep your eye on it constantly. You will note that small bubbles form on the surface. These bubbles give way to larger bubbles. At this point, the color of the custard will deepen and the large bubbles will disappear (165 degrees on candy thermometer). Immediately take custard off the stove. Turn into bowl and beat with spoon until cool. Flavor with vanilla, sherry or whiskey to taste.

If custard curdles in spite of your best efforts, beat 1 tablespoon of the curdled mixture into 1 tbsp. of milk or cream. Beat in the curdled mixture very gradually.

Keep in mind the fact that custard is most perishable. Never let it sit in a hot kitchen. Refrigerate as soon as possible. Never cover until custard is cool.

You will note that the small bubbles which appear on the surface of the custard are replaced by large bubbles. When these large bubbles disappear and the color deepens (165 degrees on candy thermometer), take immediately off stove and beat to cool. Strain.

If custard curdles in spite of your best efforts, either put it through a fine sieve into a cold bowl. Or try putting it through the blender to take out the lumps.

Cuisinart Fresh Fruit In Jelly

3 tsp. unflavored gelatin
3 tbsp. of cold water
½ cup orange juice
1 ¼ cups grapefruit juice
½ cup unsweetened white grape juice
3 tbsp. sugar
1 halved cantaloupe, 2 lbs.
1 kiwi, sliced

Sprinkle unflavored gelatin over cold water in small cup. Let stand for 2 or 3 minutes. Mix orange juice, grapefruit juice, unsweetened white grape juice, sugar and bring to boil. Take off heat and add gelatin mixture. Chill until syrupy, about 1 hour or more.

With melon scoop, scoop out flesh from cantaloupe. Place in colander to drain. Slice 1 cup of washed and hulled strawberries. Add to syrupy gelatin. Pour into 6cup ring mold. Chill until firm, 2 hours. Unmold and garnish with sliced kiwi.

Cuisinart Chocolate Icing (1 ½ cups)

12 oz. Baker's sweet German chocolate
6 tbsp. light cream
1 cup sour cream

Break chocolate into 1-inch pieces and process 1 minute. Heat cream just to boil and with motor running, slowly pour through feed tube and process until chocolate melts, 30 seconds. Cool to room temperature, about 3 minutes. Add sour cream and again process 30 seconds

Cuisinart Chocolate Cake

Use a 2 9-inch layer pans.

4 eggs
2 cups sugar
1 cup cocoa
1 1/3 cups butter
1 cup milk
2 tsp. vanilla
2 cups flour
1 1/3 cup flour
4 tsp. baking powder
1 cup seedless raspberry jam
Preheat oven to 350 and prepare pans.

Process eggs and sugar until light in color and fluffy, about   90 seconds. Add cocoa and process to combine 25 to 30 sec. Scrape down bowl and add butter cut into 1-inch pieces and process until creamy, 15 sec. With motor running, pour milk and vanilla through tube. Again scrape down. Add flour and baking powder and pulse 2 or 3 times or until flour disappears. Pour batter into prepared pans and bake 30 to 35 minutes, or until toothpick comes clean. Cool on rack for 10 minutes. Spread jam between layers and frost. To reduce calories and cholesterol and calories, substitute egg beaters for the eggs, margarine for the butter and skim milk for the milk.

Cuisinart Strawberry Bavaria (4 Cups)

1 envelope gelatin
2 tbsp. water
6 oz. strawberries (use whole, frozen unsweetened berries, defrosted in refrigerator or you can use fresh if in season)
4 tsp. raspberry jam
2 tsp. raspberry liqueur
1 egg white
½ cup whipping cream
1 tbsp. non-fat dry milk.

Stir gelatin and water into Pyrex cup and place in lightly simmering water for 5 minutes or so until it dissolves. Stir and cool.

Process berries, jam and liqueur until smooth -60 sec. Add egg whites and process until mixture thickens and rises to top of work bowl, 2 or 3 min. With motor running, add gelatin mixture and process 20 seconds to mix.

Beat cream and dry milk to stiff peaks, by hand. Fold fruit mixture into this. Chill for at least 4 hours in fancy cups or soufflé dish. Can be made a day ahead.

Peach Gratin

Any type of soft fruit can be used. Harder fruits such as pears should be first poached.

3 ripe peaches
1/3 cup brown sugar
1 egg, lightly beaten with fork
½ cup heavy cream
½ cup sliced almonds
1 cup heavy cream,
1 tsp. powdered sugar
1 tbsp. powdered sugar

Slice peaches and arrange in circular pattern in round, flat, shallow dish. Complete circle and place remaining slices in decorative pattern to simulate center of a flower. Sprinkle with the brown sugar. Mix beaten egg whites with the cream and pour on top of peaches. Sprinkle with the sliced almonds and bake at 375 degrees for 35 to 40 minutes.

Peaches should be browned and slightly caramelized. Sprinkle with powdered sugar and serve lukewarm.

Apple Strudel

1 cup or 6 ½ oz. pecans chopped into small pieces
2 tbsp. lemon juice (1 lemon)
2 lbs. (about   4) Granny Smith apples, peeled, cored and thinly sliced
¾ cup sugar
2 tsp. cinnamon
½ cup raisins
1/3 cup butter, melted
10 phyllo sheets

Put apples in bowl and toss with lemon juice. Add sugar, cinnamon and raisins. Mix. Preheat oven to 375 degrees. Grease baking sheet with butter. Melt butter and do the 10 phyllo sheets as above, brushing with the melted butter plus a tbsp, finely chopped nuts per page. (If sheets are laid out individually, use 2 per page.)

If using above directions, the "book" should be opened to the center, top sheet unbuttered. Spread and even 3-inch layer of the filling over the dough 1 inch from bottom. Do the same thing up both sides but this time, 2 inches from edge. Do not do top edge. Fold in both sides and the bottom and roll up as for a jelly roll. Spread over any remaining butter. Bake for about 30 min. or until crisp and golden. Cool for 10 minutes before slicing, with serrated knife. Can be made a day before and refrigerated in which case, bring to room temperature.

Craig Claiborne's Cheesecake

Crust:

Coat 8-inch cake pan with 1 tbsp. soft butter followed by 2 oz. (cup) processed graham crackers, shaking off excess.

Filling:

½ tbsp. butter, at room temperature
3 tbsp. lemon juice
1 tbsp. grated lemon peel
2 lbs. soft cream cheese
4 eggs
1 ¾ cups sugar
1 tsp. vanilla extract

Mix this filling and beat until light and fluffy. Bake in middle level of oven preheated to 325 degrees for 1 ½ to 2 hours or until set and golden. Should be baked in an improvised bain marie with boiling water coming halfway up sides of cake pan. Cool completely on rack. Cover and chill at least 4 hours before inverting. The size of cake pan, 8 inches, is important to this recipe.

Cheesecake Sauces

1 10 oz. jar fruit jam
¼ cup sugar
1 tbsp. rum or fruit liqueur

Heat preserves, sugar and cup of water in saucepan. Simmer until slightly thickened, about 4 min. Strain. Stir in liqueur and chill for an hour.

Strawberry Sauce

½ cup sugar
1 tbsp. quick cooking tapioca
1 tbsp. brandy
1 tsp. lemon juice
1 pint strawberries

Sprinkle sugar over berries and let stand for hour. Drain and add enough water to drained juice to make ¾ cup. Put juice in small saucepan and add a ¼ tsp. of salt, tapioca. Let this stand for a few minutes and cook until it comes to the boil. Take off heat and stir in brandy, lemon juice and berries.

Cream Cheese Pastries

The first is better but harder to handle.

8 oz. package cream cheese, softened
2 sticks butter
2 cups of flour, sifted
1/3 tsp. salt

Beat cheese and butter until smooth in mixer at medium speed. Now at low speed, slowly add flour and salt. Knead only enough to mix. Wrap and chill for at least 2 hours. Makes enough for 2 8-inch shells.

Other proportions:

½ cup softened butter
3 oz. package cream cheese, softened
½ cup flour
1/3 tsp. salt
Christmas Pudding
Cream together:
½ cup margarine
1 cup brown sugar
3 to 4 eggs
2 cups flour
¾ cup each currents and white raisins
¾ cup brown raisins
¾ cup cherries – glace or maraschino
1 cup nuts, walnuts or almonds
¼ cup brandy or rum

Divide into Pyrex bowls of desired size. Above amount should make 3 puddings for 1 1/2 pint bowls.

Tie on wax paper lids tightly. Steam for 1 ½ hours.

Ceel's Black Truffles

Pastry:

½ lb. butter
½ tsp. vanilla extract
½ cup confectioner's sugar
2 cups sifted flour

Cream butter preferably with mixer. Add vanilla and sugar, mixing until smooth. On low speed, add flour until mixture just holds together. Transfer to piece waxed paper. Flatten slightly. Shape into oblongs.

Chill while preparing the following:

Filling:

8 oz. blanched almonds
8 oz. dark, sweet chocolate
1 tsp. butter, melted
½ tsp. vanilla extract
5 oz. heavy cream
4 oz. sugar
2 cups sifted flour

With hands make ball of blanched almonds and chocolate, both finely ground, melted butter, cooled until mixture just holds together. Divide into 40 pieces, rolling each piece between your hands to form a ball. Remove pastry from refrigerator. It should not be hard. Flatten each piece in palm of your hand and wrap around chocolate truffle, covering it completely.

Dust hands with sugar and roll into ball between palms. Put on ungreased cookie sheet, 1-inch apart. Preheat oven to 300 degrees and bake 25 to 30 or until very lightly colored. Cool on paper.

Margaret's Truffles

12 oz. chocolate
4 egg yolks
2 tbsp. Kalua liquor
2/3 cup softened butter
½ cup espresso coffee
2 ¼ cups boiling water
4 oz. semi-sweet chocolate
½ stick unsalted butter

Melt the chocolate in a double boiler, remove from heat and cool to room temperature. Add egg yolks one at a time. Mix in liquor while smoothing it in the double boiler. Put in the Cuisinart; beat in the butter one tablespoon at a time. Pour into glass dish and refrigerate. Melt chocolate in double boiler with coffee and water, when just melted remove from heat. Beat in 2 tbsp. at a time, and let it cool. Pour on top of truffle.

Crème Brulée

Should you wish, you can continue on to crème brulée in which the mutual caramelizing can be omitted, proceed exactly as above. Chill and invert custard on plate but this time, pack surface of custard with brown sugar. Continue to chill for several more hours. When ready to serve, run custard briefly under hot broiler; brown sugar will melt. Watch this procedure carefully.

Bombes

A bombe is a fancy frozen party dessert made by lining a melon-shaped mold with different kinds of ice cream. When cut into serving pieces, you have a multi-colored effect, the more contrasting the better. I like pistachio next to raspberry, chocolate next to orange ice.

The center could be filled with a mousse, whipped cream beaten into Italian meringue or perhaps simply grated chocolate. It makes a great Christmas present for a friend's holiday dinner.

A plus is that not only should it be made the day before, it has to be. I use a melon mold but it could be made in a stainless steel bowl. I doubt if you will make 2 or 3 kinds of ice cream, so use the best commercial variety you can find. Begin by oiling mold with a tasteless salad oil. Put in freezer for an hour or so. Spread an inch or so of ice cream on sides and bottom. If too cold, the ice cream is unspreadable, if too warm, it will slide down sides. Return to freezer for an hour or so. Add another layer of ice cream and freeze again. Make and add center. Again freeze. Take out of freezer and refrigerate half hour before serving. Run knife around inside of mold and unmold by inverting on chilled plate. If bombe does not slide out, wrap base in dish towel wrung out in hot water.

Italian Meringue and Whipped Cream

1 cup sugar
1/3 cup water
1 tsp. cream of tartar

2 egg whites
¼ tsp. vanilla

Combine sugar, water and cream of tartar.

Set over moderately high heat but instead of stirring to dissolve sugar, swirl pan around. As you have egg whites to be beaten at the same time, turn down heat under syrup as soon as it boils and liquid is clear. Cover and beat egg whites with ¼ tsp. of salt until stiff. Add vanilla. Uncover pan, turn up heat and boil until it reaches 238 degrees, soft boil stage, on candy thermometer, a must. Above mousses could be described as follows: pour hot sugar syrup over egg yolks while beating rapidly so that hot syrup cooks the yolks. Mixture will triple in volume. Lighten by folding in whipped cream.

Tried Cookie Recipes

Macaroon Jam Tarts (makes 14, 3-inch)

½ cup butter
2 tbsp. sugar
2 tbsp. lemon rind
1 ½ tsp. lemon juice
1 egg yolk
1 ½ cups sifted flour
2 tbsp. cold water
3 egg whites
1 ½ cups sifted 4xxx, confectioner's sugar
1 tsp. vanilla extract
½ ground blanched almonds
1 grated rind of lemon

Cream butter and sugar. Beat in rind, juice and yolk. Stir in flour gradually with the water. Chill dough for 24 hours.

Roll out dough to 1/8-inch and cut into 3-inch rounds.

Beat whites until stiff. Gradually beat in 4xxx and vanilla. Fold in nuts. Make border around each cookie and bake 20 minutes or so until done. Fill centers with jam.

Pecan Rolls (makes 40)

½ cup butter
2 tbsp. cup sugar
1 cup pecan meats
1 tsp. vanilla
1 cup sifted cake flour
4 tbsp. xxxx sugar

Preheat oven to 300 degrees. Cream butter, sugar and add vanilla. Mix pecans and flour and add sugar. Grease baking sheet and make balls. Bake for 30 minutes. While hot, roll 4 times. Put back in oven for 1 minute.

Macaroon Jam Peck

Makes 38

1 ½ cups ground nuts
1 to 2 unbeaten egg yolks
1/3 cup sugar
¾ cups jam

Mix eggs and sugar and only enough egg whites, a little at a time, to make a paste firm enough to be shaped. Form into a 1 ½ -inch in diameter roll and place on well greased baking sheet. Make trench in center. 15 or 20 mm. in 350 degree oven or until lightly browned. The minute it comes out of the oven, fill trenches with hot jam which has been heated to the boil. Cool a bit and loosen with spatula. Slice when cool.

Bake at 350 degrees.

Jelly Cookies

Makes 48

2 sticks butter
2 tsp. vanilla extract
2/3 cup sugar
2 cups sifted flour
2 egg yolks

¼ cup currant jelly

Cream butter and sugar. Add yolks, one at a time. Mix well and stir in vanilla. Add flour, ½ cup at a time. Make tiny balls and make indentation with finger. Fill with current jelly. 8 minutes in oven or until edges are slightly golden. Space on rack.

Bake at 375 degrees.

Almond Spritz

Makes 5 to 6 doz

2 sticks butter
½ cup plus 2 tbsp. 4xxx (confectioner´s sugar)
3 oz. almond paste
2 cups flour
¼ tsp. salt
1 tsp. each almond extract and vanilla
1 large egg, beaten
sliced cherries or coarsely chopped nuts

Cream butter, sugar, almond paste. Gradually add flour, then flavorings and salt. Blend completely. Use cookie press tube with star attachment. Decorate with sliced cherries or nuts. Bake at 375 degrees, 8 to 10 min. or until edges curl.

Viennese Chocolate Walnut Bars

Crust

1 stick butter
¼ cup dark brown sugar, firmly packed
1 ¼ cups sifted flour

Cream butter in mixer. Beat in sugar. Add flour at low mixing speed - only enough to blend. With fingers, spread dough on ungreased 9-inch square cake pan. 10 min. at 375 degrees. Prepare filling:

Filling

¼ cup apricot preserves

1 cup sugar
6 oz. powdered walnuts
¼ cup dark brown sugar, firmly packed
2 eggs
½ tsp. salt
2 tbsp. unsweetened cocoa

Beat eggs with mixer at high speed for 2 or 3 min. Add salt, vanilla and then on low speed, sugar and cocoa. On high speed again, beat for 2 or 3 min. more. Again back to low speed, add nuts and beat only enough to incorporate. Spread preserves on dough, filling on top. Bake 25 min. When completely cool, make icing.

Icing:

1 cup semi-sweet chocolate bits
2 oz. walnuts, ground medium fine
¾ cup Karo corn syrup
3 tsp. each rum, boiling water

Melt chocolate in double boiler. Add Karo, rum and boiling water while still over heat. Stir until smooth. Spread on cake and press in nuts.

Leslie's Father's Rice Pudding

2 cups water
3 qts. milk
1 cup rice
¾ cup sugar
¾ tsp. cinnamon
Boil 20 minutes, and then bake for 25.
Pepin's Rice Pudding
½ cup mixed candied fruit
4 tbsp. kirsch
1 qt. milk
2/3 cup long grain rice
4 egg yolks
¾ cup sugar
2 tsp. vanilla
2 tbs. lemon rind
2 grated tsp. orange rind
2 envelopes gelatin
1 ½ cups heavy cream, whipped to Chantilly stage

4 tbsp. vegetable oil

Macerate fruits and kirsch overnight in bowl.

Bring milk to boil. Scatter in rice. Cover tightly and cook in preheated 400 degree oven for ½ hour. Stir, recover and cook for another half hour.

Mix   together   yolks, sugar, vanilla, grated lemon, orange rind and gelatin. Stir quickly and thoroughly into rice. Cover and put back in oven for 5 min. Transfer rice to bowl. Cover with plastic and chill. Fold cream, into rice mixture.

Oil 2-qt. mold. Add rice mixture, cover with plastic, wrap and chill overnight. Unmold, serve.

Sauce

10 oz. jar current jelly
2 tbsp. sugar
¼ cup water

Combine current jelly, sugar, ¼ cup water. Bring to boil, turn down heat and simmer 5 or 6 minutes. Strain,   chill. Pour around rice.

Perfect Cake Proportions

1 cup flour
½ cup sugar
1 egg
4 tbsp. butter
1/3 cup liquid
1/8 tsp. salt
1 ½ tsp. baking powder

Procedure is to mix dry ingredients and beat 1 min. at low speed. Add butter and 1 cup of the liquid - medium speed for 1 ½ minutes. In another bowl, beat yolks, vanilla, 1/3 cup liquid lightly. Add flour in 3 sections, beating 20 seconds each time. 2 buttered, floured, 9 by 2-inch cake pans (or line with greased wax paper). Bake in center of 350 degree oven for 25 to 30 minutes, turning pans once. Cool pan on rack for 10, then invert on rack.

Best Cake

4 cups sifted cake flour
2 cups sugar
5 tsp. baking powder
1 ½ tsp. salt
2 sticks softened butter
1 1/3 cups room-temperature milk
1 tsp. vanilla
8 egg yolks
Mix and bake in 375 degree oven.
Chocolate Cake
1 cup boiling water
¾ cup Dutch processed cocoa
3 cups sifted cake flour
4 eggs, separated
2 cups sugar (14 oz.)
1 ½ tsp. salt
2 tbsp. baking powder
1 ½ tsp. vanilla
1 cup soft butter

Procedure is to dissolve cocoa in boiling water. Cool to room temperature. In another bowl, whisk vanilla into yolks and whisk in ¼ of cooled chocolate mixture. Set aside. In mixer bowl, mix flour, sugar, salt, baking powder at low speed for 1 minute. Add remaining cocoa/water mixture to above dry ingredients with butter and beat at medium speed for 1 ½ minutes. Add egg/cocoa mixture to above in 3 parts, beating each addition for 20 sec. Whisk egg whites until stiff and fold gently into the cake mixture. Divide into two equal portions and transfer to the cake tins. Bake as above.

Fudge Frosting

1 cup heavy cream
1 lb. extra bittersweet chocolate
3 tbsp. cognac, flavored with vanilla bean

Scald heavy cream and off heat, stir in bittersweet chocolate. When melted, season to taste with vanilla bean flavored cognac. They point out that this recipe is not quite enough for proceeding chocolate cake. Make half again as much.

Cook's White Buttercream

1 cup sugar
6 tbsp. water
3 egg whites
2 tbsp. sugar
¼ tsp. cream of tartar
¼ tsp. salt
1 cup chopped-up butter
3 tbsp. corn syrup
1 tsp. vanilla

In small saucepan, bring sugar and to the boil, stirring constantly to 238 degrees to 240 degrees. Beat whites until stiff, add cream of tartar and salt, and slowly add boiling syrup. With mixer at high speed, beat 3 or 4 min. or until bowl is cool. Still on high speed, add, piece at a time. When butter lumps disappear, beat in and finally, tsp. vanilla. Beat 3 egg whites until frothy before adding sugar cream of tartar and salt. Beat whites until stiff and slowly add boiling syrup.

With mixer at high speed, beat 3 or 4 min. or until bowl is cool. Still on high speed, add 1 cup chopped-up butter, piece at a time. When butter lumps disappear, beat in 3 tbsp. corn syrup and finally, 1 tsp. vanilla.

Cook's Basic Frozen Parfait

Serves 2 to 4

The procedure is to stabilize the parfait, by beating egg yolks, sugar and liquid over simmering water until thick, continuing beating off heat until cool at which whipped cream is folded in.

4 egg yolks at room temperature

½ cup sugar
½ cup orange juice
½ cup berry puree
1 cup cream
2 tsp. vanilla extract

Place egg yolks in beater bowl. Beat in sugar, a tbsp. at a time. Gradually beat in orange juice, berry purée. Place this in top of double boiler over simmering water and beat until thick, pale yellow and tripled in volume, 7 to 10 min. If improvising a bain marie, do not let water boil.

Take pan off heat and continue to beat until mixture is cool, 5 or 10 min. Beat cream with either vanilla or liqueur, to Chantilly stage and fold into above mixture in 4 additions. Either pour into bowl or 4 individual cups. Cover with plastic, wrap and freeze for at least 4 hours, 30 to 40 minute in refrigerator just before serving. Chocolate variation: use milk for liquid. Melt 4 oz. semi sweet chocolate in double boiler. Gradually beat into mixture right after removing heat, before beating to cool. Before freezing, stir in scant 1/3 cup raisins that have been plumped overnight in 2 tbsp. dark rum.

Trifle

Line bottom of pretty glass dish with macaroons, ladyfingers or sliced sponge cake. Sprinkle with sherry and spread lavishly with raspberry jam. Add defrosted and drained raspberries and pour over a thin custard sauce. Scatter over a few chopped almonds.

Chocolate Pie Sinatra

Pre-bake pie shell and bake meringue over it.

Pie shell

2 egg whites
½ cup sugar
½ tsp. each vanilla and cinnamon.

Mix. Bake at 350 degrees 15 or 20 min.

Filling

2 egg yolks
¼ cup rum
1 ½ cups heavy cream

Melt chocolate, add yolks, rum and cook until. Beat until cool and fold in heavy cream.

Lemon Sponge Pudding

Top is almost like a cake, the bottom gooey. Begin by greasing 1 ½ qt. casserole.

¼   cup flour
1 cup sugar
¼   tsp. salt
3   tbsp. softened butter and cream until blended
2 egg yolks
¾ cups milk
¼ cup of lemon juice and zest of 1 lemon.
2 egg whites
¾ cup chopped nuts

Top is almost like a cake, the bottom gooey. Begin by greasing 1 ½ qt. casserole. Sift together flour, sugar, salt. Add softened butter and cream until blended. Beat egg yolks until light. Add milk and blend in lemon juice and zest of lemon. Beat whites until stiff and gradually fold into above mixture. Add chopped nuts. 3500 for 50 to 55 minutes degrees. It can be served hot or cooled and refrigerated for an hour.

Chocolate Admonitions

Chop or process chocolate   before melting. Do not process unsweetened choc. Melt in heated double boiler and take off heat before adding choc. Can be micro waved in dish, covered with plastic for 2 ½ min.

New York Times Mincemeat Pie

Pastry dough
2 cups sifted flour
3 cups   mincemeat
½ tsp. salt
2/3   cup cold lard
3 tbsp. brandy

Preheat oven to 350. Separate dough into 2 unequal pieces. Line bottom of 9-inch tin. Cut top into 3/4-inch wide strips. Add mincemeat mixed with brandy. Adhere strips. After 10 min. of baking, reduce oven heat to

350 degrees and cook an additional 50 min. I think foil ring to protect crust goes on at beginning of baking, removed when oven is turned down.

Mincemeat

1 lb. beef round
1 bottom round pastry dough
1 tsp. salt
1 tsp. cinnamon
1 tsp. cloves
2 oz. finely chopped ginger, allspice, nutmeg
1 lb. beef suet
1 cup coarsely chopped walnuts
2 oz. each raisins, currents
1 cup dry sherry or brandy
4 candied orange and lemon peel
2 large apples, peeled, cored
7 oz. dark brown sugar

Add just enough boiling water to cover meat. Simmer an hour and let cool an hour in saucepan. Dice and put in big bowl. Add all ingredients through brown sugar. Mix well and add everything else. Add spirits and refrigerate for 3 or 4 weeks, stirring up every few days for 2 weeks.

Grace's Pecan Balls (25 balls)

1 cup butter
1 tbsp. water
½ cup powdered sugar
2 cups flour
1 tps. vanilla
¼ tsp. salt
1 bsp. water
2 cups ground nuts
 Cream butter, sugar, rest of ingredients. Chill for an hour.
Roll into balls. Bake at 250 degrees for an hour.
Wine Mousse (serves 12)
½ cup lemon juice
½ cup orange juice
1 zest for each of above

10 egg whites at room temperature
1 cup cold heavy cream
2 tbsp. candied peel
¾ cup fruity white wine
1 tbsp. gelatin plus 1 tsp.
¼ tsp. salt
1 cup sugar

Let gel soften 5 minutes in water. Beat yolks with half the sugar, too much, I say, juices and wine. Cook over heat or preferably in double boiler until thick. Add gel and stir. Chill in bowl surrounded with ice cubes and a little water. Remove when it reaches consistency of unbeaten whites. Add zest and kirsch. Beat whites plus salt to soft peaks. Add rest of sugar and beat until stiff. Stir in ¼ of the whites into custard. Now fold in balance. Fold in beaten cream. Spoon into glass bowl or bowls. Spread over candied peel and chill for at least 3 hours. Serve same day.

Sherry Jelly

2 envelopes gelatin
3 cups dry sherry
2 tbsp. brandy
¼ cup sugar
2 tbsp. lemon juice

Sprinkle gelatin over cold water. Dissolve and add boiling water. When cooled to room temperature, add sugar and sherry, lemon juice to taste. Chill for several hours.

Raspberry/ Chocolate Fool

2 10 oz. packs frozen raspberries
3 oz. semi sweet chocolate
3 tbsp. water
1 cup slightly whipped cream

Thaw and drain raspberries (reserving juice). Bring this liquid to the boil and reduce to a syrupy ¼ cup. Set aside to cool. Purge berries and strain into reduced juice. Chill covered for 2 hours.

Melt semi sweet chocolate in double boiler with 3 tbsp water. Cool to room temperature.

Fold whipped cream into berries. Drizzle over chocolate, slightly fold in and chill.

TV Pears

Melt sugar to caramel. Add good lump butter plus cream. Poach pears in this.

Baked Pears

Peel and cut pears into strips. Put in baking dish and pour over a dry white wine. Sprinkle over cake or cookie crumbs. Bake 25 min. at 350 degrees, or until tender, basting now and then.

Charlotte Malakoff

8 ladyfingers split in half vertically
½ cup softened butter
½ cup sugar.
¾ cup ground, blanched almonds
2 tbsp. of kirsch
¾ cup of heavy cream
½ cup heavy cream
2 cups sugar
½ tsp. vanilla

Line   bottom of 4-cup charlotte mold with waxed paper, sides with ladyfingers. If there are any left over, sprinkle with kirsch. Cream cup softened butter and sugar. Stir in almonds and another tbsp. of kirsch. Beat heavy cream lightly and fold into almonds. Spoon half of almond mixture into prepared mold. Put any reserved, sprinkled ladyfingers on top and top with rest of almond mixture. Cover and chill 4 hours. Trim ladyfinger sides so that they are level. Unmold almond mixture onto serving plate. Remove waxed paper circle. Beat until stiff, heavy cream and sugar and vanilla. Spoon over.

Christmas Butter Cookies

Yields 2 ½ dozen

1 stick butter at room temperature
½ cup sugar
2 egg yolks, room temperature
2 tsp. vanilla extract
1 cup flour

Grease baking sheet. Cream butter, sugar in electric mixer. Beat in yolks and vanilla, stopping to scrape down bowl. Add flour and continue to beat only until mixed. Shape. Chill on greased baking sheet and then put in center of 350 degree oven -one sheet per oven- 8 to 10 minutes or until edges start to brown and centers are firm to the touch. Place on rack. Chill before rolling out or make indentation.

Cake Pan Measurements

Substitute sizes for cake pans

All cake recipes call for baking pans of a specific size. If you do not have the proper size on hand, you can make these substitutions (make sure that the pan is the same height):

Sizes called for in recipe:	Substitutions:
9" round	8" square
13" by 9" by 2"	two 9" round or
	two 8" square
15" by 10" by 1"	two 8 " round
	two 9" square

(It is pointed out that in the last two substitutions, cake may rise a little higher and may require a little extra baking time)

Oven Placement

Never have 2 filled racks. Cakes, cookies, unfilled pie shells, puff paste all go on second shelf from bottom. Filled pies go on bottom rack as they need heat from underneath. Highest rack is useful only for a tart that needs last minute browning.

18

ENTERTAINING

A Brief Note on Parties

What makes a good party is anyone's guess. Is it good food, a relaxed atmosphere coupled with peppy music, the cocktail hour, guests who are fun? I, for one, wish I had the answer. Sometimes they fail, sometimes they succeed and when they do, it is rewarding. On the other hand, a Spanish party will almost invariably take off right from the start. Could this be due to the supposed euphoric effects of their sherry?

There is, of course, the relatively easy convivial type in which guests have drinks and hors d'oeuvres in the kitchen while you put the finishing touches on the meal and then on to the dining room as opposed to the more formal which begins in the living room.

No matter how carefully you plan, the latter will entail a last 10-minute stint in the kitchen. In either case, if your guests exceed the number of dining room chairs, guests can help themselves and carry plates to living room. After dinner, you will remove plates and pass dessert and coffee.

Both of the above require careful planning on your part. Sit down with paper and pencil a few days ahead. Decide on your menu and shop accordingly. Check dinnerware, silver, centerpiece, liquor, ice, club soda and even what you plan to wear. Do all you can, including all possible cooking at least a day ahead.

After many years of cooking, a first course is still beyond me. When both working and keeping house I would go so far as to set the table a day ahead. I once made the mistake of hanging out guest bathroom hand towels in advance, pinning a note on them which stated sternly - you know what will happen to you if you touch these - (aimed of course at my husband). The mistake was in neglecting to remove the note.

No matter how careful the planning, as pointed out above, a last minute stint in the kitchen is almost impossible to avoid, particularly if you are working alone, with no help whatsoever. Of course you could serve a series of baked casseroles directly from oven to table, but that would be extremely boring.

As my entertainment is now quite informal, guests will accompany me with their drinks while I attend to these last minute chores. Even in the limited content of this book, there are several dishes suitable for parties, namely gumbo and lamb curry. What are the criteria? You should be able to prepare these dishes a day ahead, re-heating them without loss of flavor, and they should of course be elegant.

I find gumbo an excellent and much appreciated party dish. It can be frozen ahead and defrosted or it can be made a day ahead of the party and reheated at serving times. It will still require ten minutes of cooking time after the last minute shrimp is added. I like to serve this with boiled rice and Cole slaw. As pointed out under rice, the rice can be boiled in the morning and steamed for ten minutes in rice steamer just before serving. Cole slaw can be chopped the night before, bagged and refrigerated. It can be dressed just before guests arrive.

The lamb curry, for example, requires no last minute work other than a final re-heating of the curry. During the summer it can be served with the vegetable casserole listed under vegetables which does not require any last minute work. Roasts are certainly acceptable, as are hams, with gravy being the only last minute chore, which will take 10 minutes to make.

Rolls can be made a day ahead and reheated. There are many desserts that can be made a day or several days ahead. If your refrigerator is small, I would suggest a dessert that can be placed in a large serving bowl, rather than individual cups which can take up a great deal of refrigerator space.

Hors d'oeuvres

There are some purists who feel that hors d'oeuvres should be limited in order not to spoil dinner appetites. If you have an extended cocktail hour, I would certainly suggest something more substantial than say salted nuts, perhaps the toasted almonds, cheese appetizers and either the mushroom turnovers of the mushroom pâté. The mushroom turnovers can be made ahead and frozen but they still have to be baked just before serving. The others are disgustingly simple and most of the world can be done a day ahead which is a plus if entertaining. Of course there is always Brie served with crisp crackers.

The ever popular dish is not one of my favorites, particularly if runny. However a dip in the center of a large platter, surrounded by mounds of raw vegetables interspersed with watercress is attractive in appearance. Carrots, celery and cucumbers are good candidates as are cauliflower flowerets. Cut the first three vegetables into elongated strips, roughly two inches long and perhaps ½ of an inch wide, larger than the matchstick julienne. Salt and mound individually. They can be cut up the night before provided you refrigerate them in separate zip lock bags.

If you are going to serve drinks, accompanying hors d'oeuvres are almost a necessity. The following are all exceedingly simple and, other than stuffing the cherry tomatoes, require no last minute effort on your part.

Toasted Almonds

To save yourself the trouble of blanching, buy the pre- blanched and for this recipe, always the whole. If only the unblanched are available, drop them briefly in boiling water. Boil for a minute or two. Drain; refresh by running under cold water, slip off skins and dry with paper towel. I allow an 8-ounce package for 4. Place nuts on cookie sheet and drizzle with olive oil. Place in preheated oven. You want to turn them a golden, not a deep brown. This will take about 12 minutes. Stir up once or twice with fork. As they start to color, station yourself at oven door as they can burn rapidly. When done, drain on paper towels and sprinkle with salt. When cool, they keep well in tin box with lid.

Garlic Confit

Preheat oven to 375 degrees. One head of garlic should take care of 3. Slice top off whole head of garlic. Separate cloves and place on sheet of foil. Sprinkle with salt and a little olive oil. Fold edges of foil together and fold in ends to make a package. Place package in preheated oven, baking for 45 minutes or until cloves are softened.

Remove from oven and when cool enough, -squeeze cloves from skins. Pound cloves in mortar until pureed. Add a little more oil. Place garlic in small bowl and put in middle of serving plate and surround with crackers on which guests will spread the puree. This can be made several days ahead and refrigerated in closed glass jar.

Stuffed Cherry Tomatoes

12 cherry tomatoes
1 tbsp. lemon juice
1 tbsp. grated onion
3 tbsp. finely chopped parsley leaves

Wash cherry tomatoes. Cut out stem end with tip of soft knife. Enlarge hole with forefinger, salt and turn upside down to drain.

At room temperature, soften cream cheese. Season to taste with salt, lemon juice, grated onion and finely chopped parsley leaves. If to be served right away, tomatoes can be stuffed and served. If not, refrigerate seasoned cheese and take it out of refrigerator 1 hour before serving and stuff.

Cream Cheese and Dried Beef

2 slices dried bread
5 oz. cream cheese
10 fillets dried beef

Overlap 2 or 3 slices dried beef. Mold seasoned cream cheese into tubular shape and lay it on dried beef. Roll up and chill. When ready to serve, cut into 1-inch pieces with sharp knife. Secure with toothpick.

Brie and Sun-Dried Tomatoes

1   lb. brie without rind
2 tbsp. minced parsley
¼ cup pine nuts
4 sun-dried tomatoes in oil, reserving 1 tbsp. oil
2 tbsp. parmesan
6 leaves basil
4 garlic cloves, minced and mashed to paste
crackers

Mix everything but brie. Spread over brie and let stand an hour.

Cheese Puffs

1 cup water
1 cup sifted flour
1 tsp. each salt, mustard, white pepper
½ cup butter
4 eggs
1 cup shredded Cheddar cheese

Heat water to full boil. Add flour, seasonings, all at once. Stir until cool. Beat eggs vigorously one at a time. When shiny and smooth, add cheddar. Put on cookie sheet – rounded tsp. 1 inch apart. 25 min. at 400 degrees until they puff. Cook on rack. If frozen, heat at 250 degrees for 10 minutes
Stuffed Celery
3 celery stalks
5 oz. cream cheese

Celery ribs can be washed and chilled in plastic bag. Just before serving, fill centers with the cream cheese and cut into bite-size pieces.

One More Cream Cheese Pastry

Pastry

6 tbsp. butter
4 oz. pack cream cheese, softened
1 cup sifted flour.

Mix butter, cream cheese and stir in flour. Make into 3 balls and chill, bagged. Place on ungreased, tart shell. Press against sides and bottom. Bake at 325degrees for 25 min or until shells are set.

Pate Rustica by Bonnie Strauss

1 clove garlic
½ lb. chopped mushrooms
1 lb. chopped chicken livers
¼ cup butter

Sauté clove minced garlic with mushrooms and chicken livers in butter. Cool. Place mixture in processor and slowly add stick of softened butter. Season. Sprinkle this mixture with brandy to taste. Pour into crock and chill. Serve with toast triangles.

Guacamole (yields 2 ½ cups)

3 pitted, peeled avocados
2 cups of seeded
2 chopped tomatoes
1 sliced red onion
¼ cup of lemon juice
1/3-cup fresh, chopped coriander leaves
¼ tsp. cayenne

Mash avocados. Add seeded, chopped tomatoes, sliced red onion, lemon juice, chopped coriander leaves, cayenne to taste.   Can   only be made ahead if covered.

The evening before, you might cut out neat long slices of carrots and/or zucchini, cauliflower and perhaps broccoli flowerets. Salt them and refrigerate each separately in closed zip-lock bags for the night. Just before serving, arrange vegetable slices in neat individual piles on large plate with guacamole in center.

Chicken Liver Spread

2 cloves of minced garlic
½ chopped mushrooms
1 ½ lbs. chopped chicken livers
3 or 4 tbsp. of chopped parsley
¼ cup of butter
I tbsp. sherry to taste

Sauté minced garlic with chopped mushrooms and one pound of chopped chicken livers and chopped parsley leaves in of butter. Cool. Place mixture in processor and slowly add stick of softened butter. Season. Sprinkle this mixture with sherry to taste. Pour into crock and chill. Serve with toast triangles or the above sliced vegetables.

Cuisinart's Food Processor Pizza

1 pack yeast
1 cup warm water
1 1/3 cups flour
2 tbsp. vegetable oil

Stir yeast and sugar into water and let stand 10 minutes. Put the flour into work bowl and with machine running add water and yeast mixture. Process 45 sec. Add oil and process 60 sec. If dough sticks, add more flour, 2 at a time, processing 10 sec. after each addition, until is soft and leaves sides of bowl.

Divide dough into 4 equal portions and roll each into an 8-inch circle using more flour if necessary to keep dough from sticking, dusting off excess. As these are designed for grilling, the circles are first browned on grill, 2 minutes on one side, 1 on the other. Topping is put on brownest side. It is then covered and put back on grill for 2 minutes or until bottom is done and topping hot.

A topping: 4 parsley leaves, 3 oz. mozzarella, (well chilled, and chunked), 3 oz. Gorgonzola, 6 oz. ricotta, 6 pimientos, 4 tsp. good olive oil. Process parsley for 30 sec. Add mozzarella and pulse 8 times. Add other cheeses and mix well, for 8 sec. Does this mean pulse chopping? Divide among the 8 crusts and top with pimiento strips.

Another topping: 1 ½ lb. zucchini, 12 0z. plum tomatoes, 3 oz. chilled mozzarella, 1 tsp. each salt and pepper, 5 tbsp. oil.

Slice both zucchini and tomatoes with slicing disk. Switching to metal blade pulse-chop cubed cheese 8 times or until coarsely chopped. In small bowl, mix salt and pepper with 1 tbsp of the oil. Brush vegetables with this and grill 1 minute to heat through. Divide among 4 shells and sprinkle each with tsp oil.

Dough for 12-inch Pizza, not made in Cuisinart: 1 ¼ cups flour, 3/4 dry yeast, cup plus 1 warm water, 1 tbsp. olive oil, cornmeal.

Barley Mushroom Pilaf

Yields 6 Cups

1 ½ oz. dried mushrooms, rinsed, soaked in hot water
¾ cup parsley
1 medium onion, chopped
2 celery ribs, chopped
4   tsp. butter
¾   white onions, caps chopped, if large
1 cup pearl barley
4   tbsp. dry sherry
3 cups beef broth
salt and pepper

Heat up butter in large skillet. Soften celery and onions, about 8 minutes. Drain. Pulse-chop the mushrooms, 10 to 12 times, remove the stems from the white. Add mushrooms and all the other ingredients to skillet. Cover and cook over medium low heat until all liquid is absorbed, 35 to 40 min.

Another of the Above - Williams & Sonoma,

Serves 4 to 6

½ sticks butter
1 medium carrot
1 medium onion, both chopped
1 cup pearl barley
2 cups chicken stock

1 celery rib
6/8 strips cooked bacon

Sauté onions and carrots in butter until soft. Add barley and cook until grains are golden, about 5. Now add warmed stock and bring to boil. Simmer for an hour, covered.

Add 1 stalk very finely chopped celery. Let stand 5 min. uncovered, before serving.

Favorite Cheese Dish

Neither a fondue nor soufflé.

6 slices bread, buttered, decrusted
5 whole eggs
2 ½ cups milk
½ cup grated
dried mustard

Layer bread in greased baking dish, sprinkling with cheese.   Rest of ingredients in another bowl. Pour over milk and let stand for 2 hours or overnight in refrigerator. Bain marie for an hour at 350 degrees.

Alter this by adding more cheese, Tabasco, Worcestershire

Cucumber Sandwiches (serves 12)

½ medium cucumber
1   oz. smoked salmon
3   light cream cheese
½   grated lemon zest
pepper to taste
6 slices white bread

Wash and trim off ends of cucumber. Peel in ½ strips, giving striped effect. Put in processor slicer upright with light pressure. Pat dry and set aside.

Watercress Sandwiches

2 sticks softened butter
2 tbsp. minced parsley
1 cup watercress, blanched for 5 minutes. drained, squeezed, minced
1 tsp. fresh tarragon
1   tsp. Dijon mustard
1   tsp. lemon juice
1 tsp. Worcestershire sauce
5 or 6 slices bread

Cream   butter. Blend in rest plus salt and pepper and let stand in cool place for an hour. Spread half of bread with this. Top and halve.

Soufflés

A soufflé might be defined as a flavored sauce - a thick béchamel - into which egg yolks have been beaten and egg whites folded. The egg whites cause the soufflé to rise and puff. They are excellent Sunday supper or brunch dishes or the perfect answer for anyone who has dropped in for a drink and has been persuaded to stay for supper.

In some quarters, a soufflé is synonymous with trouble. The reputation is undeserved. I have always contended that it is more difficult to sauté than it is to make a soufflé. As long as the egg whites are beaten to the proper amount of stiffness, folded in delicately and if you are successful in getting your guests to the table before the soufflé falls, you will have no problems.

Egg Whites

There is no better time to talk about egg whites. We all know that even a speck of egg yolk in the whites will prevent them from mounting. A trace of grease or dampness in bowl or beater will have the same effect. It is easier to separate eggs when cold but whites can be beaten to a greater volume if at room temperature. Using a whisk, a rotary beater or hand-held electric beater, beat whites until frothy and add ¼ tsp. of salt or cream of tartar if called for. Continue to beat until whites are just stiff. How is this determined?

Test by holding up beater. If whites that cling to it stand up in vertical peaks, they have been beaten sufficiently. Do not beat so thoroughly that they lose their wet, glossy look, Dry, overbeaten whites are almost impossible to fold into a sauce.

The beaten whites must be folded quickly and delicately into the sauce. Start by stirring a big spoonful of the beaten whites into the sauce to lighten it. Turn the bowl of whites onto top of the sauce. Center a rubber spatula on top and cut right down to the bottom of the bowl, coming back up against the sides. As you do this, turn your wrist so that contents of the spatula fall onto the surface.

Continue to do this, at the same time, rotating bowl with your other hand. The object is of course to blend whites into sauce but not too thoroughly. It does not matter if there are flecks of white on the surface. The whole procedure should not take more than 1 minute.

Soufflé Base:

3 tbsp. butter
1 cup filling
3 tbsp. flour
1 cup milk
5 egg whites (always 1 more egg white than yolk)
4 egg yolks

Preheat oven to 400 degrees. Make roux (see roux), melting butter, adding flour and then off heat the hot liquid. After cooking roux, take pan off heat and stir in egg yolks, one at a time. Beat whites and stir in the big spoonful into the sauce. Add filling and fold in whites. Place in middle level of preheated oven and bake until it browns and puffs. Give it 5 minutes before taking it out of the oven. You have roughly 5 minutes before it falls.

The well-known cheese soufflé is made in exactly the same way. Use 1 cup grated Swiss cheese or a combination of Swiss and parmesan, reserving a couple of tbsp. to sprinkle over the top just before it goes in the oven. There are many fillings such as lightly sautéed mushrooms plus a tablespoon or so finely minced ham, cooked shrimp, mashed or crab.

Cheese Ramequins

Butter individual baking dishes heavily.   Preheat oven to 375 degrees. Mix ¼ cup of flour, 2/3 of the grated gruyere (2 cups in all), salt,   and pepper. Scald 1 cup milk and off heat, immediately add flour/cheese mixture. Add 2 tbsp. soft butter and stir until smooth. Back on heat, beat until it no longer sticks to the sides. Let it cool slightly and beat in 3 yolks, one at a time. Spoon into dished. Sprinkle with rest of cheese and tbsp butter and sprinkle with remaining cheese. 15 to 20 minutes for ramekin.

Garlic Soufflé plus Garlic Purge

2 garlic heads, separated
½ cup oil
½ cup water
¼ tsp. thyme
1 bay leaf
6 tbsp. butter
5 tbsp. flour
1 ½ cups of half-in-half
1 cup heavy cream
bouquet garni. (bay, ¼ tsp. dried thyme, 2 onion slices, 2 garlic cloves, 10 peppercorns, 4 sprigs parsley).

8 oz. mixture of parmesan and gruyere

Cover 2 broken heads with oil and water. Add thyme and bay. Cover and bake at 250 for 1 ½ hours, basting now and then. Strain off liquid and puree.

Should you wish to make a garlic soufflé, make roux butter, flour, half-in-half and heavy cream, both scalded. Cook roux 5 to 8 minutes. Let cool a bit before adding bouquet garni. Cook 1 hour in double boiler. Remove bouquet garni. Add eggs, heaping tbsp. garlic puree, beaten whites. Bake in top shelf, 450 for 10 minutes.

Crab Soufflé Varenne

3 tbsp. butter
2 tbsp. flour
Soufflé Base
¼ cup heavy cream
4 egg yolks
6 egg whites
4 oz. cooked crab meat
1 cup milk
1 sliced onion

1 bay leaf
6 peppercorns
2 shallots, minced
¼ cup cream

Infuse boiling milk with onion. Add bay and pepper. Let it sit covered. Let it sit in warm place. Make roux after sautéing the shallots, after adding milk; add cream, salt, pepper, cayenne and nutmeg. Boil 2 min. for 12 to 18 min. at 425 degrees.

Frittata

9 eggs
2 cloves
1 medium onion

Cook minced garlic and onion, both minced, in oil. Add thinly sliced small zucchini, skinned tomato and fresh herbs. Cover and cook until tender. Cool and season.

Beat 9 eggs lightly and mix with the above. Pour back into skillet and cook slowly until eggs pull away from skillet. Run under broiler.

Curried Fruit

Must be made a day ahead. Drain all fruit. You can substitute. You will need:

1 large can peaches
1/3 cup melted butter
3 small cans pineapple
¾ cup packed brown
3 small cans apricots
1 cup sugar
10 Maraschino cherries
4 tsp. curry

Preheat oven to 325 degrees. Fruit, hollow sides up, then place in shallow baking dish. Pour mixture of sugar, curry and butter into hollows and bake an hour, basting now and then. Chill overnight and reheat for 35 minutes at 350 degrees

Preheat oven to 325 degrees. Fruit, hollow sides up, goes in shallow baking dish. Pour mixture of sugar, curry and butter into hollows and bake an hour, basting now and then. Chill overnight and reheat 35 minutes at 350 degrees.

INDEX

Table of Contents

Made in the USA
Middletown, DE
24 April 2022

64718582R00186